# Nurturing Essence

## A Compass for Essential Parenting

John Harper

Copyright © 2025 by John Harper

All rights reserved. No part of this publication may be reproduced, distributed, or transmitted in any form or by any means, including photocopying, recording, or other electronic or mechanical methods, without the prior written permission of the publisher, except in the case of brief quotations embodied in critical reviews and specific other noncommercial uses permitted by copyright law. First Edition: September 2025

ISBN: 979-8-9924438-4-4 (Paperback)

HarpGnosis Books

Back cover image by John Harper. Almaas' *Loss of Essence* graph used with permission of Hameed Ali (A.H. Almaas).

Online image here: Nurturing-Essence.com

# Dedicated to the Curious

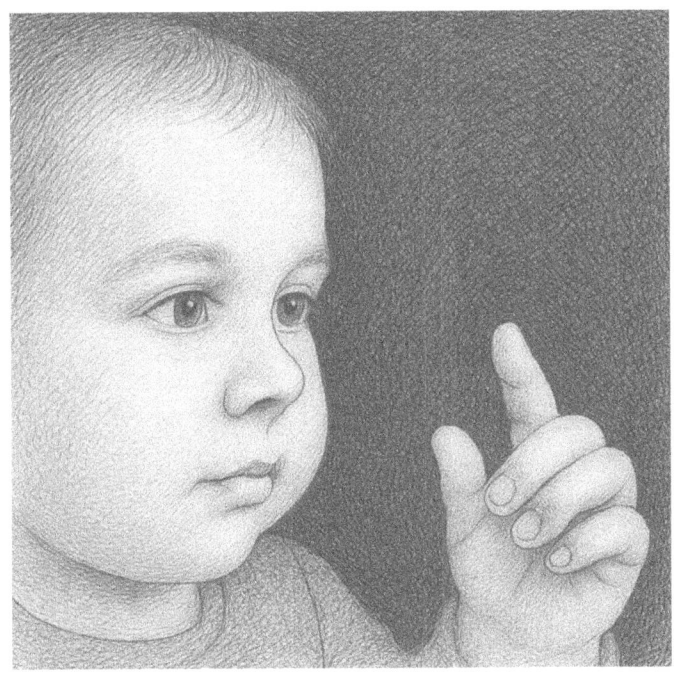

# Acknowledgements

Without Catherine Harper's (Big Sis) editing skills and feedback, I'd be lost.

Many thanks to Jessica Britt, Sandra Maitri, Linda Krier, Karen Johnson, and Alia Johnson.

A deep bow to Hameed Ali (A.H. Almaas)

# Table of Contents

Foreword .......................................................................................................... iii

Preface .............................................................................................................. v

Author's Note on Scope ................................................................................. vi

How to Use This Book .................................................................................. vii

Why? ................................................................................................................ ix

Introduction .................................................................................................... xi

SECTION 1: The Foundation and Broadstrokes .......................................... 1

    Chapter 1 The Developing Child—A Multifaceted View .......................... 1

    Chapter 2 The Council of Nine Theorists ................................................ 10

    Chapter 3 The Developing Self in Childhood ......................................... 14

    Chapter 4 The Dance of Learning ............................................................ 20

    Chapter 5 The Social Mirror ..................................................................... 32

    Chapter 6 Language and Labels ............................................................... 43

    Chapter 7 The Authority of Culture ........................................................ 57

SECTION 2: The Essential Journey .............................................................. 74

    Chapter 8 Essence and Ego ....................................................................... 74

    Chapter 9 Understanding Essence ........................................................... 86

    Chapter 10 Inherent Wholeness—The Unsculpted Self ........................ 96

    Chapter 11 Emergence of the Individual .............................................. 106

    Chapter 12 Learning Through Joyful Expression ................................ 110

    Chapter 13 Preserving the Spark ............................................................ 127

SECTION 3: The Developmental Lens ...................................................... 139

    Chapter 14 Birth to 6 Months ................................................................. 139

    Chapter 15 6 to 12 Months ...................................................................... 147

    Chapter 16 12 to 18 Months .................................................................... 156

    Chapter 17 18 to 24 Months .................................................................... 166

    Chapter 18 24 to 30 Months .................................................................... 177

    Chapter 19 30 to 36 Months..................................................................188
SECTION 4: Essential Qualities..................................................................200
    Chapter 20 Merging Gold Essence.........................................................202
    Chapter 21 Essential Strength...............................................................212
    Chapter 22 Essential Will.......................................................................224
    Chapter 23 Essential Joy........................................................................236
    Chapter 24 Value, Peace, Space, and Nourishment............................251
    Chapter 25 When Essence Becomes Holes.........................................257
    Chapter 26 The Integrated Child..........................................................266
    Chapter 27 When Development Becomes Emergence.....................275
    In Conclusion............................................................................................278
    Glossary......................................................................................................280

# Foreword

There are moments when a child teaches us more about life than any textbook ever could. A laugh that bubbles up for no reason. A gaze that sees without judgment. A tiny hand reaching in trust. These are not just milestones—they are glimpses of essence.

John Harper's book, *Nurturing Essence,* reminds us not to overlook them. Not to rush past them. Not to cover them with layers of expectation or fear. Instead, we are invited to see these moments as the very ground of becoming.

What unfolds in these pages is a map of both stories: the visible growth of the child through developmental stages, and the quieter, often hidden arc of essence—the joy, strength, will, and presence that form the child's deepest nature. Too often, one story drowns out the other. We celebrate skills and achievements, while overlooking the quiet spark of being that makes all growth meaningful. This book restores that balance.

As the developer of *The Attuned Parent Project*, I have witnessed how profoundly parenting is shaped by awareness, attunement, attachment, and authenticity. These four ways of becoming echo throughout these chapters. To see a child clearly (awareness). To meet them where they are, not just where we want them to be (attunement). To offer relationship as the secure ground from which they grow (attachment). To honor who they are, rather than molding them into what culture demands (authenticity). These are not lofty ideals; they are daily practices. And they align seamlessly with the vision offered here.

What strikes me most is how this book refuses to romanticize essence as something fragile to be preserved in a glass case. Instead, it shows us how essence can flow into development itself, how personality structures can remain permeable rather than rigid, and how parents can help their children grow into adults who are both capable and whole. This is the work of integration, not perfection.

The invitation to parents is simple yet profound: mirror essence, not just behavior. See the strength in persistence. The will behind a firm "no." The joy behind wild play. Speak to the heart, not only to performance. In doing so, you honor not only the child before you, but also the child within you—the part of you that still remembers what it felt like to be whole, alive, and free.

Parenting is never just about raising children who function well in the world. It is about raising beings who remain in contact with what is most true. When parents engage their histories, meet their lost places with compassion, and recommit to their unfolding, they create the very space in which a child's essence can stay alive and accessible.

This is not an easy path, but it is a sacred one. Each pause to notice, each choice to attune, each willingness to honor essence over expectation is a step toward raising not only a child, but consciousness itself.

As you enter these pages, may you read not only with your mind but with your heart. May you discover a deeper way of seeing your child and yourself. And may this book remind you, again and again, that the quiet spark behind the eyes of every child is not something to perfect, but something to honor.

—Mary Filice, PhD (Dr. Mary)
Co-Founder, The Attuned Parent Project

# Preface

The inspiration for this book came in 1998 or 1999, during my teacher training for the Diamond Approach. At that time, I considered psychology to be a bunch of bunk—thanks, Dad. Unlike many of my fellow students, I hadn't arrived at the Diamond Approach through a background in therapy or psychology. I came via mysticism, although I had stepped off that path in hopes of learning how to become a real human being.

That search led me to the teachings of A.H. Almaas and to the psychodynamic work that is integral to the Diamond Approach. As I began studying pioneers in psychology and child development, a question kept surfacing: Why isn't this knowledge more available and accessible to parents?

Textbooks and academic studies certainly existed, but I hadn't encountered a book that answered: What's happening in your child's developing brain/body self? What's unfolding in their sense of self? And, perhaps most essentially, how does all of this relate to essence and the loss of essence as the personality develops over time?

Around 2006, I began working on this book. It's taken a while, but here it is.

I hope the book helps parents better understand what's happening with the mysterious being who has landed in their arms. And in some small way, I hope it supports them in recognizing, nurturing, and celebrating the essence of that soul adapting to this world.


John Harper, September 2025

# Author's Note on Scope

This book explores typical childhood development through the lens of essence and the unfolding sense of self. It does not attempt to address the nuanced needs of neurodivergent development, including autism, ADHD, or other diagnoses that have become central to modern psychological understanding.

I offer this work not as a clinical manual, but as a contemplative and developmental map, a way of seeing how essence weaves through the emergence of personality in early life. Those seeking in-depth guidance on developmental differences are encouraged to consult the many experts dedicated to those fields.

This book is a general exploration of what it means to become a functioning self in this world, and how, even in that becoming, the deeper nature of who we are may still be remembered.

## A Note on Redundancy and Interpretation

You may notice that some ideas and insights reappear throughout the book, sometimes in slightly different contexts or with renewed emphasis. This repetition is intentional. Rather than sending you flipping back and forth to reassemble the thread, I've chosen to let the ideas breathe where they naturally arise. Development itself is recursive, not linear. So too is the flow of this book—returning, deepening, circling back with fresh insight. The aim is not efficiency but transmission.

What you are reading is not a textbook, nor a neutral presentation of psychological theory. It is a lived, contemplative understanding of ten powerful frameworks, each filtered through decades of personal experience, teaching, and deep inner work. I make no claim to academic precision. My aim has not been to quote the theorists verbatim, but to digest and integrate what they point to, what they awaken in the heart, the body, and the soul of parenting.

If you're looking for a footnoted analysis of the literature, you won't find it here. What you'll find instead is an invitation to feel into these perspectives as living inquiries: How do they illuminate your experience? What awakens in you as you read? What is truer in you now than before? That is the real curriculum of this work.

# How to Use This Book

There's no one right way to read this book, just as there's no one right way to parent. *Nurturing Essence* is designed to meet you where you are. Whether you're a new parent, a seasoned caregiver, a therapist, or a curious soul longing to understand the mystery of human development, this book can serve as a companion, a reference, or a mirror.

For your convenience, a glossary is provided at the end of the book and PDF of Childhood Stages of Development can be found on our website: Nurturing-Essence.com. (include the hyphen)

**Here are a few ways readers have found helpful:**

- **Start at the Beginning and Read Chronologically:** This approach allows you to follow the natural arc of early development from birth through age 6. You'll trace how the child's sense of self unfolds, how essential qualities emerge and retreat, and how psychology and essence intertwine through the stages of life.
- **Begin with the Age Your Child Is:** You might be most interested in what's happening with your two-year-old's tantrums or your five-year-old's need for independence. Each chapter stands alone, so feel free to jump in wherever your child currently is, and then circle back later to earlier or later stages.
- **Use it as a Developmental Reference:** This book can serve as a guide or mirror when things become confusing. If your child is behaving in ways you don't understand, scan the developmental themes and essential qualities to see what may be surfacing. Often, what appears as "bad behavior" is a quality of essence emerging in a distorted or frustrated form.
- **Follow the Essential Qualities:** Some readers are drawn not to the chronological structure, but to the presence of specific essential qualities, such as Strength, Joy, or Will. You can trace these qualities across chapters to see how they evolve in expression as your child grows, and how your relationship to those qualities may impact how you respond.
- **Read Reflectively, Not Just Informationally:** This isn't just a book of knowledge; it's an invitation to inquiry. Each chapter includes reflective questions that can deepen your understanding of your developmental history, your reactions as a parent, and your child's deeper being. Let yourself pause. Journal. Notice.

- **Use It in Community:** Whether in parenting groups, study circles, or therapeutic settings, this book is intended for discussion. You'll find that others' insights often mirror or deepen your own. The experiences of parenting and being parented are rarely solitary affairs.

Whatever path you take, trust your rhythm. Let this book be not an authority, but a companion, one that honors both the complexity of development and the simplicity of presence.

# Why?

If your first child were born today, you have about three years to prepare yourself for the experience of *Why?* Three-year-olds are an insatiable embodiment of curiosity, whose endless demand and mantra is: Why? They are relentless in their pursuit of the infinite answers to this simple question.

There's no time to waste! You need to start preparing right now. But wait, hold on! Before you get to *Why?*, there are the *Terrible Twos*. And you can never do enough to prepare yourself for them!

These stages in childhood development are just two of the tsunamis heading your way as parents. And, like tsunamis, no amount of preparation will prepare you for the actual *lived experience*. But, just like preparing for a tsunami, an early warning system can save lives. For soon-to-be parents, our hope is that this book will help to accomplish that, at least metaphorically.

Today's body of wisdom on childhood development can help prepare and forewarn you for one of the most challenging and rewarding experiences possible for human beings—parenting.

Becoming a parent is relatively easy for most human beings. Parenting, on the other hand, is a more challenging endeavor. Parenting is full-throttle life. Even when you're taking a break, there is no off switch. Your mothering, or fathering, brain and instincts are in a state of constant vigilance. General knowledge and an overview of childhood development are like preparing for a tsunami, earthquake, or power grid failure by having an emergency survival kit handy. It's not optimal to wait for an emergency and get a kit.

Believe it or not, human beings are not born as adults. We undergo a developmental process that involves not only physical growth but also brain and mind development, along with the expansion of our neural network and associated processes, ultimately leading to the development of a *sense of self*.

When we're born, we have no sense of self. We have not yet developed the capacities needed for a sense of self. And yet, many parents interact with their newborns and young children as if the child is a self with adult resources, such as fully functional and discriminated multi-modal perception and self-reflective cognition.

It is this insight and wisdom into the developmental process of the sense of self where the treasure lies for prospective parents. However, while amazing and valuable, knowledge of the developmental process can be even more revelatory and supportive when combined with an understanding of **essence**. Essence is what we are at our core. Essence exists before the developmental process, during the developmental process, and is that which *gets lost* to consciousness because of the developmental process.

We enter the developmental process as essence and exit it as an ego/personality with little conscious awareness of our essential nature. We are lost to ourselves while we spend our lives seeking what was lost—our authentic self, our essence.

Very little, if anything, is done in the first 6 to 7 years of life to help the child recognize and maintain awareness of their essential nature because few parents have an experiential understanding of essence and its relationship to psychological development.

> *From the problem, you can't see the solution.*
> *But from the solution, the problem is apparent.*

This is what this book is about.

# Introduction

**Parenting as Presence, Not Perfection**

Becoming a parent can feel like being handed the lead role in a play for which you've never seen the script. One moment, you're anticipating a child's arrival; the next, you're in the thick of something raw, beautiful, disorienting, and all-consuming. There are books, of course, and advice from every direction. But nothing prepares you for the real, lived experience of parenting: a daily invitation to show up, again and again, often without knowing how.

This book is not a manual. It's not a list of parenting strategies or best practices. *Nurturing Essence* is something different. It's a way of seeing your child, yourself, and the sacred unfolding that happens between you. It's about understanding development not just through milestones and behavior, but through the deeper movements of the soul.

In the early years of life, your child is building a sense of self. But they're also bringing something in with them, something essential, unconditioned, already whole. Most parenting approaches focus on shaping behavior or guiding development. This book asks a different question: *How do we support our child's growth without losing touch with what was never missing to begin with?*

We draw here from the great developmental theorists—Piaget, Erikson, Bowlby, Mahler, Vygotsky, and others—each offering insight into how the child's mind, emotions, and relationships take shape. However, we also include the often-overlooked dimension of essence —the quiet presence, joy, strength, and will that reside in each child before their personality develops.

When you understand both the development and essence of your child, you begin to see them not just as someone to shape or guide but as a being to meet. A mystery to welcome. A soul finding its way into this world, through your love, your attunement, and your willingness to be changed in the process.

Parenting is not about getting it right. It's about becoming more real. As your child grows, so do you—not by mastering techniques but by learning to be present in the unknown.

This book is for those who sense that there's more to parenting than surviving the early years. It's for those who want to understand not just what's happening on the outside, but what's unfolding on the inside of your child, and of you. May it serve as a mirror, a compass, and a companion on this sacred path.

# SECTION 1: The Foundation and Broadstrokes

## Chapter 1
## The Developing Child—A Multifaceted View

Childhood development is one of the most remarkable transformations in life. In just a few years, a newborn who can't hold up their head becomes a young child who walks, talks, plays, asks questions, solves problems, and begins to understand themselves as a separate person. This unfolding touches every area of growth—physical, emotional, cognitive, and social—and all of it contributes to the formation of the child's emerging sense of self.

This chapter provides a comprehensive overview of these early years and introduces how different developmental theorists help us understand the changes occurring in a young child's world. The goal isn't to memorize the theories but to see how they illuminate different aspects of your child's growth.

**From Newborn to Young Child: What's Unfolding**

The first 6 years of life are marked by rapid and complex changes that can be challenging to track. However, we can begin to make sense of them by examining the four primary areas of development.

**Physical Development**

Babies start with almost no control over their movements. They gradually learn to lift their heads, roll over, sit up, crawl, stand, and eventually walk and run. As their bodies strengthen and coordination improves, children become more confident and capable in navigating their world. Fine motor skills also develop. Skills such as grasping, drawing, and feeding oneself begin to emerge. This physical growth follows a general sequence from head to toe and from the center of the body outward.

**Cognitive Development**

Early thinking begins with the senses. Infants learn through touch, sight, taste, and movement. As they grow, their ability to think symbolically, solve problems, and understand cause and effect increases. Language develops quickly. What begins as babbling quickly becomes complete sentences and stories. By the preschool years, children can remember, imagine, and begin to reason, even if their logic is still childlike.

**Emotional Development**

Newborns feel and express pleasure and distress. Over time, children develop a wider emotional range and begin to identify, express, and regulate their feelings. They begin to understand that others have feelings too, which leads to the development of early forms of empathy. They also start to experience more complex emotions, such as pride, embarrassment, and guilt. Emotional development is closely tied to relationships; it depends on how feelings are met, named, and supported.

**Social Development**

From the earliest preference for faces and voices, a child's social world gradually expands. They move from watching others to playing alongside them, and eventually to playing with them. Social development includes learning to share, take turns, follow simple rules, and respond to group expectations. These early relational patterns shape how the child will connect with others for years to come.

**Developmental Timelines**

While each child develops at their own pace, there are general windows of time during which specific patterns tend to emerge. Here is a simple outline of what typically unfolds in the first 6 years.

**Birth to 1 year: Foundation**

This is a time of rapid change. Babies go from primarily reflexive reactions to more intentional interaction with the world. Physically, they gain head control, learn to roll over, sit, and may begin walking near their first birthday. Cognitively, they begin to lay the foundation to understand object permanence, the idea that people and things continue to exist even when they're not in sight. Socially, they form strong attachments, develop preferences, and enjoy simple games like peek-a-boo. They also begin to express a unique temperament.

**1 to 3 years: Emergence of Independence**

Toddlers want to do things by themselves. Language grows quickly. Children go from a handful of words to hundreds, and from simple requests to complete sentences. Physically, they gain confidence in walking, climbing, and handling objects. Emotionally, they begin to assert themselves, experience strong feelings, and test limits. Socially, they transition from solitary or parallel play to more intentional interactions, although cooperation is still a work in progress.

**3 to 6 years: Expansion and Integration**

During the preschool years, children take more active roles in the social world. Their play becomes more collaborative, their conversations more complex, and their thinking more imaginative. The question "why" becomes central as they seek to understand the world. Physically, they refine coordination and balance. Cognitively, memory and language flourish. Socially and emotionally, they navigate friendships, group dynamics, and an increasing awareness of social expectations.

These years are not just a time of growth but of profound becoming. The child is not only acquiring new skills; they are forming a sense of who they are. And at each step something more profound is moving too—the quiet presence of essence, still visible beneath the emerging personality.

To help us understand the many layers of child development, this book draws on the insights of nine major thinkers in developmental psychology. Each one brings a unique lens to the unfolding process of how a child becomes a person. When taken together, these perspectives provide a more comprehensive understanding of what is truly happening in your child's inner and outer world.

**Introduction to Our Nine Developmental Theorists**

To help us navigate this complex terrain of child development, we'll be drawing on the wisdom of nine influential thinkers in developmental psychology. Each brings a unique perspective that illuminates different aspects of how children grow and develop:

- **Jean Piaget** showed how a child's thinking evolves from raw sensory exploration to more abstract reasoning, with each stage building on the last.
- **Lev Vygotsky** emphasized the social and cultural context of learning, reminding us that children grow in relationship with parents, teachers, and the world around them.
- **Albert Bandura** highlighted the importance of imitation. Children learn a tremendous amount by simply watching and mimicking the people in their lives.

- **Lawrence Kohlberg** mapped out the development of moral understanding over time, beginning with simple notions of right and wrong and progressing to more nuanced ethical thinking.
- **Margaret Mahler** explored the psychological birth of the self, how a child gradually separates from the caregiver to become a distinct individual.
- **Erik Erikson** described development as a series of emotional and psychological tasks, each with its challenge to be worked through and integrated.
- **Sigmund Freud** introduced the idea that early experiences shape personality in deep and lasting ways, often outside our conscious awareness.
- **D.W. Winnicott** provided us with powerful concepts, including the "good-enough parent," the "true and false self," and the emotional holding environment necessary for healthy development.
- **John Bowlby** established attachment theory, showing how early bonds lay the groundwork for emotional security and future relationships.

These nine perspectives will give us a multifaceted view of your child's development. But there's a tenth perspective that will help us understand something most developmental theories miss—the essential nature of your child and how it interacts with their developing personality.

**The Perspective of Essence**

The Diamond Approach®, developed by **A.H. Almaas**, offers a distinctly different perspective on childhood development. Instead of focusing solely on how the ego or personality takes shape, it asks a deeper question: What is present in the child before any of that forms?

Almaas describes this as essence. Essence is our original nature—qualities like joy, will, strength, peace, and presence that are not learned or developed but are already there. They don't need to be earned or taught. They simply are.

As the child grows, these qualities tend to fade from conscious awareness. Not because they disappear, but because the developing personality becomes the louder voice. The child learns language, rules, roles, and strategies for navigating the world. This is necessary and important. But it also comes at a cost.

The graph on the back cover of this book tells a story in two parts (online image here: Nurturing-Essence.com). Above, a detailed map of developmental stages charts the intricate architecture of personality formation across the first seven years—from Vygotsky's zones to Erikson's crises to Bowlby's attachment phases.

Below, a different story unfolds—the gradual fading from consciousness of essential qualities. Watch the lines descend—Essence, Joy, Strength, Merging, Will—each tracing its trajectory as these capacities dim in the child's awareness while the complex scaffolding of selfhood assembles itself.

This isn't one line rising as another falls. It is multiple essential capacities slowly fading from conscious access as the child gains tools for navigating the world—language, boundaries, and social awareness. The qualities don't disappear; they become background music to the louder melody of becoming someone.

The qualities remain. The child's awareness of them grows faint.

This is where parents come in. The invitation is to support both movements. Yes, children need to build a personality, learn to name things, and understand boundaries. But they also need help staying connected to what was there before all of that, to the part of them that doesn't need to be earned or proven.

Joy supports curiosity and exploration. Strength fuels movement and persistence. Merging allows for deep bonding. Will carries the child through moments of frustration. These aren't abstract ideals. They are essential capacities that live inside the child and support development from the inside out.

To nurture essence is not to bypass development. It is development. It is what allows the child to grow into a self that is both functional and deeply real.

**Figuring It Out as We Go**

Let's be honest. No matter how many books we read or theories we learn, parenting is an improvisation. The moment those two pink lines show up or we first hold that child in our arms, we are launched into a role that no amount of preparation can fully cover.

Most of us enter parenting with a mix of hope, excitement, and quiet apprehension. We guess, we try, we fail, we learn. We look for clues. We call our parents or search parenting blogs in the middle of the night. We want to do it right, but the truth is, most of it feels like learning to swim while already in deep water.

And just when we think we've figured out a routine, bam, it changes. The baby who finally slept through the night starts teething. The toddler who loved broccoli now throws it at the wall. The preschooler who was so affectionate one day becomes a mystery the next.

Parenting is not a role we master. It's a relationship we grow into. And even the most prepared among us end up improvising, adjusting, doubting, and trying again. We bring with us our history, our wounds, and our unconscious scripts. Sometimes we parent out of love. Sometimes out of fear. Sometimes out of sheer exhaustion.

That's why this book doesn't offer a one-size-fits-all answer. Instead, it provides a way of seeing. A way of being with your child that honors both their developmental needs and their deeper nature. It invites you to grow alongside them, not by becoming perfect, but by becoming more present.

You're not expected to know it all. None of us does. But you can learn to recognize what's unfolding, to meet your child where they are, and to stay connected to what's real in both of you.

The rest of this book builds on that foundation. We'll explore what's happening at each stage of development, from the inside out, drawing from both psychological theory and the lived presence of essence. Together, these perspectives can help you see your child more clearly, respond more wisely, and maybe even recognize parts of yourself that you'd forgotten were there.

**What Children Need Beyond Love**

Love is essential, no question. But there's something children need even more than love, and that's acceptance. Not permissiveness, not indulgence, but a deep kind of seeing. A way of meeting your child that says, "I see who you are." Not who I want you to be. Not who I think you should be. But you.

This kind of acceptance allows something quiet and powerful to unfold in the child. It gives their essence space to breathe. It tells them, without words, that their being is welcome here.

The trouble is, we often bring our hopes and dreams into our parenting without realizing how much weight they carry. We want our children to thrive, to shine, to become something beautiful. But even our most loving intentions can cast a shadow. When we imagine who our child might become, we subtly communicate that who they are now isn't quite enough.

Children don't know what that something else is supposed to be. They just feel the pressure to be different. So they watch us. They listen. They try to twist and stretch themselves to fit the shape they think we're asking for.

This shaping isn't always overt or harmful. It can be as subtle as a hopeful glance when they excel, or a quiet sigh when they don't. It can come from our wish for them to be gifted, spiritual, successful, kind, whatever it is we value. But even in a loving environment, a child can begin to feel like who they are isn't quite right, like they need to become someone else to be fully loved.

Facing this as parents isn't easy. We're not just responding to our children; we're responding through layers of our conditioning. Through ideas we absorbed in our childhoods about what's acceptable, what's strong, and what's lovable. Many of these ideas operate outside our awareness. That's why parenting, at its best, becomes a path of self-inquiry.

It's through that inquiry, by slowing down, reflecting, and noticing our patterns, that we create space for our child to be fully themselves. When we meet them without needing them to change, we offer something that love alone can't always provide. We offer wholeness.

That kind of presence can save a child years of internal confusion. It can spare them the painful journey of having to unlearn someone else's version of themselves. When we accept their essence now, as it is, we invite them to grow from the inside out. And something surprising happens along the way; they begin to show us who they really are. Not the version we imagined, but the one that's been there all along.

This is how parenting becomes a path of awakening, not just for the child but for the parent. When we allow the child to guide us back to presence, we remember something about our forgotten essence. We become students again. The child becomes the teacher.

As we delve deeper into this book, we'll continue to weave together the perspectives of our nine developmental theorists. Their insights often overlap in illuminating ways. During a child's first year, for example, a parent might be holding all of the following at once:

- Erikson's view of trust versus mistrust
- Bowlby's attachment theory
- Piaget's sensorimotor learning

- Mahler's symbiotic stage
- Freud's oral phase
- Winnicott's concept of the holding environment

These aren't conflicting ideas. They're different angles on the same unfolding. Like instruments in an orchestra, each one adds something essential to the symphony.

In upcoming chapters, we'll explore each developmental stage through this integrated lens. We'll look at what's happening in the child's world—emotionally, cognitively, socially, and essentially—at different stages of growth: from birth to 6 months, 6 to 18 months, 18 months to 3 years, and 3 to 6 years.

By weaving these threads together, we create a clearer, more compassionate view of what's unfolding in the child and what's being asked of us as parents.

## Practical Ways to Support Growth and Essence

Bringing these insights into daily life isn't about doing things perfectly. It's about showing up with presence and care. Here are a few simple, grounded ways to support both development and essence:

- Offer sensory experiences. Young children learn through their bodies. Let them explore textures, movement, sounds, and sensations. Unstructured play is powerful.

- Support their growing edge. Vygotsky referred to this as the zone of proximal development, the area just beyond what individuals can accomplish independently. Give just enough support to help them stretch without doing it for them.

- Be mindful of your modeling. Your child is watching more than they're listening. How you handle frustration, express affection, or relate to yourself teaches them what's possible.

- Encourage effort, not just results. Let them feel the satisfaction of trying, practicing, and persisting. This builds inner strength and self-belief.

- Mirror essence, not just behavior. When you notice qualities like joy, strength, or curiosity emerging, name them. Reflect them. This helps your child recognize who they are beneath what they do.

This balanced approach, honoring both the personality that's forming and the essence that is always there, lays the foundation for a child who can function in the world without losing touch with their inner truth.

In the chapters that follow, we'll examine each theoretical perspective in greater detail. But more importantly, we'll keep returning to the real question: What's unfolding in the soul of the child, and how can we meet it, moment by moment?

# Chapter 2
# The Council of Nine Theorists

This chapter isn't a second introduction to developmental theory; it's a refinement. In Chapter 1, we met our ten guiding perspectives. Here, we clarify why each of them matters. Rather than outlining full models or detailing stages already mentioned, we'll focus on what each lens helps us *see* and what it invites us to *do*.

Each theorist observed something vital about how children grow. No single framework holds the whole truth, but together they help us respond more wisely to the everyday questions of parenting: Why is she clinging today? What's going on beneath his tantrum? How do I guide without imposing?

These are not abstract questions. They're the ones that show up at breakfast, in bedtime battles, in the silence after a slammed door. The theories that follow offer tools for meeting those moments, not with perfect technique but with growing presence.

## Jean Piaget: Understanding Misunderstanding

Piaget offered a structure for how thinking evolves, not just what children know, but how they know. From reflexive responses to symbolic reasoning, he charted the unfolding mind through stages. His work helps us understand why children can't "just see it our way"—not out of stubbornness, but because their minds aren't yet structured to do so. Concepts like object permanence and conservation help decode children's thinking.

A three-year-old bursts into tears when her sandwich is cut in half, convinced it's now less. She's not being irrational; she's at a stage where "more" still means "bigger," and "whole" means "one piece." Piaget provides us with a map to understand how cognition develops in complexity.

## Lev Vygotsky: Growth Happens Between Us

Where Piaget saw the child as a lone scientist, Vygotsky saw the child in relationship. His concept of the Zone of Proximal Development (ZPD) highlights the fertile space between what a child can do alone and what they can do with support. This space is where learning flourishes when scaffolding is offered, then gradually removed.

A toddler struggles to fit a puzzle piece. You sit beside them, narrate, encourage, and offer just enough help. The puzzle is completed but so is something larger: the child's confidence. Vygotsky's model turns our attention to this co-created learning.

**Albert Bandura: You Are the Curriculum**

Bandura's social learning theory revealed how children internalize what they observe. His concept of self-efficacy, the belief that "I can do this," is nurtured through modeling, mastery experiences, and encouragement.

Your child watches you handle a setback with composure. They absorb it. Later, facing their frustration, they try again rather than giving up. Bandura reminds us that every moment models something: persistence, helplessness, empathy, or blame.

**Lawrence Kohlberg: Morality as a Journey**

Kohlberg mapped moral reasoning as an unfolding process, from avoiding punishment to following rules to internalizing universal values. His stages suggest that what appears to be "bad behavior" may actually be the roots of ethical development.

A child tattles on a sibling not to be mean, but because they believe in fairness. Another begins to question rules, not to rebel, but to understand justice more deeply. Kohlberg helps us understand that morality develops gradually, and each stage has its logic.

**Margaret Mahler: The Push-Pull of Becoming**

Mahler focused on how a child gradually separates from the caregiver and forms a sense of self. Her stages, from symbiosis to individuation, illuminate why toddlers seem so contradictory as they crave both closeness and independence.

"I do it myself!" quickly turns into "Carry me!" Mahler shows that this isn't inconsistency; it's the dance of differentiation. Her work helps us honor the inner push-pull of becoming a separate self.

**Erik Erikson: Identity Through Challenge**

Erikson proposed that development unfolds through psychosocial tasks: trust, autonomy, initiative, and industry. Each stage poses a challenge, and how it's met shapes future identity.

A defiant "No!" is more than defiance; it's a step toward autonomy. Erikson reframes these moments as developmental thresholds. For parents, his model becomes a mirror: What's being asked of me here? What was modeled to me in my childhood?

## Sigmund Freud: The Echo of the Unseen

Freud introduced the idea that unconscious patterns formed in early life influence later behavior. His psychosexual stages—oral, anal, phallic—link development to bodily experience, pleasure, and identity formation.

A parent overreacts to their child's messiness or defiance. Freud helps us ask: Is this about the present, or something from the past? His work points us toward our inner history and how it might echo through the present.

## D.W. Winnicott: Presence Over Perfection

Winnicott introduced the concept of the "good enough" parent, offering reassurance. Consistent, attuned presence, not perfection, is what fosters a child's true self. Without that presence, a "false self" may emerge as a survival adaptation.

A child melts down, and instead of fixing it, the parent simply stays near, breathing slowly. This is "holding." Winnicott reminds us that containment—emotional availability—can be more healing than words or solutions.

## John Bowlby: Attachment as Blueprint

Bowlby emphasized that early emotional bonds form internal working models of the self and others. Secure attachment builds a foundation of safety and trust.

At preschool drop-off, a child clings. Rather than rushing them inside, the parent pauses, crouches, and connects. That gesture says: You matter. You are safe. Bowlby reframes separation not as a problem to be fixed, but as a threshold to be honored.

## A.H. Almaas: Essence Is Already Here

Almaas brings a spiritual perspective, reminding us that children are not blank slates. They come into the world with essence—qualities like will, joy, strength, and love—that shine through in unguarded moments.

A toddler bursts into song, eyes wide with aliveness. No agenda, no performance. Just being. Almaas helps us recognize these moments, not as anomalies, but as reminders of what's most real. And perhaps what we, too, have forgotten.

**Entering the Child's World**

Each of these theorists opens a window into how children grow cognitively, emotionally, relationally, and essentially. But no child lives in theory. They live in time, in bodies, in families, in moments that defy neat categories. Development doesn't follow a checklist; it flows like weather, predictable in pattern, surprising in detail.

That's why, in the chapters ahead, we'll move from general frameworks to the felt texture of specific developmental stages. We'll ask, "What is happening in the child's world?"—not in abstract terms, but in the real, everyday dance of sensation, emotion, behavior, and presence.

We won't simply track milestones. We'll look at what's awakening in the child, and what might be dimming. We'll explore how to support both the development of a functional self and the preservation of essential qualities.

Let's begin where all development starts: at the threshold of life itself.

# Chapter 3
# The Developing Self in Childhood

If we're going to be honest about parenting, we have to discuss how the "self" takes shape in our children. Contrary to what it may seem, babies aren't born with a fully developed sense of identity.

As much as we chatter away about little Jimmy's cute button nose or baby Ella's adorable giggles, that's us mapping our ideas of identity onto a mostly blank slate. Their "self," that innate sense of I-ness we take for granted as adults, actually unfolds over time.

## How the "Self" Takes Shape

Let's break this down a bit. Jean Piaget's observations highlighted that infants and young toddlers, rather than being self-aware philosophers, interact with the world primarily through pure sensation.

Psychoanalyst Donald Winnicott described infants as an "unintegrated matrix" with no defined self-other boundary. They don't know where they end and the world begins. Spiritual teacher A.H. Almaas describes the infant soul as an "undifferentiated field of conscious awareness" brimming with essence long before a solid self-concept emerges.

Yet, despite having no clue they even exist apart from Mom's nourishing arms, we talk to babies like fully formed friends, complete with bold preferences, quirky personalities, and thinking much deeper than poop schedules.

This means that the sense of self we assume is innate is more of a mental construct that gradually develops over the first 2–3 years as babies begin to distinguish between their internal world and the external environment. Through hundreds of thousands of interactions, they begin to discern sensations, emotions, and desires that are unique to them, as opposed to those belonging to their caregivers. In short, selfhood originates relationally.

## Cognitive Stages and What They Mean in Everyday Terms

Piaget's theory helps us understand how a child's cognitive development shapes their emerging sense of self. During the sensorimotor stage (birth to 2 years), the infant's understanding of the world is based entirely on sensory experiences and motor actions. Babies can't yet think symbolically or understand that they exist as separate entities from what they're experiencing.

Object permanence, which typically develops between 8 and 12 months, is a crucial milestone in this process. When babies realize that objects (including people) continue to exist even when out of sight, they're beginning to form mental representations, the foundation for understanding themselves as separate, continuous beings.

Mahler extends this view by highlighting that while Piaget situates object permanence around 8–12 months as a cognitive milestone, its fuller emotional significance emerges later, between 15 and 18 months, when the child not only knows the mother exists when absent but also struggles with her separateness during the individuation process.

As children enter the preoperational stage (2–7 years), they develop symbolic thinking and language, giving them new tools to construct their sense of self. However, their thinking remains egocentric, making it difficult to see things from another's perspective. This cognitive limitation influences how they perceive themselves, primarily through their immediate perceptions, without fully understanding how others perceive them.

In everyday terms, this means your 3-year-old genuinely believes that everyone experiences the world just as they do. When they hide by covering their eyes, they genuinely think they're invisible to you. This isn't selfishness; it's a cognitive limitation that gradually gives way to more sophisticated understanding as the brain develops.

**Psychological Birth of the Individual**

Mahler's theory guides us step by step through this psychological birth. For those first symbiotic months, the baby knows itself simply as a nonconceptual sense of "we" intertwined so closely with the mother that separation is nonexistent for the baby. But around toddlerhood, babies venture bravely into the beginning awareness of a distinct "I," testing out their agency in that glorious repetition of "No!" and "Mine!"

Mahler outlined several distinct phases in this journey:

- **Normal Autism** (First Few Weeks): In the beginning, newborns exist in what Mahler called "normal autism, " a self-contained, dream-like state where they're minimally aware of external stimuli, focused primarily on their internal sensations.

- **Symbiosis** (1–5 Months): As infants become more aware of the outside world, they enter a symbiotic relationship with the mother (or primary caregiver). The infant and caregiver form a psychological unit, with the infant experiencing the caregiver as an extension of themselves.
- **Separation-Individuation** (5–36 Months): This primary phase represents the psychological birth of the individual and consists of several subphases:
  - **Differentiation** (5–10 months): The infant begins to emerge from the earlier sense of fusion with the mother, showing heightened alertness and interest in the external world. This phase is marked by visual exploration—studying faces, turning toward new stimuli, and using gaze to test boundaries between self and other—signaling the first stirrings of separateness.
  - **Practicing** (10–16 months): With the development of walking, the toddler joyfully explores the world, periodically returning for "emotional refueling."
  - **Rapprochement** (16–24 months): The child becomes aware of their separateness, creating anxiety. They seek independence but also reassurance. This phase often includes "shadowing" and "darting away."
  - **Consolidation and Object Constancy** (24–36 months): The child develops a more stable sense of self and the ability to maintain emotional connection even when physically separated.

## The Role of Parents in Supporting Healthy Cognitive Development

Parents play a crucial role in supporting this emerging selfhood:

- Create a secure attachment base
- Support autonomy with boundaries
- Mirror and validate inner experience
- Use language to develop self-concept
- Respect emotional and physical boundaries

## Other Voices in the Orchestra

While Piaget and Mahler offer invaluable frameworks, the emergence of self is a polyphonic process enriched by many theoretical voices.

Erik Erikson's stages offer a powerful lens here. His first three conflicts—trust vs. mistrust, autonomy vs. shame and doubt, and initiative vs. guilt—directly parallel a child's journey into selfhood. The self doesn't emerge in a vacuum; it wrestles its way into clarity through these very developmental tensions.

John Bowlby complements this by showing how a secure attachment, what he called a "secure base," frees the child to explore independence. A child's sense of self grows not through detachment but through confident returning.

Lev Vygotsky's contributions come into play as the self begins to internalize. His concept of the Zone of Proximal Development illustrates how adult scaffolding evolves into inner dialogue. The voice of the parent becomes the voice of the child's mind—guiding, judging, narrating.

Sigmund Freud's early stages (oral and anal) can also be viewed through this lens. These early struggles with bodily control, pleasure, and frustration shape one's sense of boundaries, mastery, and identity.

Lawrence Kohlberg's early moral stages add yet another layer, where obedience and avoidance of punishment form the first glimmers of self as a moral agent. Right and wrong initially live outside the self but are slowly absorbed into the architecture of identity.

**The Secret Ingredient**

Beyond stages and milestones lies the child's essence, their inherent qualities of being. These shine through as curiosity, joy, strength, and will. Supporting development means honoring both structure and essence.

From the practicing toddler's radiant strength to the 4-year-old's eruptive imagination, essence isn't taught; it's revealed. The parent who sees it, mirrors it, and supports it gives their child not only a healthy ego but a bridge to their true nature.

The path of parenting is not just managing behavior or promoting achievement. It's witnessing a miracle: the emergence of a self that remembers where it came from.

As we've seen, the development of self in childhood is not a mechanical unfolding but a living dialogue between inner potential and outer environment. Identity doesn't simply arrive; it emerges through contact, reflection, and resonance. But this emergence doesn't happen all at once. It comes in waves, in stages, in subtle shifts of awareness and capacity.

What, then, is actually happening in the child's world as they move through those early stages? How does development feel from the inside out, not just through theory but through the lived experience of the child?

**Stage-by-Stage: The Emergence of Self**

**Birth to 6 Months**

In this earliest stage, the infant lives in a fluid, nonconceptual awareness. Winnicott's "unintegrated matrix" and Almaas's undifferentiated field describe this well. There's no sense of separation from the world or caregiver. Erikson's trust vs. mistrust is already in motion, with every holding, feeding, or missed cue laying foundations. Mahler's normal autism and early symbiosis reside here, alongside Bowlby's pre-attachment behaviors. The child's essence often manifests as peace, radiant presence, or a gurgling sense of pleasure.

**6 to 12 Months**

Differentiation begins. Mahler notes that infants begin to show visual checking behaviors, glancing back at their caregiver to orient themselves. Piaget's object permanence also begins to emerge. Curiosity, will, and vitality rise into view. Vygotsky would highlight early vocal mirroring, while Bowlby identifies clear attachment preferences. This is the quiet emergence of agency.

**12 to 24 Months**

Now practicing begins. The toddler is on the move—climbing, running, exploring. Mahler's practicing phase radiates joy. Autonomy vs. shame and doubt (Erikson) enters center stage. Freud's anal stage begins as the child gains bodily control and boundary awareness. Will and strength as essential qualities become apparent. This is a time of delight and power struggles.

**2 to 3 Years**

Rapprochement surfaces. The child wants to be separate but still held. Anxiety and volatility rise. Language acquisition accelerates. Vygotsky's scaffolding deepens. Kohlberg's first stage of moral understanding takes shape; authority is initially external but begins to be internalized. Object constancy (Mahler) becomes possible. Essence shows up as strength, vulnerability, and emotional clarity (Almaas).

**3 to 5 Years**

The self becomes increasingly symbolic. Magical thinking dominates (Piaget), and imaginative play blooms. Erikson's initiative vs. guilt appears as children try on roles and test impact. Freud's phallic stage begins, focused on identity and self-perception. Kohlberg's instrumental morality surfaces. The child's world is a dance between grandeur and insecurity.

**5 to 6 Years**

Cognitive structure stabilizes. Social referencing increases. The child begins to see themselves through others' eyes. Vygotsky's internal dialogue strengthens. The superego consolidates. Brilliancy and discernment often begin to show through. This is the beginning of social selfhood—identity embedded in a field of meaning.

In the chapters that follow, we'll step into the child's world more intimately. Stage by stage, from infancy to early childhood, we'll explore not only what's happening developmentally, but what the combined lens of the nine theorists reveals when we ask: Who is this child becoming, and how can we meet them as they are?

Chapter 4 picks up with one of the child's earliest drives: to learn. But before school subjects and grades shape our understanding, we return to a deeper question: What is learning, before it becomes schoolwork?

# Chapter 4
# The Dance of Learning

Before learning becomes schoolwork, grades, and expectations, it begins as something more primal: a reaching. The infant reaching for light, the toddler repeating a sound, the preschooler asking "Why?" fifty times in an hour. Learning, at its core, is the soul's way of exploring existence.

Jean Piaget described the early stages of learning as sensory and motor exploration, as well as cognitive engagement through action. But beneath that, something more essential is at play: curiosity. Not curiosity as a mental function, but as an essential quality of being. The child doesn't just want to know; they *burn* to discover. This fire is intrinsic, not assigned.

Vygotsky understood that learning arises in relationship through dialogue, modeling, and shared tasks. But if we look closer, his "Zone of Proximal Development" is not just a pedagogical zone; it's a sacred space. It is the gap between what the child *can* do and what they *might* become, and it is crossed through connection.

Erikson reminds us that initiative is central to this age; the child must feel safe to try, to fail, and to imagine. But initiative doesn't arise from performance pressure. It emerges when a child feels the right to *exist creatively*. To learn is to risk, and the ego cannot take that risk if shame and fear dominate the stage.

Before we discuss school readiness, academic pressure, and the social complexity of learning environments, we need to revisit the question: What is learning, when no one is measuring it? What is learning when it is still a wonder?

## Learning as More Than Accumulation of Knowledge

When we think about learning, we often picture the acquisition of information and skills—a child mastering the alphabet, counting to ten, or reciting the names of animals. But learning in early childhood is far richer and more complex than this accumulative model suggests.

Authentic learning involves integrating experiences into the child's developing understanding of themselves and the world. It encompasses not just what children know but how they come to know it—the processes of exploration, discovery, and meaning-making that shape their cognitive, emotional, and social capacities.

For young children, learning is a holistic and embodied experience. A toddler discovering how to stack blocks isn't just acquiring spatial reasoning skills; they're experiencing the relationship between intention and outcome, developing persistence, calibrating their movements, and perhaps experiencing joy in creation or frustration in collapse. All of these dimensions are part of the learning process.

This multidimensional view of learning aligns with our understanding of brain development. Young children's brains are creating neural connections at an astonishing rate, up to one million new neural connections per second in the first few years of life. These connections form not in isolated cognitive compartments, but across regions that support emotion, memory, attention, motor control, and higher-order thinking.

By recognizing learning as this rich tapestry of development rather than a simple accumulation of knowledge, parents can better support their children's growth in ways that honor both their developmental needs and their essential nature.

**Zone of Proximal Development**

Lev Vygotsky's zone of proximal development opens the dance floor, inviting the child to reach just beyond their grasp to learn in collaboration with others. This concept illuminates the space between what a child can accomplish independently and what they can achieve with guidance from a more knowledgeable partner.

Imagine a four-year-old attempting to complete a puzzle. Working alone, she might manage to connect a few obvious pieces but struggles with the more complex sections. With gentle guidance from a parent, perhaps suggestions about looking for corner pieces first or focusing on matching colors, she accomplishes what would have been impossible on her own. In this collaborative space, learning thrives.

The zone of proximal development isn't about pushing children beyond their capabilities or leaving them to struggle with tasks they cannot yet master. It's about finding that sweet spot where challenge meets support, the growing edge where development happens most naturally.

For parents, understanding this concept means recognizing when to offer help and when to step back. Too much assistance can create dependency and rob children of the satisfaction that comes with mastery; too little can lead to frustration and disengagement. The art is in providing "just-right" support—what Vygotsky called "scaffolding"—that enables success while fostering growing independence.

This balance shifts constantly as children develop new capabilities. What required substantial guidance yesterday may need only a gentle reminder today and might be accomplished independently tomorrow. Attentive parents notice these shifts and adjust their support accordingly, gradually transferring responsibility to the child as their competence grows.

It is here, in the interplay of guidance and exploration, that the child's innate joy can either be nurtured or stifled. At its best, learning within the zone of proximal development is a joyful affirmation of life's possibilities, not a rigid imposition of facts and figures.

Parents who understand this concept can transform everyday interactions into opportunities for joyful learning:

- Preparing dinner becomes a lesson in measurement and chemistry
- A walk in the park becomes an exploration of biology and seasons
- Bedtime stories become journeys into language, emotion, and imagination

In these moments, learning doesn't feel like work; it feels like dance, with the parent and child moving together in a rhythm of discovery.

## Observational Learning and Its Impact

As Albert Bandura's observational learning takes center stage, it becomes clear that strength is more than just muscle; it is the robustness of character and the resilience of the spirit. Children learn not just skills and facts but ways of being in the world by watching those around them.

Children don't just listen to our instructions; they absorb how we live. Bandura emphasized that for learning to take root, children must first notice us, remember what we do, be able to imitate it, and feel a reason to. These four dimensions—attention, memory, capacity, and motivation—aren't just theoretical; they're pulsing through everyday life. When a child watches you persist with a difficult task or repair after a mistake, you're not just teaching a skill; you're transmitting strength.

This framework helps us understand why children often adopt the mannerisms, phrases, and problem-solving approaches of the significant adults in their lives. A two-year-old who sees her father speak kindly to a stranger, a three-year-old who watches his older brother persist at a challenging task, a four-year-old who observes her mother standing up for what she believes in—these children are absorbing lessons about the nature of strength that go far beyond what could be explicitly taught.

The models to which the child is exposed will shape not only what they do but who they become.

*The strength they observe is the strength they will embody or regret.*

This profound truth carries a responsibility for parents. When we model resilience in the face of setbacks, courage in the face of fear, or integrity in the face of temptation, we are showing our children what strength looks like in lived experience.

But strength isn't always about powering through or standing firm. Sometimes it's expressed in vulnerability, in admitting mistakes, in asking for help. When parents demonstrate this more nuanced manifestation of strength, they support their children to access the full spectrum of this essential quality.

Observational learning extends beyond discrete behaviors to include attitudes, values, and emotional responses. Children learn how to approach challenges, treat others, and interpret their experiences primarily by observing the adults around them. This social learning not only shapes what children know but also influences who they become.

### Learning Environments Shape Both Skills and Essence

The environments we create for children, both physical spaces and emotional atmospheres, profoundly influence not only what they learn but how they experience the learning process. These environments can either support or hinder the expression and development of their essential qualities.

**Physical environments** send powerful messages about what we value in learning:

- Spaces filled with closed-ended toys with single "correct" uses suggest that learning is about following predetermined paths to correct answers.
- Environments rich in open-ended materials, such as blocks, art supplies, and natural objects, communicate that creativity, exploration, and multiple solutions are valued.

- Areas organized for independent access tell children they are trusted as capable learners.
- Outdoor spaces that allow for vigorous movement, sensory exploration, and connection with nature support holistic development and essential vitality.

**Emotional environments** shape children's relationship with learning even more profoundly:

- Atmospheres of judgment and evaluation teach children that learning is about pleasing others and avoiding mistakes.
- Environments characterized by curiosity and wonder communicate that learning is a joyful journey of discovery.
- Contexts that emphasize competition over mastery can disconnect children from their intrinsic motivation to learn.
- Relationships that offer both high expectations and high support foster the essential qualities of confidence and perseverance.

The most supportive learning environments honor both developmental needs and essential qualities. They provide appropriate challenges while allowing authentic expression, create structure while valuing spontaneity, and offer guidance while respecting autonomy.

When learning environments are aligned with essence, children can develop skills and knowledge while maintaining connection to their essential joy, strength, curiosity, and will. Their learning becomes not just an acquisition of capabilities but an expression of their deepest nature.

## Role of Joy, Strength, and Will in the Learning Process

Joy, strength, and will are not just pleasant additions to the learning process; they are essential qualities that animate and sustain meaningful learning. When these qualities are recognized and supported, learning becomes not just more enjoyable but more effective and integrated.

**Joy** infuses learning with delight and vitality. When children experience joy in discovery, they develop positive associations with learning that motivate them to continue exploring. Joy isn't about making learning "fun" through external entertainment; it's about tapping into the natural excitement that comes from mastery, discovery, and connection.

A child who experiences joy in learning:

- Approaches new challenges with enthusiasm rather than anxiety
- Persists through difficulties, sustained by the anticipation of discovery
- Integrates information more deeply through the neurological benefits of positive emotional states
- Develops a lifelong love of learning rather than seeing it as a chore to be endured

**Strength** provides the foundation for tackling challenges and overcoming obstacles in the learning process. This isn't just about physical strength but also about the inner resources that allow children to try, fail, and try again without being defeated by setbacks.

A child learning with strength:

- Approaches complex tasks with confidence rather than fear
- Bounces back from mistakes with resilience
- Maintains focus and persistence in the face of distraction
- Advocates for their needs and communicates their ideas clearly

**Will** enables focused attention and intentional action in the learning process. This essential quality helps children direct their energy toward goals and maintain engagement with challenges over time.

A child whose will is engaged in learning:

- Sustains concentration on self-chosen activities for extended periods
- Sets and works toward meaningful goals
- Navigates distractions and impulses to stay on course
- Takes initiative rather than waiting to be directed

These essential qualities don't need to be taught as separate skills; they are inherent aspects of the child's being. The parents' role is to recognize, reflect on, and create environments that support their child's natural expression throughout the learning process.

## Observational Learning and Will

The relationship between observational learning and the essential quality of personal will deserves special attention. Bandura's research demonstrates that children develop a significant portion of their sense of self-efficacy—their belief in their ability to succeed—by observing others overcome challenges.

When children witness others demonstrating will in learning contexts, they internalize powerful messages:

- Seeing a parent persist through a difficult task shows that challenges are normal parts of learning, not indications of failure.
- Watching a sibling recover from a mistake demonstrates that setbacks are temporary, not defining.
- Observing a teacher acknowledge their limitations models that strength includes vulnerability and honest self-assessment.
- Noticing how others manage frustration provides templates for emotional regulation during difficult learning experiences.

The quality of strength that children observe in learning contexts shapes not just what they know how to do but what they believe is possible for themselves. A child who regularly witnesses others demonstrate perseverance, resilience, and courage in learning develops an internal representation of themselves as someone capable of these same qualities.

Parents can intentionally model will in learning by:

- Letting children see them tackle challenging projects
- Verbalizing their problem-solving processes when facing difficulties
- Acknowledging struggles while demonstrating persistence
- Celebrating effort and growth rather than just achievement
- Sharing stories of overcoming obstacles in their learning journeys

Through these observations, children develop not just specific skills but the personal will that supports all future learning.

**Moral Development and Will**

The will, that deep current of intentionality and perseverance, is honed through the practices of Lawrence Kohlberg's stages of moral development. Here, the child learns to navigate the waters of right and wrong, of justice and fairness.

Kohlberg showed us that moral reasoning evolves, from avoiding punishment to acting from principle. As children grow, they don't just follow rules; they begin to develop an inner sense of direction. This maturation of morality mirrors the development of will, shifting from compliance to a more intentional approach. When we honor this shift, we help children move from "what will get me in trouble?" to "what feels right in my being?"

At this age, the child's sense of right and wrong lives in the immediacy of consequences—praise, punishment, reward. But beneath that simplicity is a moral compass in the making. How we guide, how we correct, and how we affirm–all shape the roots of a child's conscience. Before they know "right," they feel it.

Yet, in teaching morality, we must be cautious not to impose a will upon the child that silences their will. It is a dance as delicate as lace, where the will must be channeled without being dominated, guided without being suppressed.

When parents consistently override a child's will—"because I said so" becoming the default answer to "why?"—they may inadvertently teach that the child's will is invalid or ineffective. This can lead to passive resignation or rebellious defiance, neither of which represents a healthy development of will.

Conversely, when parents invite children into age-appropriate decision-making and honor their preferences when possible, they strengthen the child's sense of agency and efficacy. A three-year-old choosing between the red shirt or the blue, a four-year-old deciding which vegetable to have with dinner, a five-year-old determining how to solve a problem with a friend—these are all opportunities to exercise and develop will in a supported context.

Moral development and the development of will are intricately connected. As children progress through Kohlberg's stages, they move from being guided primarily by external authorities to developing internal principles that guide their choices. This internalization represents a maturation of will, from simply following directions to making decisions based on considered values and principles.

Parents can support this development by:

- Providing clear, consistent boundaries that help children understand the impact of their choices
- Explaining the reasons behind rules and expectations
- Engaging children in age-appropriate discussions about ethical dilemmas
- Respecting the child's growing capacity for moral reasoning
- Modeling ethical decision-making in their own lives

Through these approaches, parents help children develop a will that is both strong and guided by ethical principles, a will that expresses the child's essential nature while honoring the rights and needs of others.

**Parental Role in Nurturing Essence**

In these critical years, parents are the child's most influential teachers and the architects of the learning environment. The parental challenge is to inspire learning that amplifies the child's essence rather than diminishing it. It is to encourage a joy that resonates with the child's spirit, to foster a strength that supports their true nature, and to guide a will that aligns with their innermost self.

This is not just a treatise on developmental stages; it is an invitation to parents to reflect on their role in their child's learning. It is a call to cultivate an environment where joy is not a rarity but the norm, where strength is drawn from authenticity, and where will is understood as a powerful expression of the child's essence, an extension, and expression of what is moving the cosmos.

Parents nurture essence through learning when they:

- **See learning as discovery rather than acquisition:** Viewing learning as a process of uncovering what's already there rather than filling an empty vessel honors the child's innate wisdom and capacity. This perspective invites parents to act as guides who help children tap into their natural curiosity and intelligence, rather than instructors who impart knowledge.
- **Follow the child's lead and interests:** Children naturally gravitate toward learning experiences that resonate with their essential qualities and developmental needs. By observing closely and following these interests, parents support learning that aligns with essence rather than imposing adult agendas that may disconnect children from their authentic motivations.

- **Create rhythm and flow in learning:** Learning flourishes when it moves between different energies—concentration and relaxation, structure and freedom, individual and collaborative work. Parents who create rhythmic patterns that honor these natural cycles support both learning and essential connection.
- **Value process over product:** When parents focus on the quality of engagement rather than the outcome, they help children maintain connection to the essential joy of learning rather than becoming fixated on external measures of success. This doesn't mean ignoring results but instead seeing them as natural outgrowths of meaningful process.
- **Recognize essence in learning moments:** Parents who are attuned to essence can spot when essential qualities are emerging through learning activities—the will that manifests in determined problem-solving, the joy that bubbles up in discovery, the strength that initiates action and engagement. By noticing and naming these qualities, parents help children recognize and value their essence expressing through learning.
- **Model essence-connected learning:** When parents approach their child's learning with joy, strength, and will, when they demonstrate curiosity, persistence, and authentic engagement, they show children that these essential qualities remain vital throughout life. Children learn not only from what their parents teach them, but also from how their parents approach learning.

*Parents can benefit by allowing their children to reeducate and reconnect the parents to play.*

In teaching their children, parents learn about life, their children, and themselves. In the embrace of learning, remember that essence is not only preserved in what we allow the child to experience but also in what we encourage them to express.

**Essence and Learning**

From the perspective of essence, learning is not merely the acquisition of skills or information but an opportunity for the expression and integration of essential qualities. When learning aligns with a child's essential nature, it feels natural, engaging, and meaningful.

Consider how different essential qualities might manifest in learning:

- **Joy** infuses learning with delight and curiosity. A child connected to their Essential Joy approaches new experiences with enthusiasm rather than anxiety.

- **Will** provides the capacity to persist through challenges and setbacks. A child in touch with their Essential Will doesn't give up easily; instead, they approach difficulties with resilience.

- **Strength** enables focused attention and intentional action. A child who expresses Essential Strength engages deeply with subjects that capture their interest, displaying remarkable aliveness and expansiveness.

- **Clarity** allows for penetrating understanding. A child accessing Essential Clarity sees through confusion to grasp fundamental principles.

- **Value** fosters appreciation of both the learning process and one's capabilities. A child connected to Essential Value approaches learning with self-respect rather than seeking external validation.

When these Essential Qualities are recognized and supported, learning becomes not just more effective but more aligned with the child's true nature. Rather than imposing an external curriculum on the child, this approach allows learning to emerge from the meeting point of the child's essence and the world around them.

**The Dance Continues**

The dance of learning continues, a *pas de deux*, a dance for two, of growth and essence, where every step taken in joy, every display of strength, and every act of will is both a testament to the child's development and a homage to their unadulterated self.

As we move forward in our exploration of essence and development, we'll turn our attention to the social mirror: how children see themselves reflected in others and how these reflections shape both their developing self-concept and their connection to essence. But first, take a moment to reflect on your experience of learning:

- When have you experienced learning as a joyful, natural expression of your essence?

- How was will supported or suppressed in your educational experience?

- What models of strength did you observe as a child, and how have they shaped you?
- How might your experience influence how you approach learning with your child?

These reflections can help you become more conscious of how you dance the learning dance with your child, creating development opportunities that honor and preserve their essential nature.

In a world increasingly focused on academic achievement at earlier ages, this perspective offers a countercultural invitation to trust in the power of play, to value joy as much as knowledge, and to see learning not as preparation for some future accomplishment but as the natural unfolding of the child's essence in the present moment.

# Chapter 5
# The Social Mirror

In the heart of childhood, nestled between the innocence of infancy and the independence of adolescence, lies a critical stage of development: the child's discovery of the social mirror. This chapter examines how children, through their interactions with others, begin to perceive reflections of themselves and how these reflections influence their developing sense of self. It explores the nuanced interplay between individual essence and social identity, informed by the theoretical frameworks of Vygotsky, Erikson, and Bandura.

**Children See Themselves Through Others' Eyes**

As children grow beyond the initial stages of self-development, they enter a world of increasingly complex social relationships. These interactions create what sociologists call "the social mirror," a phenomenon in which children begin to see themselves reflected in the responses, judgments, and interactions of those around them.

Charles Horton Cooley's concept of the "looking-glass self" helps explain how children develop self-understanding through social reflections. According to this theory, we develop our sense of self through three steps:

1. We imagine how we appear to others
2. We imagine how others judge that appearance
3. We develop feelings about ourselves based on these imagined judgments

Children are particularly susceptible to this process as they're actively constructing their identity. Their developing cognitive abilities enable them to consider how others perceive them, but they may not yet possess the perspective-taking skills necessary to interpret these perceptions accurately.

Consider a two-year-old who has just completed a tower of blocks. She looks up expectantly at her father. If he responds with enthusiasm—"Wow, look at that tall tower you built!"—she not only registers his approval but also begins to see herself as someone who can accomplish things, who can create. If, instead, he barely glances up from his phone, she learns something quite different about her worth and capabilities.

This simple interaction illustrates how the social mirror works. Each response, each reaction from others, particularly significant caregivers, adds another brushstroke to the child's developing self-portrait.

The reflections children receive come in many forms:

- Verbal feedback and explicit statements ("You're so helpful!" or "Why are you always so difficult?")
- Facial expressions and body language (smiles, frowns, open arms, or turned backs)
- Attention or its absence (engaged presence or distracted dismissal)
- Comparisons with others ("Why can't you be quiet like your sister?")
- The roles they are assigned or allowed to take in play and family life

These reflections accumulate over time, creating patterns that shape how children see themselves and what they believe is possible for them.

**True and False Selves**

D.W. Winnicott's concept of the "true self" and "false self" provides profound insight into how social reflections influence identity development. According to Winnicott, the true self emerges when a child's spontaneous gestures and authentic expressions are met with attunement and responsiveness from caregivers. It represents the authentic core of the personality, the source of creativity, spontaneity, and genuine feeling.

The false self, in contrast, develops as a protective covering when the environment requires the child to comply with external demands at the expense of their authentic feelings and needs. Rather than responding to the child's genuine expressions, caregivers might impose their expectations, leading the child to develop a compliant façade that hides and protects the vulnerable, true self.

This distinction helps us understand the potential impact of the social mirror. When children consistently receive reflections that honor their authentic expressions, their true selves develop and flourish. But when the reflections they receive demand conformity to expectations that don't align with their inner experience, they support the developing sense of a false self designed to gain approval and avoid rejection.

The development of a false self isn't always pathological. We all develop social personas that help us function effectively in various contexts. The problem arises when the false self becomes rigid and disconnected from the true self, when children learn that only certain aspects of themselves are acceptable. In contrast, others must be hidden or denied.

Parents can support the development of the true self by:

- Responding to the child's actual expressions rather than to what they wish the child had expressed

- Creating space for authentic emotion, even when it's inconvenient or uncomfortable

- Valuing the child's unique way of being in the world rather than trying to shape them to match predetermined expectations

- Allowing the child to develop at their own pace rather than pushing them toward milestones for parental validation

When children feel their true self is seen, accepted, and celebrated, they develop a solid foundation for authentic living—one that can withstand the inevitable pressures toward conformity they will face as they move into broader social contexts.

**Mirrors of Development**

Erik Erikson's stages of psychosocial development remind us that societal expectations influence each stage of a child's growth. For example, the crisis of *initiative versus guilt* is profoundly shaped by the cultural narrative around autonomy and conformity. Here, the child learns either to embrace their innate drives for exploration and expression or to curb these impulses in favor of social approval.

Erikson's psychosocial theory offers a lens through which to view the child's burgeoning identity against the backdrop of societal expectations. The stages most relevant to early childhood include:

- **Trust vs. Mistrust (Birth to 1 Year):** During this stage, infants develop a sense of whether the world is fundamentally trustworthy, primarily based on the consistency and quality of caregiving they receive. The social mirror here is primarily the parents' responsiveness, which reflects to the baby whether their needs matter and will be met. This sets the foundation for all later development.

- **Autonomy vs. Shame and Doubt (1-3 Years):** As toddlers begin asserting their independence, they look to caregivers for reflections on their growing autonomy. When parents respond to their child's self-help attempts with patience and appropriate support, the child develops confidence in their capabilities. When met with excessive control or criticism, children may internalize a sense of shame about their impulses and doubt about their abilities.
- **Initiative vs. Guilt (3-6 Years):** During the preschool years, children's ventures into new activities, leadership, and creative play are either encouraged, leading to a sense of initiative, or derided as disruptive or inadequate, leading to feelings of guilt. The social mirror here reflects whether the child's ambitions and imagination are valued or viewed as problematic.

At each stage, how others respond to the child's developmental strivings shapes not just their immediate behavior but their enduring sense of who they are and what they can become. The reflections they receive through the social mirror directly influence how they resolve each stage's central crisis.

When a four-year-old eagerly volunteers to help set the table and is met with "You're too little, you'll break something," the mirror reflects an image of incompetence and limitation. If instead, the response is "I'd love your help! Here's how we can do it together," the mirror reflects capability and value. These reflections accumulate over time, forming the foundation of the child's self-concept.

The social mirror, in this sense, is not only reflective but directive, guiding the child toward a self-concept that aligns with or rebels against these external judgments.

## Parental Reflection Impacts a Child's Self-Perception

As the primary figures in the child's early life, parents hold a unique position in front of the social mirror. The way parents view and respond to their child not only reflects an image of the child but also sets the stage for how the child perceives themselves. It is here that essence—the child's innate qualities of joy, strength, and will, among others—face its greatest challenge and opportunity.

Parental reflections shape a child's self-perception through several mechanisms:

- **Direct Verbal Messages:** The words parents use to describe their children become internalized as self-definition. Labels like "shy," "difficult," "smart," or "helpful" don't just describe behavior; they suggest essential characteristics that children incorporate into their identity. Even casual remarks can have a lasting impact when they come from such significant figures.
- **Emotional Responses:** A parent's emotional reactions provide powerful feedback about a child's worth and acceptability. When a parent responds to a child's excitement with shared joy, the child learns their enthusiasm is valued. When met with consistent irritation, they may conclude there's something wrong with their natural exuberance.
- **Attention and Interest:** What parents pay attention to signals what they value. A child whose artistic efforts are met with genuine interest develops different self-perceptions than one whose artwork is barely acknowledged while academic achievements are celebrated.
- **Interpretation of Experiences:** Parents help children make meaning of their experiences through how they discuss and frame events. "You were so brave when you fell but got back up" versus "You're always so clumsy" offer very different templates for self-understanding after the same incident.
- **Physical Interaction:** The quality of physical contact—gentle or rough, frequent or rare, responsive or intrusive—communicates powerful messages about the child's body and being. Respectful, attentive touch helps children develop a positive sense of embodiment; disrespectful handling teaches very different lessons.

These parental reflections are particularly influential because they occur within a relationship of profound attachment and dependency. Children are biologically predisposed to absorb and internalize the messages they receive from their primary caregivers, making these early reflections especially formative.

Parents, through their interactions, have the power to affirm or obscure the child's essence. A parent's recognition and encouragement of the child's intrinsic qualities can strengthen their connection to their essential self, even in the face of external pressures to conform or adapt. Parents need to be mindful of the reflections they offer and to strive for images that honor the child's individuality while also preparing them for the realities of social integration.

**Essential Mirroring**

A child's developing sense of self is dependent upon parents for mirroring and reflecting what they see in the child. If the parent only sees the body, or focuses on the parent's hopes and dreams, or views the child as a boy named Joe or a girl named Lucy, then this is what the child internalizes into their sense of self. If we want our children to stay connected to their essence, then we need to mirror their essence back to them. This nurtures the connection between the developing sense of self and its essential ground.

This *essential mirroring* presents a direct challenge for parents to discern and appreciate the essence in their experience. Essence is not an idea, concept, or emotion. It is deeper, more fundamental, and subtler than our usual realm of experience.

Consider these everyday opportunities for essential mirroring:

- **When a child displays natural joy**: Rather than just saying "You're so happy today!" a parent might recognize and reflect the essential quality with "Wow, you seem full of yellow bubbles."

- **When a child persists at a challenging task**: Instead of only praising the outcome ("Good job finishing that puzzle!"), a parent might mirror the Essential Will with "You figured it out! You kept trying different approaches until you found what worked."

- **When a child expresses a clear preference for trying something**: Rather than dismissing it, a parent could acknowledge the Essential Strength with "Give it a go, let's see what you can do!"

This form of mirroring doesn't just validate behaviors; it recognizes and affirms the deeper qualities from which those behaviors arise. It helps the child maintain awareness of these qualities as aspects of their being, not just as things they do.

Essential mirroring differs from conventional praise or feedback in several important ways:

- It focuses on being rather than doing
- It reflects qualities rather than behaviors
- It acknowledges what is already present rather than evaluating performance

- It connects to deeper aspects of self rather than just external actions
- It is descriptive rather than judgmental

By practicing essential mirroring, parents help children maintain conscious connection to their authentic nature even as they develop the personality structures necessary for social functioning. This connection becomes a resource they can draw upon throughout their life, particularly during times of challenge or pressure to conform.

## Social Interaction in Identity Formation

Bandura's social learning theory further enriches our understanding by highlighting the power of observation and imitation. Children learn about themselves by mirroring the attitudes and actions of those around them. Through this process, they also develop an understanding of their will and the limits of their agency. The social mirror, thus, becomes a tool for self-definition as children adopt, adapt, and sometimes reject the behaviors they observe.

A five-year-old who sees her mother stand up for herself in a difficult conversation learns something about assertiveness and self-respect. A child who watches his father apologize after making a mistake learns about the importance of humility and accountability. These observed behaviors become potential templates for the child's self-expression.

Beyond the family, children's social circles gradually expand to include peers, teachers, extended family members, and community figures. Each of these relationships provides additional reflections that contribute to the child's developing self-concept:

- **Peer Relationships:** By around age 3, children begin developing genuine friendships based on mutual interests and enjoyment. These relationships provide powerful social reflections as children compare themselves to peers and receive direct feedback through play interactions. Being chosen or excluded, copied or criticized by peers creates strong messages about social acceptability and value.
- **Teacher Relationships:** Early childhood educators and caregivers become significant figures who provide authoritative reflections on the child's abilities, behavior, and social standing. A teacher's belief in a child's capabilities can profoundly influence their self-concept and academic trajectory.

- **Cultural Messages:** Even young children absorb messages from books, media, and cultural celebrations about what is valued, who belongs, and which characteristics are considered desirable. These broader social mirrors often reflect limited images that may not represent the diversity of human essence and potential.

Through these varied social interactions, children gradually construct a sense of identity that incorporates aspects of how they see themselves reflected in different relationships and contexts. This process isn't simply passive absorption; children actively interpret, sometimes resist, and ultimately integrate these reflections into their evolving self-concept.

The quality of these social interactions significantly influences whether children develop a self-concept that remains connected to their essence or one that becomes increasingly alienated from their authentic nature. Adults who interact with children from a place of essence-awareness can provide reflections that affirm rather than obscure essential qualities.

**Navigating the Social World While Preserving Essence**

The journey through the social mirror is fraught with both perils and possibilities. As children navigate their social worlds, they encounter a spectrum of reflections, some that resonate with their essence and others that challenge it. Parents can guide and support their children in this navigation, encouraging them to discern which reflections to internalize and which to let pass.

During the preschool years, children begin to engage more actively with peers, expanding their social mirror beyond the family. This brings new challenges and opportunities. Other children, teachers, and extended family members all contribute their reflections, some of which affirm and others potentially distort the child's self-image.

Parents can help children navigate this complex social landscape by:

- **Creating a Secure Base:** A strong, loving relationship with parents provides an emotional anchor from which children can explore social relationships without losing themselves in the process. This secure base enables children to venture into the social world with confidence, knowing they have a haven to return to when social waters become rough.
- **Discussing Social Experiences:** Talking with children about their social interactions helps them process and make sense of the various reflections

they encounter. When a child comes home upset because a peer criticized their drawing, parents have an opportunity to help them interpret this experience. Rather than simply dismissing the criticism ("Don't listen to them, your drawing is beautiful!"), parents can engage in a deeper conversation:

- "How did that make you feel when they said that?"
- "Do you think all drawings have to look the same to be good?"
- "What do you like about your drawing?"

These conversations help children develop the capacity to evaluate social reflections rather than simply absorbing them without question.

- **Offering Alternative Perspectives:** When children receive negative or limiting reflections, parents can offer different viewpoints that more accurately reflect the child's capabilities and essence. This doesn't mean denying difficult realities but providing a more balanced perspective that includes the child's strengths and intrinsic worth.
    - If a child has a learning difficulty that affects school performance, they may begin to see themselves as "stupid" based on social feedback. Parents can acknowledge the challenge while offering an alternative mirror: "Learning to read is taking a bit longer for you, but I notice how persistent you are and how you never give up even when things are hard. That determination is a powerful quality."
- **Modeling Authentic Relationships:** Children learn about relationships by watching the significant adults in their lives. By demonstrating respectful and authentic connections with others, parents show children how to interact in ways that honor both their essence and the essence of others.

Parents provide children with a template for relationships that support rather than diminish authentic self-expression when they model:

- Open communication
- Empathetic listening
- Healthy boundary-setting
- Conflict resolution
- Genuine appreciation of others

- **Teaching Social Skills Without Social Masks:** There's an important distinction between teaching children the social skills they need to function effectively in groups and encouraging them to develop a "social mask" that hides their true selves. Parents can help children navigate this distinction by:
    - Explaining the purpose behind social conventions rather than just enforcing rules
    - Acknowledging that different situations call for different behaviors without requiring personality changes
    - Validating their child's feelings even when those feelings need to be expressed appropriately
    - Distinguishing between behavior and identity ("That action wasn't kind" rather than "You're not being a nice person")
    - Creating home environments where authentic expression is welcomed and valued
- **Building Empathy Alongside Identity:** As children develop a stronger sense of self, they also need to develop awareness of others' perspectives and feelings. This dual development of identity and empathy creates the foundation for healthy social relationships.

    Parents can nurture this development by:
    - Encouraging perspective-taking: "How do you think your friend felt when that happened?"
    - Reading stories that explore different viewpoints
    - Discussing emotions in everyday situations
    - Pointing out the impact of actions on others
    - Validating the child's emotions while helping them understand others' feelings

    When children develop both a secure sense of self and empathy for others, they're equipped to build relationships that honor everyone's authentic being.

**Dance of Reflection and Essence**

The task ahead for parents is both delicate and profound: to guide their children in balancing the external influences of the social world with the internal guidance of their essential qualities. In doing so, they foster the development of a self that is not only capable of navigating the social landscape but also true to the unique essence that shines within.

This dance between reflection and essence is beautifully illustrated in the graph of essence and personality development introduced earlier. As children progress through early childhood, their personality structures naturally develop and strengthen through social interaction and mirroring. Without conscious attention to essence, this process can lead to a diminishing awareness of essential qualities.

Parents who engage in essential mirroring can help moderate this trend, maintaining a stronger connection between personality development and essence. The goal isn't to prevent the development of a functional personality, which is necessary for navigating the social world, but to ensure that this personality remains grounded in and informed by the child's essential nature.

Parents are encouraged to be mindful of their relationship with essence, recognizing how social conditioning has shaped their self-concept and perhaps obscured aspects of their essential nature. Through this self-awareness, parents can become more intentional about the reflections they offer their children, striving to mirror not only socially valuable behaviors but also the deeper, essential qualities that underlie them.

By creating a home environment that values both social competence and essential authenticity, parents provide their children with the best of both worlds—the skills they need to thrive in society and the connection to essence that allows them to live with meaning, purpose, and joy.

As we move forward in our exploration of childhood development, we'll turn our attention to the power of language and how the words we use shape our children's understanding of themselves and their world. The social mirror provides reflections through actions and responses. Language gives those reflections form and permanence, further influencing the delicate balance between essence and personality.

# Chapter 6
# Language and Labels

Language, the bedrock of human connection and understanding, unfolds its power in the early years of a child's life, not just as a medium of communication but as a tool for shaping reality. In this chapter, we explore the profound impact of language and labels on the child's developing sense of self and their perception of the world. Through the lens of developmental theories and the essence of Being, we examine how the words we use and the names we give become the foundational elements of identity and consciousness.

**Power of Naming in Shaping Reality**

As children acquire language, they begin the intricate process of categorizing and defining their experiences. Piaget's stages of cognitive development emphasize how language not only fosters cognitive growth but also contributes to the construction of reality. Each word a child learns is a thread in the tapestry of their understanding, a label that distinguishes, connects, isolates, and integrates.

Consider the moment when a child first learns to name emotions. Before having the word "sad," they experience a complex set of sensations—a heaviness in the chest, tears welling up, a sense of loss. Once they can label this constellation as "sadness," they gain a tool for communicating their experience. They also begin to package the experience into a neat category that may not fully capture its richness and uniqueness.

Language doesn't merely describe reality; it actively shapes it by determining what we notice, how we categorize experiences, and what we consider significant. For young children, this power is especially profound as they simultaneously acquire language and construct their understanding of the world.

When a parent points to a flower and says "rose," they're not just teaching vocabulary but directing attention to particular distinctions in the world. This flower (rose) is different from that one (daisy). When they describe a behavior as "helpful" or "mean," they're teaching ways of interpreting social actions. These linguistic patterns gradually become the child's frameworks for understanding.

As language philosopher Ludwig Wittgenstein observed, "The limits of my language mean the limits of my world." For children, the words they acquire quite literally determine what aspects of reality they can consciously perceive, remember, and communicate about.

Labels serve essential purposes in cognitive development and social functioning. They help children:

- Organize information into manageable categories
- Communicate experiences efficiently
- Develop conceptual frameworks for understanding
- Connect with shared social meanings

Yet with each label comes the potential for confinement. Words, in their necessity, can limit as much as they liberate. Language inherently involves abstraction, replacing direct experience with symbols that represent but can never fully capture that experience. Consider how differently a child experiences a sunset before and after learning the word "beautiful." Before acquiring the label, the experience might be a flood of sensations—vivid colors, changing light, and an emotional response. After acquiring the label, the same sunset might be quickly categorized as "beautiful" without the same immersion in its unique qualities.

**Words Define and Potentially Limit Experience**

Language also introduces cultural and conceptual filters. The words available in a particular language shape what children notice and how they interpret experience. Some languages have multiple words for types of snow, others distinguish between different kinds of love, and still others have terms for emotional states that have no direct equivalent in other languages. The vocabulary children acquire influences the distinctions they make in their experience.

The categories established through language can become rigid, creating artificial divisions in what might be more accurately understood as a continuum. When we teach children that emotions fall into discrete categories, such as "happy," "sad," and "angry," we may inadvertently limit their ability to recognize the complex blends of feelings that often characterize emotional experiences.

Perhaps most significantly, language introduces evaluation alongside description. Words like "good," "bad," "right," and "wrong" not only identify experiences but also judge them. These evaluative labels, particularly when applied to a child's behavior or characteristics, can have a profound impact on self-concept and emotional well-being.

For parents, the challenge is to use language in ways that expand rather than constrict their child's experience:

- Introducing rich, nuanced vocabulary that allows for subtle distinctions
- Being cautious about definitive labels, especially those that seem to define the child's character or potential
- Acknowledging the limitations of language by sometimes pointing to experiences that words can't fully capture
- Recognizing and respecting experiences that might be pre-verbal or beyond verbal expression

By approaching language with an awareness of both its gifts and its limitations, parents can help children develop linguistic tools that serve, rather than restrict, their understanding of themselves and their world.

**Moral Development and Right and Wrong**

Lawrence Kohlberg's stages of moral development help us understand how children's moral reasoning evolves, from simple obedience to rules to more complex ethical understanding. How we discuss right and wrong plays a crucial role in this development.

Children in the early years often make moral choices to avoid punishment or gain approval, which Kohlberg referred to as the pre-conventional stage. But even these simple decisions are formative. They're where the child's will is being sculpted—tested, thwarted, encouraged. How we respond at this level shapes whether their will becomes compliant, defiant, or empowered with inner guidance.

The language parents use to discuss moral issues significantly influences how children develop their understanding of right and wrong. When parents exclusively use punishment-focused language ("If you hit your sister, you'll go to time-out"), they reinforce Stage 1 moral reasoning, which is based on avoiding negative consequences rather than understanding the inherent reasons for moral behavior.

As children develop, language that emphasizes the impact of actions on others helps them move toward more sophisticated moral understanding. "When you take your brother's toy, he feels sad because he was playing with it" focuses attention on the effects of behavior rather than just the rules or consequences.

Kohlberg's framework reminds us that young children aren't capable of understanding complex ethical principles abstractly. They learn through concrete examples, clear explanations, and consistent modeling. The words parents use to explain moral concepts should match the child's developmental level while gradually introducing more complex understandings.

Parents can support moral development through language by:

- Explaining the reasons behind rules in terms that children can understand
- Using language that focuses on impact rather than just obedience
- Gradually introducing more complex moral concepts as children develop
- Engaging children in age-appropriate discussions about fairness and care for others
- Narrating moral decisions in daily life to make moral reasoning visible
- Using stories to explore moral dilemmas in accessible ways

By being mindful of how they discuss moral concepts, parents can help children develop a moral understanding that goes beyond simple rule-following to encompass empathy, fairness, and eventually principled reasoning.

**Impact of Labels on Self-Concept**

Labels become particularly powerful when applied to the child's identity rather than just their experiences or behaviors. Being labeled as "the shy one," "our little athlete," or "the smart one" may initially seem affirming, but it can also create pressure to maintain that identity or make it difficult to explore other aspects of oneself.

The language we use to describe children doesn't just reflect our perceptions; it actively shapes how they perceive themselves. When a parent repeatedly describes a child as "my sensitive one" or "our little troublemaker," these characterizations become internalized as core aspects of the child's identity, rather than temporary behaviors or states of being.

Research in psychology has demonstrated the profound impact of labeling on self-concept and behavior:

- Children labeled as "smart" often become more concerned with preserving that image than with learning, avoiding challenges that might threaten their "smart" identity.

- Children described as "shy" tend to behave more cautiously in social situations, living up to the label even if they might otherwise be more outgoing.

- Labels that attribute behavior to fixed traits ("You're so impatient") lead to less improvement than language focusing on specific behaviors ("You interrupted before I finished explaining").

The most limiting labels are those that suggest fixed, global traits rather than specific behaviors or temporary states. "You're a bad listener" conveys something fundamental and unchangeable about the child, while "You're having trouble focusing right now" acknowledges a temporary challenge that can be addressed.

These identity labels are powerful because children naturally look to significant adults for help in understanding who they are. Parents represent authoritative sources of information about the child's self, and their characterizations carry tremendous weight.

Parents can minimize the limiting effects of labels by:

- Describing behaviors rather than assigning trait labels: "You worked persistently on that puzzle" rather than "You're so smart."

- Using temporary language for challenging behaviors: "You're having a hard time sharing today" rather than "You're selfish."

- Avoiding comparisons that create fixed identities: "Sam enjoys quiet activities while Alex prefers active games" rather than "Sam is our shy one, and Alex is our outgoing one."

- Noticing when children begin to define themselves through labels and gently expanding those self-definitions: "You enjoy drawing, and you're also exploring music now."

- Being aware of subtle labeling in everyday language: "Are you being shy again?" reinforces shyness as an identity

By becoming more conscious of the labels they use, parents can create space for children to explore different aspects of themselves without being confined by premature or limiting definitions.

## Using Language that Preserves Connection to Essence

In recognizing the power of language, parents and caregivers are called upon to wield it with conscious intent. The challenge is to use language that nurtures the child's essence, celebrates their unique qualities, and supports their burgeoning sense of self. This involves moving beyond fixed labels to a language of possibility and open-endedness that embraces the child's potential for growth and change.

The role of language in connecting to the essential self, as explored by A.H. Almaas, suggests that our words can either bridge the gap between immediate experience and essence or widen it. By choosing words that resonate with the child's intrinsic qualities, such as strength, joy, and curiosity, we can help maintain their connection to essence, even as they learn to navigate the social constructs of language.

Here are practical strategies for using language that nurtures essence:

- **Describe rather than evaluate:** Instead of saying "Good job!" try "You worked hard on that" or "I notice how carefully you placed each piece." Description helps children develop their internal standards rather than becoming dependent on external approval.

- **Use process language:** Focus on the journey rather than just the outcome. Acknowledging the process of learning and the development of strategic thinking, "You tried several different ways to solve that problem," highlights the journey.

- **Offer specific feedback:** Replace vague praise, such as "You're so smart," with specific observations, like "You found a creative solution to that challenge." Specificity helps children recognize particular strengths and capabilities.

- **Acknowledge feelings without judgment:** Validate emotions without labeling them as good or bad. Saying, "You seem frustrated right now," helps children recognize and name their feelings without suggesting that the feelings themselves are problematic.

- **Avoid absolute labels:** Words like "always," "never," and permanent trait labels ("You're shy") limit the child's sense of possibility and change.

Instead, use language that acknowledges the temporality of states: "You're feeling shy in this situation."

- **Recognize essence directly:** When you observe essential qualities manifesting, name them. "I see your joy bubbling up" or "Your strength is shining through right now" helps children maintain awareness of these deeper aspects of themselves.

- **Use wondering questions:** Questions like "I wonder what would happen if..." invite exploration rather than demanding answers. They open possibilities rather than narrowing focus.

- **Share your experience:** "When I look at that sunset, I feel a sense of peace." This model connects language with direct experience rather than reducing experiences to labels.

These approaches help children develop a language that connects rather than separates, that expresses rather than reduces, and that remains fluid rather than becoming rigid.

## Language Acquisition and Its Impact on Self-Concept

Language acquisition represents a significant advancement in a child's capacity for self-awareness. When children master language, they gain powerful tools for self-reflection, self-description, and self-regulation.

Around 18 months, most children begin using their names to refer to themselves. By age 2, they regularly use "I," "me," and "mine," indicating a growing awareness of themselves as distinct individuals. This linguistic milestone both reflects and reinforces their developing self-concept.

Vygotsky emphasized the importance of private speech, the child's talking to themselves out loud, as a precursor to inner speech, the silent self-talk that becomes a powerful tool for self-regulation and reflection. As children internalize language, they develop the ability to reflect on their thoughts, feelings, and actions—a critical component of self-awareness.

As language skills continue to develop in the preschool years, children begin constructing personal narratives, stories about their experiences that connect past, present, and future. These narratives help organize and make meaning of their experiences, contributing significantly to their sense of a continuous, coherent self over time. When parents engage in memory-sharing conversations with their children, they support this vital aspect of self-development.

The quality of language children acquire during these formative years has a significant influence on how they understand themselves. Children who develop rich emotional vocabulary can identify and express subtle feelings, while those with limited emotional language may experience emotions as confusing or overwhelming. Similarly, children who learn varied and nuanced ways to describe personal qualities develop more complex self-concepts than those limited to simple, binary descriptions.

Parents play a crucial role in this process by:

- Engaging in rich, responsive conversations that extend the child's language
- Narrating experiences in ways that help children integrate them into their self-understanding
- Providing language for internal states that might otherwise remain unclear
- Supporting the development of autobiographical memory through reminiscing conversations
- Modeling self-reflection and self-description in their speech

Through these interactions, children gradually internalize not only vocabulary but also ways of organizing their experiences and understanding themselves, which will influence their self-concept throughout life.

**Self-Expression Through Language**

As children develop language skills, they gain powerful tools for expressing their authentic selves. Language enables them to communicate their preferences, share inner experiences, advocate for their needs, and connect with others through the exchange of ideas and emotions.

Self-expression through language evolves dramatically during early childhood:

- **18-24 months:** Children begin expressing ownership and preferences with simple phrases like "mine" and "no," asserting their emerging sense of self through language.

- **2-3 years:** More complex sentences allow for the expression of feelings, desires, and straightforward explanations. "I sad when daddy go" or "I want big truck" give voice to inner states and intentions.

- **3-4 years:** Language becomes a tool for sharing imaginative ideas, negotiating with others, and explaining their thinking. "Let's pretend we're dragons living in a cave," or "I'm drawing a rainbow family because they make me happy," reveal the richness of inner life.

- **4-6 years:** Children begin using language to position themselves in their social world, narrate personal experiences, and express more complex emotions and thoughts. "I'm not afraid of the dark anymore because I have my special flashlight," demonstrates growing self-reflection and the expression of identity.

Through these stages, language becomes an increasingly nuanced instrument through which children can express their essence. The child who declares, "I love feeling the wind in my hair when I swing high!" is sharing not just a preference but a direct experience of joy and aliveness that reflects their essential nature.

A child's capacity for self-expression depends significantly on the linguistic environment that adults create. When adults rush, interrupt, correct, or dismiss children's verbal expressions, they may inadvertently teach children to censor or doubt their authentic communication. Conversely, when adults listen attentively, respond thoughtfully, and value children's verbal expressions, they foster the development of confident and clear self-expression.

Parents can support authentic self-expression by:

- Creating unhurried opportunities for conversation
- Listening fully without interrupting or immediately correcting
- Asking open-ended questions that invite elaboration
- Validating children's verbal expressions, even when disagreeing with the content
- Modeling honest, respectful self-expression in their communication

When children experience language as a reliable means of expressing their authentic selves, they develop confidence in both their voice and their inner experiences. This foundation supports not only social communication but also the ongoing dialogue with themselves that shapes their identity and enables self-understanding.

**Nurturing Essence Through Mindful Language**

The words we use with children don't just describe reality; they help create it. By cultivating mindful language practices, parents can nurture their child's connection to essence while supporting healthy development.

Mindful language starts with conscious presence. When parents communicate from essence themselves—speaking from a place of authenticity rather than reactivity or habit—they model the connection between language and being. This presence is felt beyond the words themselves, creating a context where essence can be recognized and expressed.

Parents can nurture essence through language in everyday interactions:

- **In moments of achievement:** Instead of: "Good job! You're so smart!" Try: "I notice how focused you were on figuring that out. Your determination really showed through."

    This acknowledges the essential quality (will) rather than labeling the child or evaluating the outcome.

- **In difficult moments:** Instead of: "Stop being so difficult!" Try: "I see you're having strong feelings right now. It's okay to feel frustrated; let's find a way through this together."

    This separates behavior from identity while acknowledging the authenticity of the child's experience.

- **In moments of exploration:** Instead of: "Be careful! Don't make a mess!" Try: "I see your curiosity taking you on an adventure. What are you discovering?"

    This affirms the essential quality of curiosity rather than focusing on potential problems.

- **In quiet moments:** Instead of: "Why are you so shy?" Try: "You're taking your time to observe before joining in. I appreciate how thoughtful you are."

    This reframes perceived shyness as the positive quality of thoughtfulness.

- **In moments of connection:** Instead of: "You're such a good helper!" Try: "When you helped set the table, I felt your kindness and care for our family."

    This acknowledges the essential quality (kindness) expressed through the behavior rather than labeling the child.

These language practices don't require extraordinary effort but rather a shift in awareness and intention. By bringing mindfulness to our words, we help children maintain connection to their essence even as they navigate the complexities of language and social meaning.

The impact of mindful language accumulates over time, creating patterns of communication that either support or diminish essential connection. When children consistently hear language that recognizes and affirms their essential qualities, they develop the capacity to recognize these qualities in themselves, even when external reflections might not acknowledge them.

**Impact of Cultural Narratives and Language**

Beyond individual interactions, children are immersed in broader cultural narratives and linguistic frameworks that shape their understanding of themselves and the world. These include:

### Gender Narratives

The language used to describe boys versus girls often contains subtle or overt messages about appropriate behaviors, interests, and qualities. Research shows that adults use different language with children based on perceived gender, using more emotional words with girls and more achievement-oriented words with boys, creating linguistic environments that shape gender identity development.

Parents can counter limiting gender narratives by:

- Using similar emotional vocabulary with children of all genders
- Avoiding gender-based generalizations ("boys will be boys")
- Providing exposure to counter-stereotypical language and stories
- Consciously expanding the adjectives used to describe children beyond gender-typical traits

**Achievement Narratives**

Cultural messages about what constitutes success and how it should be pursued influence children's goals and self-evaluation. The prevalent achievement-oriented language in many educational and family settings creates particular pressures and expectations.

Parents can create more balanced narratives by:

- Discussing multiple forms of success beyond academics and competition
- Using language that values effort and learning, not just results
- Acknowledging the role of collaboration alongside individual achievement
- Explicitly valuing character qualities alongside performance

**Identity Narratives**

Stories about who we are as a family, community, or cultural group provide templates for self-awareness and understanding. These narratives, passed through language, help children locate themselves within meaningful traditions and collective identities.

Parents can foster healthy identity narratives by:

- Sharing family and cultural stories that provide roots and meaning
- Using language that connects children to positive aspects of heritage
- Creating space for children to develop their relationship to collective identities
- Avoiding language that creates rigid boundaries between groups

**Moral Narratives**

Language around "good" and "bad" behavior shapes children's ethical framework and often their sense of self-worth. The way we discuss morality can foster either rigid judgmentalism or thoughtful ethical awareness.

Parents can nurture healthy moral development through language by:

- Separating behavior from identity ("That word wasn't very kind" versus "You're not a kind person")
- Discussing impacts rather than just rules ("When you hit, it hurts")
- Using language of repair and growth rather than punishment and shame
- Modeling moral reasoning through their language about ethical choices

By becoming aware of these cultural narratives embedded in everyday language, parents can help children navigate them more consciously, accepting helpful aspects while questioning limiting or harmful messages.

**Words as Bridges, Not Barriers to Essence**

Language, at its best, serves as a bridge connecting inner experience, essence, and shared understanding. When used consciously, words can help children articulate their authentic experience without reducing or restricting it.

As shown in our graph of essence and personality development, language acquisition coincides with a period when the connection to essence typically diminishes as personality structures strengthen. By cultivating language that honors essence, parents can help moderate this trend, maintaining a stronger connection between verbal expression and essential experience.

The goal isn't to limit language development, which is crucial for functioning in the world, but to ensure that language serves as a tool for expressing essence rather than obscuring it. By choosing words that reflect the depth and authenticity of experience, we help children develop a relationship with language that enriches rather than diminishes their connection to their essential nature.

For parents seeking to use language as a bridge to essence, remember that:

- Words don't need to replace direct experience but can point toward it
- Labeling isn't the same as understanding
- Sometimes silence or non-verbal communication better honors essence than words

- The way we speak matters as much as what we say
- Language can evoke essence as well as describe it

As language philosopher Martin Buber wrote, "All real living is meeting." When we use language that facilitates genuine meeting with others, with experience, with essence, we help our children maintain connection to the depth and wholeness of being that exists beyond words.

In our exploration of language and labels, we've seen how the words we use shape not just communication but consciousness itself. For children developing both language skills and a sense of self, the linguistic environment we create has a profound influence on their understanding of themselves and their world.

By approaching language with mindfulness, recognizing its power to both liberate and constrain, parents can create verbal environments that support both essential connection and effective communication. The words we choose become the lenses through which our children see themselves, and with conscious attention, we can ensure these lenses clarify rather than distort.

Take a moment to reflect on your relationship with language:

- What labels from childhood still influence how you see yourself?
- How do you experience the relationship between words and direct experience?
- What phrases or types of language help you feel most connected to your authentic self?

These reflections can inform how you approach language with your child, helping you create verbal environments that nurture both effective communication and essential connection.

# Chapter 7
# The Authority of Culture

In childhood development, culture acts as both a backdrop and a weave, influencing not just the patterns that emerge but the very texture of being. This chapter delves into the intricate interplay between cultural norms, societal expectations, and the child's developing sense of self, examining how these external forces shape, support, and sometimes hinder the child's essence and individuality.

**Culture Shapes Expectations and Identity**

Culture provides a context within which the child's sense of identity is nurtured, encompassing the values, beliefs, and practices that define what is expected, desirable, and acceptable within a society. Children are immersed in this cultural milieu from the earliest days of life, absorbing its nuances through observation, participation, and instruction.

From the moment of birth, cultural expectations begin to shape the child's experience. Consider how differently a newborn might be welcomed in various cultures:

- In some societies, babies are constantly held and carried, fostering a sense of close physical connection
- In others, independent sleep is emphasized from early on, promoting separate spaces
- Some cultures celebrate birth with elaborate rituals that welcome the child into a community
- Others maintain periods of seclusion for mother and baby

These early patterns establish foundational assumptions about connection, independence, community, and identity that will shape the child's perspective throughout life.

As development progresses, cultural conditioning becomes increasingly complex, shaping:

- Gender expectations and expressions

- Relationship patterns and communication styles
- Values around achievement, cooperation, and competition
- Attitudes toward authority, tradition, and change
- Relationship to time, planning, and spontaneity
- Expression and regulation of emotions
- Spiritual and existential understanding

Children are remarkably attuned to these cultural messages, internalizing not only the explicit teachings but also the implicit assumptions that permeate everyday interactions.

Cultural transmission happens through multiple channels:

- **Direct Instruction:** Adults explicitly teach children cultural values, rules, and practices through explanations, corrections, and formal education.
- **Observation and Modeling:** Children continuously observe how adults and older children behave, incorporating these patterns into their behavior. As Albert Bandura's social learning theory demonstrates, children don't need direct reinforcement to adopt culturally modeled behaviors; they naturally imitate what they see, especially from those they identify with or who hold status.
- **Narratives and Stories:** The stories, myths, and entertainment media children encounter convey powerful messages about what is valued, what is possible, and what is taboo within their culture. These narratives provide templates for understanding oneself and one's place in the world.
- **Reward and Punishment:** Children quickly learn which behaviors elicit approval and which result in correction or disapproval. Through this ongoing feedback, they internalize cultural standards and expectations.
- **Participation in Rituals and Routines:** By engaging in cultural practices, from everyday routines like mealtimes to special celebrations and ceremonies, children embody cultural patterns that shape their experience of self and community.

These processes of cultural transmission aren't necessarily problematic. Cultures provide essential frameworks that help children organize their experience, develop shared meaning with others, and navigate social interactions successfully. Cultural traditions can offer rich resources for meaning, connection, and identity.

The challenge arises when cultural conditioning becomes so rigid that it obscures or suppresses the child's essential nature. When cultural expectations demand conformity at the expense of authenticity, children may lose touch with their intrinsic qualities and potential.

**Balance Between Socialization and Individuality**

The tension between socialization—learning to function effectively within one's culture—and individuality—expressing one's unique essence and potential—is a fundamental challenge of human development. Both are necessary; neither alone is sufficient for thriving.

**Necessity of Socialization**

Adequate socialization provides children with crucial benefits:

- Language and communication skills for connecting with others
- Social norms that make interactions predictable and safe
- Shared values that create community cohesion
- Practical knowledge accumulated through cultural history
- Identity within a larger social context

Without adequate socialization, children struggle to function in social groups, access cultural resources, or develop the shared understandings necessary for cooperation and community.

**Imperative of Individuality**

At the same time, honoring individuality is essential for healthy development:

- Expression of unique talents and potentials
- Connection to intrinsic motivation and authentic interests
- Development of innovative thinking and creativity
- Psychological well-being through authenticity
- Connection to essential qualities that transcend cultural conditioning

When individuality is suppressed in the name of socialization, children may develop what psychologist D.W. Winnicott called a "false self," a compliant persona that meets external expectations while hiding authentic feelings, needs, and expressions.

**Finding the Balance**

The optimal approach is neither complete conformity to cultural expectations nor rejection of all social norms, but rather a dynamic balance that allows children to function effectively within their culture while maintaining connection to their authentic nature.

This balance looks different across cultures. Some societies emphasize collective harmony and expect greater conformity to group norms, while others place a higher value on individual expression and unique contributions. However, even within the most collectivist cultures, there remain spaces for individual variation, and even the most individualistic cultures require basic socialization.

Parents play a crucial role in helping children navigate this balance by:

- Clarifying which cultural expectations are negotiable preferences versus essential values
- Creating family cultures that both honor heritage and allow for authentic expression
- Discussing cultural messages explicitly, helping children become conscious of influences rather than merely absorbing them
- Supporting connection to essence even while teaching necessary social skills
- Modeling their thoughtful engagement with culture rather than either rigid conformity or reactive rejection

Through these approaches, parents help children develop what might be called "conscious socialization," the ability to function effectively within cultural contexts while maintaining awareness of and connection to their deeper nature.

**Attachment Theory and Cultural Context**

Attachment theory offers valuable insights into the relationship between culture and development. While the basic human need for secure attachment is universal, the specific expressions of attachment and caregiving practices vary significantly across cultures.

**Universal Attachment Needs**

Across cultures, secure attachment develops when caregivers are consistently responsive to the child's signals and needs. This responsiveness fosters an internal working model of oneself as worthy of care and others as reliable, laying the foundation for healthy relationships throughout life.

Insecure attachment patterns—avoidant, ambivalent, or disorganized—develop when caregiving is consistently unresponsive, inconsistent, or frightening. These patterns are observed across cultures, though their prevalence varies.

**Cultural Variations in Attachment Practices**

While the need for secure attachment is universal, cultures differ dramatically in how they structure early caregiving:

- In many traditional societies, infants are carried throughout the day, sleep with parents, and are fed on demand, practices that minimize separation and maximize physical proximity.

- In Western industrialized societies, independent sleep, scheduled feeding, and regular separations are more common, practices that emphasize autonomy from an early age.

- Some cultures involve multiple caregivers from birth, with extended family members, siblings, or community members sharing care alongside the mother.

- Others emphasize the primary mother-child bond, with father and other family members in supporting roles.

These variations reflect different cultural values and ecological contexts. No single approach is universally "best;" each has evolved to prepare children for functioning within a particular cultural environment.

**Culture, Attachment, and Essence**

The relationship between attachment practices, cultural context, and connection to essence is complex.

Some traditional practices that maximize physical proximity and responsive care may support secure attachment and essential connection by reducing stress and allowing for attunement to the child's authentic expressions.

However, cultures with these practices may also have rigid gender expectations or hierarchical social structures that limit authentic expression in other ways.

Conversely, Western emphasis on independence may support certain expressions of individuality while creating attachment challenges through early separations or pressure for self-sufficiency.

The key isn't adopting any particular cultural model wholesale but understanding the underlying psychological needs that transcend cultural variation:

- Children need consistent, responsive care that builds basic trust
- They need attunement to their unique temperament and essence
- They need support for both connection and developing autonomy
- They need cultural preparation without sacrificing authenticity

Parents who understand both attachment principles and their cultural context can make conscious choices about caregiving practices, adapting cultural traditions to support their child's specific needs while preparing them for their social environment.

**Role of Rebellion in Developing an Authentic Self**

Rebellion, often seen as a phase of teenage angst, begins much earlier as children test the boundaries of their identity and autonomy. Think *terrible twos*. This resistance against cultural norms and expectations is a natural part of the developmental journey, serving as a crucible for forming a robust and authentic self.

**Psychological Function of Rebellion**

Developmental psychologists recognize that rebellion serves necessary psychological functions:

- **Boundary Definition:** Through pushing against boundaries, children discover where others end and they begin. This process is essential for developing a distinct sense of self.

- **Agency Development:** By saying "no" and asserting preferences, children experience themselves as causal agents capable of affecting their environment rather than merely passive recipients of others' decisions.
- **Identity Exploration:** Testing rules and expectations enables children to discern which cultural values align with their authentic experiences and which feel foreign or imposed.
- **Competence Building:** Successfully negotiating for greater autonomy fosters confidence in advocating for oneself and navigating social systems.

Far from being merely oppositional or problematic, these moments of resistance represent essential developmental work. When parents understand the underlying needs driving rebellion, they can respond more effectively to support healthy autonomy while maintaining necessary boundaries.

**Developmental Progression of Autonomy**

The journey toward autonomy unfolds across childhood:

- **Toddlerhood (1-3 years):** The "terrible twos" represent the first significant assertion of autonomy, as children discover and frequently deploy the power of "no." This stage is characterized by the psychosocial crisis that Erikson termed "autonomy versus shame and doubt." Children are driven to establish that they are separate beings with their own will.
- **Early Childhood (3-6 years):** Children begin testing not just whether they can oppose adults but whether they can create and enforce their own rules and systems. They may become intensely interested in fairness and rule-following, often holding adults accountable to the standards they've established.
- **Middle Childhood (6-11 years):** Social groups become increasingly important, and children may begin to test family values against peer values, experimenting with different ways of being in various contexts. They develop more sophisticated negotiation strategies and may question the reasoning behind rules rather than simply opposing them.
- **Adolescence (12-18 years):** The search for identity intensifies with more fundamental questioning of cultural values and expectations. Teenagers often experiment with different identities, affiliations, and belief systems as they strive to develop an authentic sense of self that strikes a balance between individuality and social belonging.

Throughout these stages, children are engaged in the fundamental task of developing a sense of self and individuality. This developmental task involves breaking through pre-existing, externally imposed boundaries and constructing new ones that more accurately represent and express the emerging sense of self.

Through this process of differentiation and boundary formation, individuals help carve out their unique identity, learning to distinguish between who they are and who they are not, both in terms of their internal world of feelings and thoughts and their external world of relationships and societal roles. This journey toward self-definition and autonomy often involves a series of negotiations between the self and the outer world, requiring both courage and resilience to explore new territories of being and to assert one's place within them.

**Almaas's Perspective on Rebellion and Authenticity**

Almaas's work on essence provides a lens through which to view rebellion not as defiance for its own sake but as a quest for authenticity in a world that often demands conformity. This process can be understood as the soul's attempt to maintain or recover connection with its essential nature when external forces pull toward identification with limiting self-concepts.

When children resist cultural expectations that conflict with their essential qualities, they're engaged in a profound form of truth-seeking. The child who refuses to suppress their natural exuberance in settings demanding quiet compliance, or who insists on their creative approach despite pressure to follow a prescribed method, may be protecting their connection to essential joy or strength.

Supporting children through these phases of resistance requires a delicate balance, acknowledging the validity of their search for self and meaning while guiding them through the complexities of societal integration. Parents who can distinguish between resistance that serves authentic development and behavior that merely evades necessary growth can provide valuable guidance through this challenging terrain.

**Preserving Essence While Navigating Cultural Norms**

Parents, educators, and caregivers should strive to recognize and respect the powerful influence of culture on a child's development, while advocating for spaces where children can freely explore and express their essence. This involves creating home and educational environments that honor diversity and encourage critical thinking, empathy, and self-expression.

**Creating Balance Between Culture and Essence**

Finding a balance between cultural integration and connection to essence requires thoughtful attention:

- **Distinguish Between Values and Conventions:** Help children understand the difference between core ethical principles (like treating others with respect) and cultural conventions (like specific table manners). This helps them navigate which expectations are negotiable and which represent deeper, more fundamental values.
- **Provide Cultural Context:** Rather than presenting cultural norms as absolute truths, offer context that helps children understand why certain practices have developed. This cultural literacy enables children to make sense of expectations while maintaining critical thinking.
- **Create Safe Spaces for Authenticity:** Ensure that the home provides a sanctuary where children can express their authentic feelings, questions, and perspectives without fear of judgment. This creates a secure base from which they can navigate more complex social environments.
- **Model Thoughtful Cultural Engagement:** Demonstrate how adults can honor cultural traditions while making conscious choices about which aspects to embrace, adapt, or respectfully question. This balanced approach shows children that culture can be a resource rather than a constraint.
- **Encourage Reflection on Cultural Messages:** Help children develop media literacy and critical thinking by discussing the messages embedded in stories, advertisements, entertainment, and other cultural products. Questions like "What is this teaching us about what's important?" or "Who might feel left out by this story?" foster thoughtful cultural engagement.

**Supporting Children's Navigation of Cultural Expectations**

Practical strategies for supporting children include:

- **Offer choices within boundaries:** Establish clear non-negotiable boundaries around safety and core values, while providing ample space for choice within those boundaries. This combination of structure and freedom helps children learn to exercise autonomy responsibly.
- **Validate feelings while guiding behavior:** Acknowledge children's natural feelings even when their behavior needs redirection. "I understand you're feeling angry, and it's not okay to hit," teaches that emotions are acceptable while specific actions are not.

- **Encourage perspective-taking:** Help children consider different viewpoints about cultural practices by asking questions like, "Why might some families do things differently than we do?" This develops the capacity to hold multiple perspectives simultaneously.
- **Celebrate diversity:** Expose children to diverse cultural traditions, stories, foods, music, and perspectives. This helps them recognize that there are many valid ways of being human rather than a single "right" way.
- **Address stereotypes directly:** When children encounter limiting stereotypes based on gender, race, ability, or other factors, engage in age-appropriate conversations that challenge these narrow views and affirm the diversity of human potential.

## Cultural Influences on Identity Formation

Culture profoundly shapes how children understand themselves and their place in the world. From gender roles to racial identity, from religious beliefs to national belonging, cultural messages provide templates that children use to construct their sense of self.

## Gender Identity Development

Perhaps no aspect of identity is more culturally influenced than gender. From the moment of birth (or before, with gendered baby showers and nursery decorations), children are immersed in cultural messages about what it means to be a boy or a girl in their society.

These messages are conveyed through:

- Explicit statements ("Boys don't cry," "That's not ladylike")
- Clothing and appearance norms
- Toy selection and play expectations
- Media representations of gender roles
- Adult modeling of gendered behavior
- Differential treatment based on perceived gender

By age 3, most children have internalized basic cultural gender expectations and can categorize themselves and others by gender. By early elementary school, many have developed rigid ideas about appropriate gender behavior unless adults have actively countered stereotypical messaging.

Parents can support healthy gender identity development by:

- Providing access to diverse toys, activities, and role models
- Avoiding language that limits possibilities based on gender
- Discussing media messages about gender explicitly
- Supporting the child's authentic expressions regardless of traditional gender associations
- Respecting gender diversity in themselves and others

**Racial and Ethnic Identity**

Children begin to notice racial differences as early as infancy, with the recognition of distinct features solidifying between the ages of 2 and 3. By ages 4-5, many children have absorbed cultural messages about racial and ethnic groups, including potential biases and stereotypes.

For children from dominant cultural groups, these messages often remain implicit and unexamined. For children from marginalized groups, racial and ethnic identity development becomes a more conscious process of negotiating between heritage pride and societal prejudice.

Parents can support healthy racial and ethnic identity by:

- Providing books, media, and experiences that represent diverse people positively
- Discussing cultural heritage with pride and context
- Addressing stereotypes and prejudice directly in age-appropriate ways
- Creating connections with diverse communities
- Modeling respect and appreciation for cultural differences

**Religious and Spiritual Identity**

Cultural and family religious traditions provide powerful frameworks for understanding existence, purpose, and values. Children absorb religious concepts and practices through participation in rituals, stories, and community experiences.

For some children, religious identity provides continuity, meaning, and ethical guidance. For others, tension may arise between religious teachings and personal experience or between family religious expectations and broader social contexts.

Parents can support healthy religious and spiritual development by:

- Providing age-appropriate spiritual education that respects the child's questions
- Creating space for wonder and mystery alongside specific teachings
- Distinguishing between core spiritual values and cultural expressions
- Respecting the child's developing spiritual perspective even when it differs from family tradition
- Modeling authentic engagement with spiritual questions rather than rigid certainty

**Socioeconomic Identity**

Cultural messages about social class, wealth, and status have a profound influence on children's self-concept and aspirations. Even young children absorb implicit messages about the value associated with different occupations, possessions, neighborhoods, and educational backgrounds.

These influences shape not just material expectations but concepts of dignity, worth, and possibility. Children from different socioeconomic backgrounds often develop distinct relationships with authority, distinct communication styles, and other assumptions about their futures, influenced by cultural messaging.

Parents can support healthy development in this area by:

- Teaching critical thinking about materialism and status symbols
- Emphasizing values that transcend economic measures
- Exposing children to diverse socioeconomic environments and perspectives
- Addressing class-based stereotypes and assumptions
- Fostering appreciation for various types of work and contribution

## Navigating Societal Expectations

As children grow, they encounter increasingly complex and sometimes contradictory societal expectations. Learning to navigate these expectations while maintaining connection to essence requires developing critical thinking, valuing clarity, and social flexibility.

## Developing Critical Consciousness

Children benefit from gradually developing what educator Paulo Freire called "critical consciousness," the ability to perceive and analyze social structures and cultural messages rather than simply absorbing them. This capacity helps children maintain connection to their authentic experience even when it differs from cultural norms.

Parents can nurture critical consciousness by:

- Asking questions that prompt reflection: "Why do you think that story shows boys and girls that way?"

- Pointing out contradictions in cultural messages: "Notice how this ad says everyone is special while also saying you need this product to be acceptable."

- Sharing alternative perspectives: "Some people believe success means making money, while others think it means helping others."

- Discussing the historical and social context of cultural practices: "People started doing this because..."

- Encouraging children to notice how media and advertising affect their emotions: "How do you feel after watching that show?"

## Values Clarification

As children encounter diverse value systems through school, media, and broadening social circles, they need support in developing their coherent values. This doesn't mean imposing parental values, but instead helping children reflect on what truly matters to them.

Parents can support values clarification by:

- Discussing family values explicitly, explaining their importance rather than just enforcing rules

- Asking questions that prompt ethical reflection: "What do you think would be the fairest way to solve this problem?"

- Noticing when the child expresses values through their behavior: "I noticed you shared your treat with your friend; that showed generosity."

- Creating opportunities for service and contribution that connect with the child's interests

- Sharing ethical dilemmas from your own life (age-appropriately) and explaining your reasoning.

**Social Flexibility**

Children must develop the capacity to function effectively in different social contexts without losing their authentic center. This social flexibility allows them to adapt behavior appropriately while maintaining internal integrity.

So, how do we help our children grow into ethical beings with strong, grounded wills? Not through lectures, but through presence. Through the patience of daily modeling. Through listening more than correcting. Through honoring their joy and recognizing the shape of their will, even when it clashes with ours. These are not techniques; they are invitations into relationship.

These capacities—critical consciousness, value clarity, and social flexibility—help children navigate societal expectations as active, thoughtful participants in culture, rather than as passive recipients of conditioning. They develop what might be called "cultural fluency," the ability to read, interpret, and respond to cultural contexts while maintaining connection to their essential nature.

**Embracing Cultural Richness with Individual Authenticity**

We acknowledge the richness of culture in the developmental journey, imbuing it with meaning, complexity, and color. Yet, we also champion the child's right to carve out a space within this cultural tapestry that is uniquely theirs. By fostering an environment that values both cultural heritage and individual authenticity, we can support children in growing into adults who not only respect and understand their culture but also contribute to its evolution with their unique essence and perspectives.

**Culture as a Resource, Not a Constraint**

At its best, culture serves not as a rigid mold but as a rich repository of resources from which children can draw meaning, connection, and possibility. Cultural traditions, stories, and practices can:

- Provide meaningful frameworks for understanding life transitions
- Connect children to history and community across generations
- Offer symbolic languages for expressing profound experiences
- Create shared rituals that foster belonging and security
- Supply tested wisdom for navigating life's challenges

When approached with flexibility rather than rigidity, cultural heritage becomes not a limitation but a foundation from which authentic selfhood can emerge and flourish.

**Parents' Role in Cultural Transmission**

Parents serve as primary interpreters of culture for their children. How parents present cultural expectations profoundly influences whether children experience culture as nurturing or constraining:

- **Transmitting with Context:** Explaining the meaning and purpose behind cultural practices helps children connect with the underlying values rather than just following empty forms.
- **Adapting with Integrity**: Demonstrating how to adapt cultural traditions to changing circumstances while maintaining their core meaning shows cultural vitality rather than rigidity.
- **Honoring Questions:** Welcoming children's questions about "why we do things this way" fosters critical thinking and more profound understanding rather than blind conformity.
- **Acknowledging Complexity:** Sharing the nuances, variations, and even contradictions within cultural traditions helps children develop tolerance for ambiguity and appreciation for cultural evolution.
- **Living Values Authentically:** Embodying the deeper values of one's cultural heritage in daily life transmits the spirit rather than just the letter of cultural wisdom.

Through these approaches, parents can help children develop what might be called "cultural fluency," the ability to navigate cultural expectations with both respect and freedom, drawing nourishment from cultural heritage while maintaining connection to their essential nature.

**Supporting Cross-Cultural Children**

In our increasingly interconnected world, many children navigate multiple cultural contexts simultaneously. These "third-culture kids" or cross-cultural children face unique challenges and opportunities as they integrate diverse cultural influences into their developing sense of self.

Parents supporting children across cultural contexts can:

- **Validate complexity:** Acknowledge that navigating multiple cultural worlds is complex work, and affirm the child's capacity to integrate diverse influences.

- **Create cultural bridges:** Help children identify connections and shared values across the different cultural contexts they navigate.

- **Allow for cultural code-switching:** Recognize that children may express different aspects of themselves in other cultural contexts and that this flexibility is a strength rather than a lack of authenticity.

- **Process cultural tensions:** Provide a safe space for children to express confusion, frustration, or conflict arising from contradictory cultural expectations.

- **Foster cultural integration:** Support children in developing an integrated identity that incorporates elements from various cultural influences in a coherent, personally meaningful way.

These children often develop remarkable capacities for perspective-taking, adaptability, and cultural intelligence, skills that serve them well in our diverse global society. With supportive guidance, the challenge of navigating multiple cultural worlds can become a pathway to both essential connection and social fluency.

**Balance of Authenticity and Integration**

Cultural influences significantly contribute to the strengthening of personality structures, potentially accelerating the diminishment of essential connection.

However, conscious parenting that honors both culture and essence can moderate this trend, helping children maintain a stronger connection to their essence even as they develop the cultural competence needed to thrive in society.

The goal is not to raise children outside of culture, which would be neither possible nor desirable, but to help them develop a conscious, flexible, and authentic relationship with culture that serves their development. When children can engage with cultural expectations from a foundation of essential connection, they develop the capacity to participate in cultural life without becoming limited by cultural conditioning.

This balanced approach supports children in becoming what we might call "culturally fluent beings," individuals who can navigate the expectations and norms of their social worlds with skill and ease while maintaining a vital connection to their essential nature. Such individuals contribute to cultural evolution precisely because they bring their unique essential qualities into creative engagement with cultural traditions.

By providing your children with both cultural roots and authentic wings, you support their journey toward becoming individuals who can honor heritage while expressing their unique essence in the world.

# SECTION 2: The Essential Journey

## Chapter 8
## Essence and Ego

At the core of our exploration of childhood development lies a fundamental relationship—the interplay between essence and ego. This chapter examines how these two aspects of being interact during the formative years, exploring the natural process through which essence becomes veiled as personality structures develop, and offering insights into how parents can support healthy ego development while preserving their child's connection to their essential nature.

### Relationship Between Essence and Ego Development

To understand the dynamic between essence and ego, we must first clarify the meanings of these terms in the context of childhood development.

> **Essence**, as A.H. Almaas describes it, refers to our true nature, the authentic core of our being that exists before conditioning and personality formation. Essence manifests as various qualities such as joy, strength, peace, will, compassion, and clarity. These qualities are not learned or constructed but are inherent aspects of our being.
>
> **Ego** and **personality** refer to the structures of identity that develop through childhood as we interact with our environment. These structures encompass our self-concept, behavioral patterns, defense mechanisms, and the various roles we adopt in different contexts. Unlike essence, which is inherent, personality is constructed mainly through experience and identification.

The relationship between essence and ego is not inherently antagonistic; both serve important functions in human development. Essence is the ground of authentic being, while ego structures provide the necessary architecture for functioning (doing) in the physical and social world. Ideally, these aspects would develop in harmony, with personality structures remaining permeable to and informed by essential qualities.

However, what typically happens through childhood is that as personality structures strengthen, conscious connection to essence tends to diminish. This is not because essence disappears but because it becomes increasingly veiled behind the growing structures of identity and conditioning.

This process occurs through several mechanisms:

- **Identification:** As children develop a sense of self, they begin to identify with particular aspects of their experience—their body, emotions, thoughts, roles, and relationships. This identification, while necessary for forming a coherent self-concept, can lead to a narrowing of awareness that excludes the broader field of essential being.

- **Conditioning:** Through rewards, punishments, and modeling, children learn which aspects of themselves are socially acceptable and which are not. Essential qualities that aren't recognized or valued by the environment fade into the background.

- **Defense Mechanisms:** When children experience pain, rejection, or trauma, they naturally develop psychological defenses to protect themselves. These defenses, while serving a protective function, can also wall off access to certain essential qualities.

- **Conceptualization:** As language and abstract thinking develop, children increasingly filter experience through concepts and categories. This conceptual overlay can create distance from the direct, immediate experience of essence.

The result is what Almaas calls the "loss of essence," not an actual disappearance of essence but a diminishment of conscious connection to it as personality structures take center stage in experience and awareness.

**Natural Loss of Essence During Childhood**

The veiling of essence during childhood is not a mistake or pathology but a natural part of human development. To function effectively in the physical and social world, children need to develop a coherent sense of self, internalize cultural norms, and learn to navigate complex social relationships. The necessary development of personality structures inevitably obscures essential awareness in varying degrees.

We can observe this natural process unfolding across the developmental stages:

- **Infancy (0-18 months):** Newborns arrive in a state of undifferentiated being, with essence readily available but no clear sense of separate selfhood.

The merging essence quality predominates, allowing the infant to experience deep connection with caregivers. As basic trust develops through consistent, loving care, the infant begins the process of differentiation while maintaining a strong connection to essence.

- **Toddlerhood (18 months to 3 years):** As mobility and language skills develop, the toddler begins to assert independence. Essential strength and will naturally emerge to support this developmental task. However, the "terrible twos" often mark the beginning of significant conflicts between essential expression and social expectations. Parents' responses to the toddler's authentic impulses and explorations can either support continued connection to essence or accelerate its veiling.
- **Early Childhood (3-6 years):** During these years, the child develops a more complex self-concept and internalizes cultural norms and expectations. Imagination flourishes, and the capacity for symbolic thought expands. While these developments create new possibilities for expression, they also give rise to more elaborate structures of identity that can further obscure the individual's essence. As the child learns to adapt to varied social contexts, such as preschool or religious communities, they may begin to compartmentalize aspects of themselves, including essential qualities.

Throughout this process, certain essential qualities become more difficult to access as specific developmental challenges arise:

- **Essential Joy** may become veiled behind achievement orientation and conditional approval.
- **Essential Strength** may be covered by defenses against vulnerability.
- **Essential Will** may be suppressed through excessive control or punitive discipline.
- **Essential Peace** may be lost amid overstimulation and constant activity.
- **Essential Compassion** may be diminished through competition and comparison.

By understanding this natural process, parents can approach their child's development with greater awareness, recognizing both the necessity of personality development and the value of maintaining connection to essence.

**Supporting Connection to Essence While Developing a Healthy Ego**

Parents face a delicate challenge: supporting their child's necessary ego development while helping them maintain conscious connection to their essential nature. This isn't about preventing personality development, which would be neither possible nor desirable, but about fostering development that remains permeable to and informed by essence.

Here are key approaches for navigating this balance:

- **Create Space for Being, Not Just Doing**: In a culture focused on achievement and activity, deliberately creating space for simply being helps children maintain connection to essence. This might include quiet time in nature, moments of shared stillness, or unhurried play without predetermined outcomes. These experiences remind children that their value isn't tied solely to performance or production but resides in their very being.
- **Recognize and Mirror Essential Qualities:** When parents learn to recognize essential qualities as they manifest in their child, they can mirror these qualities back, helping the child maintain conscious awareness of them. "I see how joy is bubbling up in you right now," or "You showed such strength in persisting with that difficult puzzle," acknowledges the essential quality beneath the behavior, reinforcing the child's connection to their authentic nature.
- **Model Essence:** Children learn not just from what parents say but from how parents live. When parents maintain their connection to essence—expressing authentic joy, demonstrating genuine strength, accessing true compassion—they show children that these qualities remain available throughout life. Parents who are working to rediscover their essence provide powerful modeling of the lifelong journey of reconnection.
- **Offer Unconditional Positive Regard:** Psychologist Carl Rogers emphasized that unconditional positive regard—accepting and valuing the person regardless of particular behaviors—supports the development of a healthy, congruent self. This doesn't mean approving of all behaviors, but rather separating acceptance of the person from responses to their actions. When children feel accepted in their essence, they're less likely to develop a false self designed to earn approval.
- **Balance Structure and Freedom:** Both excessive control and excessive permissiveness can interfere with healthy development. Too much control

suppresses the child's essential expression, while too little structure fails to provide the containment needed for safe exploration. The art is finding the "good enough" balance that provides appropriate boundaries while honoring the child's authentic unfolding.
- **Support Integration Rather Than Compartmentalization:** As children navigate different social contexts, such as home, school, religious communities, and peer groups, they may begin to compartmentalize aspects of themselves to adapt to varying expectations. Parents can help children integrate these experiences by discussing differences openly, validating the challenge of navigating multiple contexts, and creating a home environment where authentic expression is welcomed.
- **Provide Language for Essence:** Developing a shared vocabulary for essential experiences helps children maintain awareness of these dimensions of being. Terms like "your inner strength," "that peaceful feeling," or "your natural joy" give children language to recognize and communicate about their essential experiences, making it more likely they'll maintain conscious connection.

By implementing these approaches, parents can support both healthy ego development and a continued connection to essence, helping their children develop a personality structure that serves as a vehicle for their essence rather than a barrier to it.

## Attachment and Self Connection

The quality of early attachment relationships has a profound influence on both personality development and the formation of essential connection. When Winnicott speaks of the "true self" and Bowlby discusses "secure attachment," they're addressing different aspects of the same fundamental human need—to be authentically seen, accepted, and responded to.

Winnicott observed that the true self emerges when the infant's spontaneous gestures are met with attunement from the caregiver. When a baby's expressions—whether coos, smiles, or cries—are received with appropriate, responsive care, the child develops a sense that their authentic impulses are valid and effective. This lays the foundation for the true self to develop and thrive.

In contrast, when caregivers are consistently unresponsive or impose their agendas, the child adapts by developing a false self. This protective facade complies with external expectations while hiding the vulnerable true self. This false self resembles what happens when essence becomes veiled behind personality structures developed to gain approval rather than express authenticity.

Bowlby's theory complements this understanding. Secure attachment develops when caregivers provide a reliable "secure base" for the child to explore and a "safe haven" to return to when stressed. This security allows children to venture into the world confidently, knowing they have a protective foundation to return to when needed.

The quality of attachment directly influences connection to essence:

- **Secure Attachment:** Children are more likely to express their essence freely when they feel securely attached. The security of the relationship provides a container in which authentic being can flourish without fear of abandonment or rejection.

- **Insecure-Avoidant Attachment:** Children who develop this pattern (often in response to consistently unresponsive caregiving) learn to suppress their needs and emotions. This suppression can extend to essential qualities, particularly vulnerability, connection, and need.

- **Insecure-Ambivalent Attachment:** Children with this pattern (typically developing from inconsistent caregiving) may become preoccupied with gaining and maintaining attention and approval. This can lead to exaggerated emotional expression and difficulty identifying authentic feelings and needs beneath the strategies used to secure connection.

- **Disorganized Attachment:** This is the most problematic pattern, associated with frightening or frightened caregivers, which creates fundamental confusion about seeking proximity during times of stress. Children with this pattern may struggle with both personality coherence and connection to essence, as basic safety becomes the primary concern.

Understanding these connections helps us see why early attachment experiences are so crucial for both healthy personality development and essential connection. The good news is that attachment patterns can be updated throughout life through new relationships, including the parent-child relationship itself. Parents who may not have experienced a secure attachment in their own childhood can still provide it for their children, especially if they're working on their healing.

**Healthy Personality Development and Essential Connection**

Secure attachment provides an optimal foundation for both personality development and essential connection. Like the banks of a river that channel but don't dam the flow of water, secure attachment relationships provide structure while allowing essence to continue flowing through the developing personality.

Here's how secure attachment supports both aspects of development:

- **For Personality Development:** Secure attachment fosters healthy personality structures in several ways:
    - **Emotional Regulation:** Children learn to identify, express, and manage emotions through co-regulation with attuned caregivers, developing internal resources for modulating feelings without suppressing them.
    - **Positive Internal Working Models:** Children who are securely attached develop positive mental representations of themselves as worthy and competent and others as reliable and caring, laying the foundation for healthy relationships throughout life.
    - **Cognitive Development:** The security of attachment allows children to direct their energy toward exploration and learning rather than managing anxiety about safety and connection.
    - **Identity Integration:** Secure attachment supports the development of a coherent, integrated sense of self rather than fragmented or compartmentalized aspects of identity.
    - **Stress Management:** Secure attachment provides children with effective strategies for managing stress, promoting resilience, and adaptive coping rather than rigid defenses.
- **For Essential Connection:** At the same time, secure attachment supports continued connection to essence:
    - **Safe Expression:** When children feel secure, they're more likely to express their authentic impulses, emotions, and essential qualities without fear of rejection or abandonment.
    - **Mirroring of Essence:** Attuned caregivers naturally tend to mirror not just behaviors but the essential qualities expressed through

those behaviors, helping children maintain awareness of their essence.

- o **Lower Defensive Barriers:** With a reduced need for psychological defenses against anxiety and insecurity, securely attached children maintain more permeable boundaries between their essence and personality.

- o **Authentic Presence:** The security of the attachment relationship allows both parent and child to be more fully present with each other, creating space for essence to be recognized and expressed.

- o **Integration Rather Than Splitting:** Secure attachment promotes the integration of all aspects of experience, including essential qualities, rather than splitting off parts that seem unacceptable or threatening.

Through these mechanisms, secure attachment creates the optimal conditions for personality structures to develop in service of, rather than at the expense of, essential connection. The child develops a healthy, functional ego that remains permeable to the qualities of essence flowing through it.

Parents who understand the relationship between attachment and essence can approach their caregiving with greater awareness, recognizing that by providing consistent, attuned care, they're supporting not just their child's psychological development but also their spiritual wholeness.

**Maintaining Essential Connection**

Building on our understanding of the relationship between essence, ego, and attachment, we can explore practical approaches for parents who wish to support their child's connection to essence while fostering healthy personality development.

- **Presence and Attunement:** The foundation for both secure attachment and connection to essence is the parent's present, attuned engagement with the child. This presence goes beyond physical proximity to include emotional availability and openness to the child's experience. When parents bring their full attention to interactions with their child, without distraction, preoccupation, or agenda, they create space for essence to be seen and recognized. Practical approaches include:

- Establishing regular "special time" with each child where they receive undivided attention
- Putting away phones and devices during key connecting moments
- Practicing mindfulness to develop greater capacity for presence
- Noticing when you're distracted or preoccupied and gently bringing attention back to the present moment

- **Balancing Acceptance and Guidance:** Children need unconditional acceptance of who they are and appropriate guidance about navigating the world. This balance enables the development of necessary personality structures without requiring the child to suppress their true nature to gain approval. Consider:
    - Separating the being from the doing in your responses ("I love you even when I don't like what you're doing")
    - Setting limits around behaviors while acknowledging and accepting feelings
    - Focusing discipline on teaching rather than punishing
    - Finding the "yes" behind the "no" ("You can't throw balls in the house, but let's find a place where you can throw")

- **Creating Rituals of Connection:** Regular rituals provide reliable containers for connection, supporting both attachment security and essence awareness. These predictable times for meaningful interaction help children integrate their experience and maintain awareness of deeper aspects of being. Family rituals could include:
    - Bedtime rituals that include both reflection on the day and quiet connection
    - Mealtime practices that create space for sharing and listening
    - Seasonal celebrations that connect the family to natural rhythms and larger meanings
    - Simple daily transition moments marked by presence and connection

- **Supporting Essence in Different Developmental Stages:** Different stages of development bring specific challenges and opportunities for connection to essence. Parents can tailor their approach to their child's current stage:
    - For infants:
        - Respond promptly and sensitively to needs, building basic trust
        - Provide plenty of physical holding and emotional containment
        - Create a peaceful, unhurried environment that doesn't overstimulate
    - For toddlers:
        - Support emerging autonomy while maintaining connection
        - Allow appropriate expression of will while providing clear, consistent boundaries
        - Validate emotions while helping develop regulation skills
    - For preschoolers:
        - Support imaginative play without excessive direction
        - Help navigate social relationships while honoring individual temperament
        - Introduce simple mindfulness practices appropriate for young children
    - For school-age children:
        - Balance achievement expectations with valuing process and essence qualities
        - Create a family culture that offers alternatives to materialistic and performance-oriented cultural messages
        - Provide language and concepts that help children recognize and articulate essential experiences

- **Developing Self-Awareness:** Self-awareness is perhaps the most powerful tool for supporting a child's connection to essence. When parents recognize how their essential nature has been veiled and are working to reconnect with it, they naturally create space for their child's essential expression. Parental work includes:
    - Reflecting on how your upbringing influenced your connection to essence
    - Noticing when you're triggered and how this affects your ability to see your child's essence
    - Seeking support through therapy, spiritual practice, or conscious parenting communities
    - Practicing self-compassion as you navigate the challenges of parenting

These practical approaches aren't techniques to be mechanically applied but orientations to be embodied in the unique relationship between each parent and child. With awareness, intention, and practice, parents can create environments that foster both healthy personality development and a connection to one's essence.

## Integration of Essence and Ego

The heart of the matter in child development is neither to prevent ego formation nor to sacrifice essential connection, but to foster an integration where personality structures develop in a way that remains transparent to and informed by essential qualities. This integration allows the child to function effectively in the world while maintaining connection to their authentic nature.

A healthy relationship between essence and ego might be compared to clear water flowing through a well-designed channel. The channel, or personality, provides direction and structure to the water, allowing it to move purposefully through the landscape. Without the channel, the water might disperse without impact; without the water, the channel serves no purpose. Together, they create something more powerful than either alone.

For parents, understanding this relationship transforms how we approach child-rearing. Rather than seeing our task as primarily molding and shaping our children into who we think they should be, we recognize that our deeper role is to witness, protect, and support the natural unfolding of who they already are in essence, while helping them develop the structures needed to express that essence in the world.

This understanding doesn't make parenting easier. It remains one of life's most challenging journeys, but it does make it more meaningful and aligned with the deeper purpose of human development. By supporting both connection to essence and healthy ego development, we help our children become not just functional adults but authentic human beings capable of living from their most profound truth.

As we move forward in our exploration of childhood development, we'll examine how cultural influences shape the relationship between essence and ego, looking at how societal expectations and norms can either support or hinder authentic development. But first, consider these reflections:

- How do you experience the relationship between essence and personality in your own life?

- What aspects of your parenting support your child's connection to essence, and what aspects might inadvertently obscure it?

- How does your attachment relationship with your child influence both their personality development and their connection to essence?

These reflections can help you become more conscious of how you're navigating the heart of the matter—the delicate, beautiful dance between essence and ego in your child's unfolding development.

# Chapter 9
# Understanding Essence

*In the absence of the sacred, nothing is sacred. Everything is for sale.* —Oren Lyons

*Your Self-realization is the greatest service you can render.* —Ramana Maharshi

*The essential is invisible to the eye.* —Antoine de Saint-Exupéry

*There is a voice that doesn't use words. Listen.* —Rumi

## A Path to the Core

At the heart of our exploration lies a profound understanding of the human experience —a perspective that transcends conventional psychological frameworks to encompass the wholeness of being. A.H. Almaas offers us a unique lens through which to view both the development of our children and ourselves as parents, illuminating the journey of essence as it interacts with the developmental processes described by our nine theorists.

Almaas integrates spiritual wisdom with modern psychology, recognizing that our essential nature—what we truly are at our core—undergoes significant transformations through the necessary process of development. This understanding provides parents with a map that integrates traditional developmental theory with the deeper dimension of essence, offering a more complete picture of the child's journey.

## What is Essence?

Essence is the fundamental nature of our being, what we are before conditioning, beyond personality structures, before self-concepts. It is not an abstract philosophical idea, but a living reality —a presence that can be directly experienced as the ground of our existence.

Unlike personality traits, which are constructed through learning and identification, essential qualities are inherent aspects of our being. They possess a palpable, substantial quality that can be directly experienced, characterized by distinct presence that unfolds naturally when not obscured by conditioning or psychological structures.

Consider how a young child embodies joy, not as an emotion that comes and goes in response to circumstances but as a bubbling, effervescent quality that radiates from within. This essential joy isn't dependent on external causes; it is a natural emanation of being. The same can be observed with qualities like strength, peace, will, compassion, and clarity. These are not personality traits but facets of our essential nature that shine through when not covered by layers of conditioning.

As Almaas describes, essence is "the most fundamental, true nature of the human being and the cosmos... It is not a product of the mind or human development, but rather the ground and true nature of the mind and all human faculties."

**Essential Qualities in Relation to Development**

Our essential nature expresses itself through various qualities, each with its distinct flavor, substance, and function. The graph we're examining shows how five key aspects of essence—connection to essence, strength, merging, will, and joy—manifest and transform throughout early childhood development in relation to the developmental stages described by our nine theorists:

- **Connection to Essence:** This top line represents the child's overall relationship to their essential nature, their direct, unmediated experience of being. The graph shows how this connection gradually diminishes over the first four years as personality structures develop and conditioning increases. This correlates with Winnicott's description of the shift from the "true self" to the development of a persona that meets environmental demands.
- **Merging Essence:** This quality manifests as a melting, dissolving presence that allows for deep connection and unity. The graph shows it peaking in early infancy, aligning with Mahler's "symbiotic phase" and Bowlby's early attachment processes. This quality enables the profound bonding between infant and caregiver that establishes basic trust, as described by Erikson.
- **Essential Strength:** Experienced as a solid, grounded presence that supports action and boundaries. The graph shows this quality emerging strongly between 6 and 15 months, coinciding with the development of mobility. This aligns with Piaget's sensorimotor stage and supports what Mahler refers to as the separation-individuation process.
- **Essential Joy:** A sparkling, effervescent quality that brings lightness and delight. The graph shows this quality peaking during what Mahler calls the "practicing period" (10-16 months), when children experience what she described as a "love affair with the world" as they delight in their expanding

capabilities. This period aligns with Erikson's development of a sense of autonomy and Piaget's exploration of cause and effect during the sensorimotor stage.
- **Essential Will:** Manifests as a directed, purposeful presence that enables focus and perseverance. The graph shows this quality emerging prominently around 16-24 months, coinciding with what Mahler terms the "rapprochement subphase" and aligning with Erikson's sense of autonomy versus shame and doubt. This is when children begin to assert their preferences and intentions more clearly, often expressed through what Freud noted in the anal stage as control and what Kohlberg would later recognize as the beginnings of moral awareness.

## Distortion of Essential Qualities

A critical understanding from Almaas is that essence isn't simply lost during development; it becomes distorted and transformed as ego identity strengthens. Each essential quality, when frustrated or conditioned by ego development and social expectations, morphs into a personality-level substitute that mimics but falls short of the original quality:

- **Essential Strength → Anger:** When a child's natural strength is thwarted, denied, or punished, it often transforms into anger. Unlike Essential Strength, which is a solid, grounded presence that supports healthy boundaries and action, anger is reactive, defensive, and often destructive. Where strength is a stable presence that doesn't need to prove itself, anger is a volatile reaction to perceived threats to the ego. We see this transformation during what Mahler calls the "rapprochement crisis," when toddlers face the limitations of their autonomy, as well as during Erikson's autonomy versus shame and doubt stage.
- **Essential Will → Efforting (False Will):** Essential Will is a directed, purposeful presence that flows naturally. When this quality becomes distorted through ego development, it transforms into efforting or "willpower," a strained, tense forcing of the self against resistance. Unlike essential will, which is aligned with one's true nature and therefore feels effortless even when focused, willpower requires pushing against one's own resistance. This distortion often emerges during toilet training (Freud's anal stage) and other early experiences of control and compliance with external demands.

- **Merging Essence → Dependency:** The pure Merging Essence of infancy—a natural, non-conceptual unity with others—becomes distorted into dependency when filtered through ego structures. Rather than experiencing merging as a natural state of connection that doesn't threaten one's being, the ego experiences only dependency, a needy attachment based on the fear of abandonment or rejection. This oscillation between dependency and forced autonomy continues throughout life, replacing the natural flow between connection and individuation that Mahler describes in healthy development.
- **Essential Joy → Conditioned Happiness:** The spontaneous, bubbling joy that is so evident in young children becomes increasingly conditioned and restricted as ego identity forms. Joy becomes tied to specific achievements, social approval, or the acquisition of desired objects. The natural curiosity and delight in simply being alive is suppressed in favor of meeting others' expectations. This transformation is particularly evident as children enter structured environments, such as school, where spontaneity is often sacrificed for conformity and achievement, a dynamic that both Bandura and Vygotsky note in their observations of social learning.

**Loss of Essence and the Formation of Holes**

The Diamond Approach offers a profound understanding of what happens as essence becomes veiled during development: the loss of conscious connection to essential qualities creates what Almaas terms "holes" in our experience, areas of emptiness or deficiency that correspond to the specific qualities that have been lost to awareness.

These holes are not merely empty spaces but dynamic absences that generate intense discomfort. They represent the places where essential qualities once flowed freely but have become blocked or obscured through developmental experiences. The nature of the hole corresponds to the specific essential quality that has been lost to consciousness:

- **Strength Hole:** When Essential Strength becomes obscured, the child experiences a fundamental sense of weakness, vulnerability, and inability to stand their ground. This hole manifests as a persistent feeling of inadequacy in the face of challenges, a sense that one lacks the inner resources to meet life's demands.

- **Value Hole:** The loss of connection to inherent value creates a hole characterized by a profound feeling of worthlessness or deficiency. Regardless of the achievements or recognition they receive, the child (and later the adult) feels fundamentally unworthy at their core.
- **Love Hole:** When the essential quality of love becomes veiled, a yawning emptiness forms in the heart, characterized by a sense of being unlovable or incapable of real connection. This hole drives a desperate seeking for external validation and affection that can never truly fill the absence of essential love.
- **Will Hole:** The obscuration of essential will creates a hole experienced as helplessness, lack of direction, or an inability to persevere. Without connection to this quality, the person feels at the mercy of circumstances, unable to direct their life with clarity and purpose.
- **Hole of Joy:** When essential joy becomes lost to awareness, a deadness or flatness pervades experience. The world loses its luster, and even pleasurable activities feel somehow hollow or unsatisfying, missing the deep, spontaneous delight that is joy's true nature.

**Essence Calls to Essence**

Perhaps the most profound insight for parents is that essence calls to essence. When essence is alive and flowing in parents, it naturally evokes and strengthens essence in their children. This reciprocal awakening works in both directions. A child's essence can call forth a parent's essence, just as a parent's essence can nurture their child's.

This dynamic is powerfully evident at childbirth, where the newborn's pure, unobstructed essence often awakens dormant essential qualities in the mother. Many mothers describe a profound shift in their state of being after giving birth—a heightened presence, an overwhelming love, and a depth of connection that transcends ordinary experience. This is the child's essence calling forth the mother's, awakening dimensions of her being that may have been veiled by years of conditioning and personality development.

This reciprocal awakening continues throughout the parenting journey. A child's spontaneous joy can dissolve a parent's heaviness and reconnect them to their joy. A child's natural strength can remind a parent of their inherent capacity for groundedness and solidity. A child's genuine will can reawaken a parent's sense of authentic purpose and direction.

For parents seeking to support their child's connection to essence, the most powerful approach is therefore to work on their reconnection to essence. Rather than treating parenting primarily as something they do to or for their child, they can approach it as a shared journey of discovery and expression.

**Parental Journey of Essential Reconnection**

For parents to effectively support their child's essential connection, they must engage in their journey of essential reconnection. This involves:

- **Exploring Personal History and Conditioning:** Examining how their essential qualities became obscured through developmental experiences and social conditioning. Which qualities were punished or ignored? Which holes formed, and what substitute structures developed to manage them? Understanding these patterns helps parents recognize how they might inadvertently perpetuate similar patterns with their children.
- **Working with Personal Holes and Substitutes:** Developing awareness of their holes (areas of essence loss) and the substitute structures they've created to manage them. This awareness helps prevent unconscious projection of their deficiencies onto their children. For example, a parent who is disconnected from Essential Strength and compensates with controlling behavior might unconsciously suppress their child's natural expressions of strength.
- **Engaging in Practices that Support Reconnection to Essence:** Regular meditation, inquiry, body awareness, and other contemplative practices. These practices can help parents reconnect with their essential nature and create space for essence to emerge through the structures of personality, gradually dissolving rigid substitute patterns and allowing essential qualities to flow more freely.
- **Creating Family Environments that Honor Essence:** Designing home spaces, routines, and interactions that value presence, authenticity, and essential qualities. This may include regular times for quiet togetherness, creative expression without judgment, or nature experiences that foster a sense of wonder and presence.
- **Seeking Support from Others on the Path:** Connecting with other parents or communities interested in essence-aware parenting. Parenting with essence awareness can feel countercultural in a society focused on achievement and conformity, making community support particularly valuable, as it provides validation, shared wisdom, and mutual support.

This work of reconnecting with essence is not separate from parenting; it is integral to it. As parents reclaim their essential nature, they naturally create environments where their children's essence can flourish. The parents' journey of healing and reconnection becomes a gift not only to themselves but to their children.

**Essential Mirroring vs. Psychological Mirroring**

A critical distinction emerges when we consider how most parenting approaches and psychological theories address the child's developing self. Conventional psychology, even at its best, tends to focus on mirroring the personality self, validating emotions, affirming competence, supporting healthy ego development, and building self-esteem. While valuable, this type of mirroring operates primarily at the level of the constructed self.

Essential mirroring is not about what you say; it's about what you are. It doesn't name or praise. It doesn't rely on carefully chosen words. Essential mirroring arises when a parent is in touch with their essence and that state of being naturally attunes to and reflects the child's essential qualities, essence calls to essence.

This is not a doing. It is a being. A parent steeped in their presence becomes like still water, reflecting the child not as a set of behaviors or achievements but as a luminous presence. The child feels seen not for what they have done, but for who they are.

Unlike psychological mirroring, which echoes the child's emotional state or actions through words, essential mirroring is wordless. It registers through tone, gaze, touch, and spaciousness. It flavors the air. The child may not recall what was said, but will remember how it made them feel. They will remember being known without being described.

Where psychological mirroring supports the development of a healthy ego, essential mirroring supports connection with essence. It is not about recognizing pride, joy, or effort; it is about resonating with strength, delight, or will as qualities of being itself.

The difference lies in what is being recognized and reflected. Psychological mirroring validates personality-level experiences and attributes, while essential mirroring acknowledges the deeper qualities of being that flow through the child regardless of specific actions or achievements.

*Essential mirroring requires parents to be present,*
*in touch with their essential nature.*
*Otherwise, the mirroring will be coming from personality, not essence.*

The soul needs essential mirroring to maintain its connection to essence. When parents can recognize and reflect the essential qualities they perceive in their child, they help the child maintain conscious awareness of these qualities even as their personality develops. This creates a bridge between essence and personality, supporting the integration of the two rather than replacing one with the other.

Traditional psychological approaches, while valuable in many ways, typically lack this dimension. Even the most enlightened psychological theories, including those of our nine developmental theorists, generally focus on supporting healthy ego development without addressing the progressive loss of essence that often accompanies it. The Diamond Approach fills this gap, offering a framework that honors both the necessary development of personality and the preservation of connection to essence.

**Supporting Healthy Development While Preserving Essence**

The developmental journey charted by our nine theorists is necessary and valuable. Children need to develop cognitive capabilities, social skills, moral understanding, and a coherent sense of self to function in the world. The goal isn't to prevent development but to support it in ways that preserve the connection to essence.

Ideally, personality would develop not in opposition to essence but as a vehicle for its expression in the world. The process mapped by our developmental theorists would unfold alongside continued connection to essence, creating what Almaas terms the "Personal Essence" or the "Pearl, a mature integration of essence and personality that allows for both authentic being and effective functioning.

For parents, this means:

- **Engaging in their essential work:** Recognizing that the most powerful way to support their child's connection to essence is to reconnect with their essential nature. As parents heal their holes and dissolve rigid substitute structures, they naturally create environments where essence can flow freely, calling forth essence in their children.

- **Supporting developmental tasks while maintaining awareness of essence:** Recognizing that learning to walk, talk, develop autonomy, navigate social relationships, and form a stable identity are important achievements that should be encouraged, while simultaneously protecting the child's connection to their essential nature.

- **Responding to behaviors with essential understanding:** Seeing the essential qualities (or their absence) beneath behaviors allows parents to address both the surface manifestation and the more profound need. A child's anger can be met with appropriate boundaries while also recognizing and supporting the underlying strength that has been thwarted.

- **Practicing essential mirroring alongside psychological support:** Complementing conventional parenting approaches with the practice of essential mirroring helps children maintain awareness of their essential qualities even as they develop necessary personality structures.

- **Creating family cultures that value both development and essence:** Establishing routines, traditions, and environments that celebrate achievements and capabilities while also honoring presence, authenticity, and essential qualities.

## Transformative Power of Parenting

Parenting offers a profound opportunity for mutual transformation. As parents support their children's connection to their essence, they also address their disconnection from it. As they work to reconnect with their essential nature, they naturally create environments where their children's essence can flourish. This reciprocal process creates a virtuous cycle of awakening and healing that benefits both parent and child.

The birth of a child often initiates this process, as the child's pure essence calls forth essence in the parent. However, for this awakening to continue and deepen, parents must consciously engage with it, working through their history and conditioning to support the reemergence of their essence in their lives.

This understanding transforms parenting from a primarily outward-focused activity of raising children to a shared journey of intimacy with essence. The parents' work on themselves becomes not a separate or selfish pursuit but an integral aspect of parenting itself, perhaps the most important gift they can offer their child.

**A Compass for the Journey**

Understanding essence, holes, substitutes, and the reciprocal nature of essential awakening provides a powerful compass for the parenting journey. It helps us recognize not just what is developing in our children but also what might be being lost in the process, while illuminating our patterns of essence disconnection and the opportunity for healing that parenting offers.

By integrating the insights of traditional developmental theory with Almaas' understanding of essence, parents gain a more complete map of both their child's journey and their own. This integrated understanding enables them to support their children in navigating the necessary stages of development while minimizing the formation of gaps and rigid substitute structures, all while engaging in their journey of essence reconnection.

As we move forward, we'll explore practical approaches to supporting essence at different developmental stages, recognizing both the challenges and opportunities that arise as children grow. We'll examine how parents can create environments that foster both healthy development and essential connection, and how they can work with their children and substitutes to become more present, attuned, and authentic in their parenting.

Almaas offers us a practical compass for this journey, a way of orienting ourselves toward what matters most as we navigate the complex terrain of raising children. By understanding how essence calls to essence and how our essential work directly supports our children's connection to essence, we gain insights that can transform our parenting from the inside out, allowing us to support our children in growing into individuals who function effectively in the world while maintaining connection to the authenticity of their true nature.

If this is stirring something in you—an interest in exploring essential reconnection—I welcome you to reach out HarpGnosisBooks@gmail.com to continue the conversation.

# Chapter 10
## Inherent Wholeness—The Unsculpted Self

*We cannot fashion our children after our desires, we must have them and love them as God has given them to us.* —Johann Wolfgang von Goethe

*The privilege of a lifetime is to become who you truly are.* —Carl Jung

*Every child begins the world again...* —Henry David Thoreau

**Newborn as Essence Incarnate**

As dawn's tender light caresses the world into wakefulness, so does the birth of a child illuminate the essence of existence. In this nascent being, we witness the unsculpted self, a tableau of potential untouched by the chisel of experience. The newborn arrives not as a blank slate awaiting inscription but as essence incarnate, embodying a completeness and wholeness that precedes personality, conditioning, and self-concept.

This inherent wholeness manifests in the infant's immediate, unmediated presence. Without the filters of language, social conditioning, or a constructed sense of self, the newborn experiences and expresses life directly. Their gaze, though unfocused by adult standards, holds a transparency that reflects the pure light of being. Their movements, though uncoordinated, flow with an authenticity untempered by self-consciousness. Their expressions, from the furrow of discomfort to the relaxation of contentment, arise spontaneously, without calculation or guile.

The newborn exists in what A.H. Almaas describes as a state of "basic trust," a non-conceptual confidence in the fundamental benevolence of reality. This trust is not a belief, but a direct experience of being held by existence —a primal orientation toward life that precedes cognitive understanding or emotional development. It is from this foundation of basic trust that all other essential qualities emerge and find expression.

**Energetic Regulation and the Formation of Identity**

At the heart of early development lies a profound and often overlooked dimension: the infant's energetic regulation and its relationship to both the expression of essence and the formation of identity. Every human being operates within an energetic range of comfort, a window of tolerable arousal that defines our sense of equilibrium and, ultimately, becomes a cornerstone of how we know ourselves.

When our system becomes too charged through stimulation, stress, or excitement, we instinctively seek discharge to return to our comfort zone. Conversely, when our energy levels fall too low due to fatigue, understimulation, or disconnection, we naturally seek activities that recharge us. This ongoing dance of charge and discharge creates a rhythmic pattern that becomes deeply familiar, establishing an energetic signature that forms part of our fundamental sense of identity.

For infants, this regulatory capacity is still developing. Their window of tolerable arousal is narrow, and they lack the skills to modulate their energetic states effectively. When overstimulated, they quickly become dysregulated, manifesting distress through crying, arching, gaze aversion, or fussiness. When understimulated, they may become lethargic, withdrawn, or irritable. In both cases, they depend entirely on their caregivers, particularly the mother, to help them return to a balanced state.

This dependency creates the perfect conditions for merging essence to manifest. As the mother attunes to her infant's energetic state and responds with regulating support—soothing when the infant is overstimulated, and engaging when understimulated—a profound energetic merger occurs. The boundary between mother and infant temporarily dissolves as their nervous systems synchronize, creating what appears as a unified field of being—the golden, honey-like experience of merging essence.

The quality of this co-regulatory relationship profoundly impacts the infant's developing sense of self and their ongoing connection to essence:

**When Co-Regulation Supports Essence**: When caregivers consistently respond with attuned regulation, neither overwhelming nor abandoning the infant, several essential qualities naturally emerge and remain accessible:

- **Merging Essence** flows freely as the infant experiences the dissolution of boundaries in states of attunement.
- **Essential Peace** manifests in the regulated state that follows successful co-regulation.
- **Basic Trust** deepens as the infant's system learns that dysregulation will be met with responsive support.

- **Essential Value** develops as the infant experiences being worth the attention and effort of attunement.

**When Co-Regulation Fails**: When caregivers consistently misread the infant's signals or respond inappropriately to their regulatory needs, either by overwhelming them with excessive stimulation or failing to provide needed engagement, the consequences for essential connection are significant:

- **Chronic Hyperarousal or Hypoarousal:** The infant may develop a chronically elevated or depressed energetic baseline, creating a foundation for anxiety or depression.
- **Constricted Comfort Range:** The window of tolerable arousal may narrow further as the infant learns that certain energetic states won't receive appropriate support.
- **Protective Contractions:** To manage unsupported dysregulation, the infant develops muscular and energetic contractions that become the foundation for ego defenses.
- **Obscuration of Essence:** Essential qualities become veiled as the infant's system prioritizes basic regulation over open presence.

For parents, understanding this energetic dimension of development offers vital guidance:

- **Recognizing Regulatory Cues:** Learning to read your infant's subtle signals of dysregulation before they escalate—changes in color, breathing patterns, muscle tone, gaze, or movement quality that indicate they're moving outside their window of tolerance.
- **Offering Regulating Support:** Providing the specific type of support your infant needs in each moment—gentle containment when overstimulated, engaging interaction when understimulated, rhythmic movement when disorganized.
- **Creating Regulatory Rhythms:** Establishing daily patterns that support natural cycles of engagement and rest, stimulation and processing, connection and solitude—allowing your infant to develop a healthy regulatory rhythm.
- **Attending to Your Regulation:** Recognizing that your regulatory state directly influences your infant's—when you're dysregulated, your capacity

for attunement diminishes and your infant absorbs your disturbed energy. Your regulatory practices become essential parenting tools.

Through attuned co-regulation, parents not only support their infant's immediate comfort but help establish patterns that will influence their essential connection throughout life. The merging essence that manifests during these regulatory exchanges is not merely a pleasant experience but a profound template for relationship with both self and other, a direct knowing of connected being that can remain accessible even as individual identity develops.

**Presence of Essential Qualities at Birth**

From their very arrival, a child emanates essential qualities that dance before our eyes, if only we have the vision to perceive them. In direct contrast to the developmental view that sees infants as incomplete beings gradually acquiring capabilities, the Diamond Approach recognizes newborns as whole beings already embodying essential qualities in their purest form.

**Merging Gold Essence** dominates the earliest days, allowing the infant to experience a non-differentiated unity with their caregiver. You might observe this when your baby completely relaxes against you during feeding or sleep, their body melting into yours without resistance or boundary. This quality supports what Mahler describes as the symbiotic phase and what Bowlby recognizes as the foundation of attachment.

**Essential Peace** can be witnessed in those moments of quiet alertness when your infant lies contentedly, neither seeking stimulation nor avoiding discomfort, simply being. Their breath flows easily, their gaze is soft yet present, and a tangible stillness emanates from them that can calm the room.

**Essential Joy** bubbles forth in the infant's first social smiles, in the full-body excitement they express when stimulated playfully, and in the delighted discovery of their hands and feet. This joy needs no reason; it is not happiness about something but the natural effervescence of being itself.

**Essential Curiosity** shines through as the infant tracks movement with growing interest, turns toward novel sounds, or explores textures with increasingly deliberate touch. This quality precedes cognitive constructs of learning or achievement; it is a pure impulse toward knowing that emerges from essence itself.

Parents who learn to recognize these qualities, not as behaviors to be reinforced but as expressions of their child's inherent nature, develop a fundamentally different relationship with their child. Rather than seeing an incomplete being that needs to be shaped, they perceive the wholeness already present, requiring only protection and nurturing to remain accessible during development.

**Embodied Formation of Ego Structure**

At its most fundamental level, the ego structure that gradually forms and obscures the infant's essential nature is not merely a psychological construct; it is embodied in the organism's tissue. The infant enters the world as pure sensitivity, a being of exquisite receptivity to every stimulus, every interaction, every environment. This sensitivity is both their greatest gift and their greatest vulnerability.

To understand this embodied process, imagine yourself deeply relaxed in a peaceful field on a perfect day. The temperature is just right, a subtle breeze caresses your skin, and gentle wildlife moves freely nearby. In this state of openness, your body is relaxed, your breath flows easily, and your nervous system remains calm and receptive. This approximates the natural state of the infant—open, undefended, completely present.

Now, imagine the sudden intrusion of a blaring car horn. Without conscious thought, your body instantly contracts; muscles tense, breath halts, the nervous system jolts into high alert. This spontaneous contraction is a protective mechanism, an attempt to defend against an overwhelming stimulus. For adults, such contractions typically subside once the threat has passed. For infants, whose nervous systems are still developing and who lack cognitive frameworks to process experience, these contractions can become persistent patterns.

The infant, being 100% an organ of sensitivity, experiences "shocks" far more readily than adults. What might seem insignificant to a parent—a sudden loud voice, a jarring transition, inconsistent responsiveness to needs—can trigger protective contractions in the infant's exquisitely sensitive system. When particular stimuli or experiences occur repeatedly, the organism begins to anticipate them, maintaining subtle contractions as a preemptive defense.

These physical contractions in the musculature and nervous system gradually solidify into what Wilhelm Reich called "character armor," which we recognize as the somatic foundation of ego structure. The infant's body shapes itself around recurring experiences, developing habitual tensions that reflect their adaptations to environmental demands and threats.

The energetic regulation pattern establishes a critical component of identity formation. As the infant establishes a familiar range of tolerable arousal, the energetic bandwidth within which they feel most comfortable, this pattern becomes a fundamental aspect of how they know themselves. "This is me" becomes partly defined by "this is how my energy feels when I'm in my comfort zone." Disruptions to this pattern feel threatening not just to comfort but to identity itself, triggering defensive contractions that preserve the familiar energetic signature.

This understanding highlights why reconnection to essence must encompass both somatic and energetic work, in addition to psychological approaches. The veiling of essence exists not just in thought patterns, emotional habits, or self-concepts, but in the very tissue of the body and the characteristic patterns of the energy system. The contractions and regulatory patterns that form in response to early experiences become the physical and energetic substrate of the defensive structures that separate us from our essential nature.

**Paradox of Development**

Parents face a profound paradox: the very processes that enable their infant to thrive in the world—cognitive development, language acquisition, self-differentiation, socialization—also tend to obscure their connection to essence. This paradox cannot be resolved but must be held in awareness, informing how we approach each stage of our child's growth:

- **The Necessary Journey of Differentiation:** The infant's journey from symbiotic unity to individual selfhood is both necessary and valuable. Through this process, they develop the capacities for autonomous action, clear boundaries, and relationship as a distinct being. Yet this same journey typically involves a growing separation from the direct experience of unity and interconnection that characterizes essence.
- **The Development of Energetic Regulation:** As the infant matures, they gradually develop the capacity to regulate their energetic states, decreasing their absolute dependence on caregiver co-regulation. This growing regulatory autonomy supports healthy functioning but often comes at the cost of the merged states that facilitate essential

connection. The very boundaries that enable self-regulation also separate the infant from the unified field of being.

- **The Dual Gifts of Language:** Language acquisition opens worlds of expression, understanding, and connection for the developing child. It enables them to name their experiences, communicate their needs, and participate in the shared reality of their culture. Simultaneously, language introduces distance from direct experience, filtering immediate reality through symbols and concepts that can never fully capture essence.
- **The Emergence of Reflective Consciousness:** As infants develop the capacity for self-reflection, observing their experience rather than simply being it, they gain crucial abilities for self-awareness and understanding. This same reflective capacity, however, creates a subtle split between the observer and the observed, introducing a layer of separation from the unified field of essential experience.
- **The Somatic Foundation of Identity:** The very bodily contractions that protect the infant from overwhelming stimuli also form the somatic basis for the separate self. These protective patterns, while necessary for functioning in an imperfect world, create restrictions in how freely essence can flow through the organism.

Parents who recognize this paradox can hold a more nuanced perspective on their child's development. Rather than seeing developmental milestones as unqualified goods or viewing essence obscuration as something to be prevented at all costs, they can approach each stage with dual awareness, supporting necessary development while creating conditions that minimize unnecessary essence veiling.

This balanced approach might include:

- **Supporting Natural Development:** Encouraging the infant's growth in cognitive abilities, motor skills, language development, and social capacities as essential aspects of human development.
- **Creating Spaces for Connection to Essence:** Alongside developmental support, deliberately creating environments and interactions that maintain the infant's connection to essential qualities, such as unhurried time in nature, moments of quiet presence together, and play that emerges from joy rather than achievement.
- **Essential Awareness and Developmental Support:** Approaching developmental tasks with awareness of the essential qualities they naturally

call forth. For example, supporting motor development not just as physical mastery but as an expression of Essential Strength and will; approaching language acquisition not just as cognitive achievement but as a means for expressing the child's essential nature.

- **Somatic Awareness and Support:** Recognizing the embodied dimension of both development and essence veiling and working with the infant's body with consciousness and care. This includes gentle, respectful touch, support for natural movement patterns, and attentiveness to signs of bodily contraction that may indicate obscuration of essence.
- **Energetic Attunement:** Maintaining awareness of your infant's energetic state and offering attuned support for regulation, while gradually helping them expand their window of tolerable arousal. This attunement preserves the merging essence that occurs during co-regulation, while supporting the development of regulatory capacity.

By holding this paradox with awareness and compassion, parents can support their child's journey toward becoming a fully functioning individual while preserving their connection to the depths of being that transcend individuality. This isn't about choosing between development and essence but about fostering their integration, allowing each to enrich rather than diminish the other.

**Parental Presence as a Protective Field**

The quality of parental presence creates a field that can either protect or accelerate the veiling of an infant's essence. When parents bring presence, attunement, and recognition of their infant's essence to their interactions, they establish an energetic environment where the essence can continue to flow, even amid necessary developmental processes.

This presence is not a technique to be mastered but a way of being to be embodied. It emerges naturally as parents work with their connection to essence, gradually dissolving the veils of conditioning and projection that obscure their perception. The more parents reconnect with their essential nature, the more they can perceive and respond to the essence in their infant.

Several qualities characterize this protective presence:

- **Non-Conceptual Awareness:** The capacity to perceive the infant beyond concepts, categories, and expectations, to see them as they are in this

moment rather than through the filter of mental constructs about who they are or should be.
- **Emotional Spaciousness:** The ability to create room for the full range of the infant's emotional expressions without being overwhelmed, defensive, or reactive. This spaciousness allows the infant's feelings to move through without becoming stuck or suppressed.
- **Embodied Attunement:** A state of presence that includes body awareness, emotional resonance, and attentiveness to subtle cues. This attunement allows parents to respond to their infant's needs and states with precision and care.
- **Nervous System Regulation:** The capacity to maintain your own regulated state even when your infant is distressed, offering them the resource of your steady presence as a template for their developing system. This co-regulatory relationship helps the infant learn to return to balance after activation, reducing the need for protective contractions.
- **Energetic Attunement:** The ability to sense and respond to your infant's energetic state, recognizing when they need help discharging excess energy or when they need stimulation to raise their energetic tone. This attunement supports the merging essence that naturally flows during co-regulation.
- **Essential Recognition:** The capacity to perceive and mirror the essential qualities flowing through the infant, acknowledging not just their behaviors or achievements but the deeper qualities of being they express.

When infants are consistently held in this quality of presence, they receive a profound message: their essence is seen, valued, and welcomed. This recognition helps essence remain accessible even as personality structures develop, creating a foundation for an integrated human being that can carry through childhood and beyond.

Parents cultivate this protective presence not by adding another item to their to-do list but by prioritizing their essential work. Practices that support essential reconnection, such as meditation, inquiry, body awareness, time in nature, and creative expression, directly enhance the quality of presence parents bring to their interactions with their infant. This makes the parents' inner work not separate from parenting but integral to it, perhaps its most fundamental aspect.

**Gift of Being Seen**

Perhaps the most vital nourishment we can offer our infants is not stimulation, praise, or even love as we commonly understand it, but the felt experience of being seen. To be seen in one's essence is to be recognized beyond behavior, personality, or need. This seeing satisfies a primal longing, not only essential for healthy ego development, but for preserving the soul's continuity with its source.

Infants come into the world with this longing already alive in them. Before they can speak or conceptualize, they are already attuned to the quality of attention they receive. They don't just register what we do; they register how we are. Are we present? Are we connected to ourselves? Are we seeing them or merely managing them?

When we meet them from our essence, we create a field of presence in which their being feels known. This is not observation; it is recognition. It's not a doing; it's a state of being that radiates through tone, touch, gaze, and stillness. It affirms: *You are here. You are whole. I see you.*

As Thomas Hübl puts it, we become "a landing place for consciousness." In that space, the infant is mirrored not just as a body or a personality in formation, but as a spark of reality, undivided and luminous. This witnessing presence helps them feel real. It supports their psychological unfolding while simultaneously anchoring them in the deeper truth of their being.

Being seen in this way is not a luxury; it is a necessity. Without it, the child begins to shape themselves around absence. With it, they remain in contact with their original fullness, even as development pulls them outward into complexity and separation.

As we conclude this exploration of the unformed self, we are invited into a radical shift in orientation: to witness our children not as blank slates or bundles of potential, but as radiant expressions of essence. In honoring their unfolding with presence instead of pressure, reverence instead of reaction, we offer them what all beings long for—the felt knowing that they are seen, known, and beloved as they are.

# Chapter 11
# Emergence of the Individual

*Do not train a child to learn by force or harshness; but direct them to it by what amuses their minds, so that you may be better able to discover with accuracy the peculiar bent of the genius of each.* —Plato

From the fluid openness of infancy emerges the distinct figure of the individual child—walking, talking, naming, and declaring: "Mine." This chapter explores the paradox of individuation: how the self that becomes more defined may also lose contact with the depth it once knew effortlessly. With every step into autonomy, something essential risks falling into the background.

This isn't a mistake. It's a necessity. But it is not without cost.

The development of a separate self is one of life's magical and mysterious achievements. But its cost is often the veiling of essential presence. What begins as playful exploration becomes patterned behavior. The body, once a channel for being, becomes a badge of identity. The mind, once luminous, begins to narrate. To compare. To judge.

This chapter considers these transitions not to pathologize them but to bear witness to them. When viewed with clarity, the arc of development becomes not a story of loss but one of invitation: Can the emerging self remember its origins?

**From Fluid Being to Bodily Identity**

Individuation begins with embodiment. The soul, once only lightly tethered to form, takes up residence more fully in the body. This cathexis, this investment of presence, follows a natural arc:

- In the early weeks, awareness flickers between hunger, comfort, and merging.

- At 4 months, delight arises as the body begins to respond: hands grasp, eyes track.

- At 8 months, crawling and cruising mark a new frontier: movement becomes intention.

- By 18 months, walking, naming, and claiming signal a deeper investment: "I am my body."

But as the child claims their body, they also begin to lose something: the spaciousness that preceded form. With embodiment comes limitation, and with restriction comes ego identity.

**Self-Reflection and the Inner Mirror**

With language and cognition comes a shift. Between the ages of 4 and 6, the child begins to reflect on themselves. They can say, "I am sad," and recognize, "You think differently than I do."

This emergence of self-reflection is a marvel, but also a narrowing. Where once experience flowed freely, now it becomes observed, commented upon, and evaluated. The narrator awakens.

By the time the superego is fully formed (around age 6), the child has developed an inner authority: a voice of judgment, inherited from early caregivers and the broader culture. This voice can guide, but it can also shame. It can protect, but it can also limit.

Here, essential qualities often become distorted:

- Essential Joy becomes "too much."
- Essential Strength becomes "defiant."
- Essential Will becomes "stubborn."

The child begins to adapt. To perform. To become the version of self that is approved and accepted. And in doing so, may lose touch with the deeper well of their being.

**Witnessing the Emergent Self**

Parents cannot prevent the rise of ego. Nor should they. What they can offer, however, is a kind of presence that mirrors more than behavior. This witnessing sees the child not only in their performance but in their essence. To witness our children with this presence is to reflect not just what they do, but what they are. We help them remember the space they once knew directly.

This witnessing is not a technique. It's a state of being. It arises from our contact with essence. The more we are in touch with our depth, the more naturally we can perceive and mirror our children's depth

## Development and the Dance of Essence

Margaret Mahler's model of separation-individuation offers a clear map:

- **Differentiation (5–10 months):** The child turns outward, seeking novelty. Here, Essential Strength supports exploration.

- **Practicing (10–16 months):** Walking brings elation and independence. Essential Joy rises.

- **Rapprochement (16–24 months):** The child longs for connection but also resists it. Essential Will emerges.

- **Consolidation (2–3 years):** A coherent self-image forms. The capacity to hold both connection and separateness stabilizes.

Each phase is not just psychological but essential. Each contains both a developmental function and an opportunity to affirm the child's deeper nature.

## Cognitive Development: A Double-Edged Gift

Piaget's preoperational stage (2–7 years) is characterized by imagination, symbolic play, and the development of early logic. Yet it also fosters egocentrism, magical thinking, and the tendency to label and categorize experiences.

Symbolic thought distances the child from direct experience. A flower is no longer a mystery; it is a "rose." The mind begins to name and tame.

Still, this stage offers rich opportunities for essence to flow:

- In imaginative play, the child may embody Freedom or Brilliance without knowing the words.

- In art or movement, essential Creativity and Flow can express naturally.

The task is not to restrict development, but to weave essence into it, ensuring that even as the mind grows, the heart remains open.

**Supporting Integration**

Parents can help preserve essence within development by:

- Valuing direct experience over performance
- Modeling self-reflection without judgment
- Naming essential qualities as they arise naturally: "I see your kindness," "I feel your strength"
- Creating spaces for unstructured presence

Most of all, they can hold the paradox: their child is becoming someone, and yet they already are.

Individuation is not the opposite of essence. It is the structure that allows essence to express more fully in the world. But without conscious support, it can become a shell, a performance of self rather than a vessel for being.

As children learn to say "I," let us remember to whisper to them the deeper truth: You are.

In the next chapter, we explore how learning environments, both structured and spontaneous, can either obscure or nourish this essential unfolding. We turn our attention to education, curiosity, and the freedom to discover from within.

# Chapter 12
## Learning Through Joyful Expression

*Children need the freedom and time to play. Play is not a luxury. Play is a necessity.*
—Kay Redfield Jamison

*We don't stop playing because we grow old; we grow old because we stop playing.*
—George Bernard Shaw

*Imagination is more important than knowledge.* —Albert Einstein

*Play is the work of the child.* —Maria Montessori

**Play as a Language of Essence**

In the labyrinth of childhood development, play stands as a beacon of light, guiding the young mind through the realms of imagination, discovery, and growth. The rituals of play are not merely acts of amusement but are fundamental processes through which children learn about themselves, others, and the world around them. Through play, a child's innate joy, strength, and will are expressed and expanded, offering a fertile ground for nurturing essential qualities.

In the temple of childhood, play stands as the primary altar where essence freely expresses itself. Unlike the constructed activities of adulthood, a child's play emerges not from planning or purpose but from the immediate flow of being. When we observe a child in authentic play, we witness essence in its purest articulation, unfettered by the constraints of expectation or the boundaries of the known.

The Diamond Approach reveals that play is not merely something children do; it is a fundamental language through which essence speaks. When the two-year-old abandons herself to the joy of splashing in puddles, when the four-year-old loses himself in crafting elaborate worlds from blocks and blankets, they are not simply amusing themselves; they are expressing the essence of what they are, of what we all are beneath our accumulated layers of personality and conditioning.

This expression often emerges with a spontaneity and freedom that can become veiled in later life. The child's play unfolds with a quality of immediacy that adults struggle to recapture in meditation retreats and spiritual practices. What seekers labor to attain—present-moment awareness, freedom from outcome, the joy of being rather than doing—children embody naturally in their uninhibited play.

What we witness in these moments is not just developmental growth but essence flowing through the vessel of the young body-mind. Parents attuned to essence can recognize the distinct qualities that manifest in different forms of play: the golden warmth of merging essence when a toddler dissolves into joyful connection, the red vitality of essential strength when testing physical limits, the crystal clarity of the intelligence of essence in focused exploration, and the steel-like determination of will essence in mastering a challenging task.

Play is not simply preparation for adult life; it is life itself, lived with a fullness and authenticity that our personality structures later learn to constrain. When we understand this, we approach our children's play not as a childish diversion but as a sacred expression, worthy of our deepest respect and most careful nurturing.

**Value of Play in Development**

While play serves as a direct channel for the expression of essence, it simultaneously drives forward the necessary developmental processes highlighted by our developmental theorists. This creates a fascinating interplay; the same activities that allow essence to flow freely also build the structures that will eventually obscure it.

As Piaget observed, play is the primary vehicle through which children construct their understanding of reality. Through sensorimotor play, the infant discovers the properties of objects and the capabilities of their body. Through symbolic play, the toddler begins to represent absent objects and events, laying the groundwork for abstract thinking. Through games with rules, older children develop social negotiation and moral reasoning skills.

Vygotsky recognized play as the primary source of development in the preschool years, a zone of proximal development in which children perform tasks that exceed their daily capabilities. The child who can barely focus for five minutes on a directed task may sustain an hour of intense concentration in self-directed play. In play, children stretch beyond their current limitations, operating in what Vygotsky called "the upper end of the zone of proximal development."

Erikson understood play as the child's way of mastering experience and resolving psychosocial challenges. The repetitive play sequences of toddlers reflect their struggle with autonomy versus shame and doubt. The imaginative play of preschoolers enables them to explore initiative without crippling guilt. Through play, children approach developmental milestones not as hurdles to overcome but as territories to explore with joy.

Winnicott perhaps came closest to bridging the developmental and essential perspectives, recognizing play as occurring in a "potential space" between inner psychic reality and the external world. This transitional space serves as both the birthplace of culture and the wellspring of creativity throughout life. In Winnicott's view, play is neither wholly subjective nor wholly objective, but exists in the fertile borderland between, where essence and personality can potentially remain in dialogue rather than opposition.

Play develops the child's capacities across all domains—cognitive, social, emotional, and physical—while simultaneously providing a protected space where essence can continue to flow even as personality structures solidify. This paradoxical function makes play uniquely valuable in supporting integrated development, which balances the necessary construction of personality with ongoing connection to one's essence.

**Essential Curiosity and Its Veiling**

Perhaps no essential quality manifests more powerfully through play than curiosity, that innate, unmediated desire to know, to discover, to understand. Essential curiosity is not the acquisition of information but a quality of being characterized by openness, wonder, and engagement with reality. It is the soul's natural inclination to explore its environment without a predetermined agenda or expected outcome.

We see this quality shine brilliantly in the young child's relentless questioning. As Sir Ken Robinson noted in his landmark TED Talk (now viewed over 26 million times), "If you're at a dinner party, and you say you work in education... if you ask [people] about their education, they pin you to the wall. Because it's one of those things that goes deep with people." Our inherent curiosity about our development runs deep; it's a quality so intrinsic to our nature that we cannot help but be interested in how we and others come to be.

The young child's cascade of "why" questions isn't merely an information-gathering strategy, but an expression of essential curiosity —a direct engagement with mystery. Children ask not to collect facts but because they are moved by an authentic desire to understand the nature of reality. Their questions emerge not from constructed identity but from essence itself.

Yet as development progresses, this quality often becomes constrained and veiled. Robinson's observation that "we don't grow into creativity, we grow out of it... we get educated out of it" applies equally to essential curiosity. The conditioning processes that diminish creativity simultaneously dampen curiosity through several mechanisms:

- **From Wonder to Utility:** Educational systems gradually shift the child's relationship with knowledge from one of wonder to one of utility. Learning becomes not an end in itself but a means to external rewards—grades, adult approval, college admission, career advancement. This transition from intrinsic to extrinsic motivation fundamentally alters the quality of curiosity, transforming it from an essential quality into a strategic behavior.
- **From Openness to Certainty:** As children internalize societal expectations, curiosity increasingly becomes channeled toward "acceptable" or "productive" questions. The boundless openness characteristic of essential curiosity gradually narrows toward questions with known or desired answers. The education system's emphasis on correct answers over exploratory thinking accelerates this constriction.
- **From Immediacy to Conceptualization:** Young children's curiosity operates primarily in the immediate present, a direct engagement with what is. As language and conceptual thinking develop, curiosity becomes increasingly mediated through mental frameworks that organize experience into categories and comparisons. While this conceptualization supports significant cognitive development, it can distance the child from the direct, unmediated curiosity of essence.
- **From Truth-Seeking to Conformity:** Perhaps most significantly, children's forthright pursuit of truth often confronts the discomfort of adults. The child who innocently asks about death at a funeral, who points out physical differences between people, or who questions logical inconsistencies in adult rules often receives signals that such direct inquiry is socially inappropriate. As Robinson notes, children "will take a chance. If they don't know, they'll have a go... they're not frightened of being wrong." Yet this fearlessness gradually diminishes as children learn that social acceptance often depends on modulating direct truth-seeking to conform to societal norms.

The dampening of essential curiosity represents a significant loss in our developmental trajectory, not just in intellectual exploration but in spiritual capacity. The quality of mind that naturally inquires into the nature of reality forms the foundation for the contemplative path in virtually all wisdom traditions. When curiosity is constrained, our capacity for direct engagement with the mystery of existence also diminishes.

Parents attuned to essence can support the continued flow of essential curiosity by creating environments where open-ended questioning is valued and where "not knowing" is recognized as fertile ground for discovery. By modeling their authentic curiosity, not performances of interest but genuine engagement with questions that matter, parents invite their children's essential curiosity to remain active and accessible.

The capacity to maintain wonder in the face of society's pressure toward certainty and conformity represents one of the most precious gifts we can offer our children. As Robinson reminds us, "If you're not prepared to be wrong, you'll never come up with anything original." Cultivating spaces where children can remain "prepared to be wrong," where essential curiosity can continue flowing freely through play and exploration, lays the foundation for lifelong creativity and essential connection.

**Impact of Screen Time on Development**

Against this backdrop of integrated development through play, the increasing dominance of screens in children's lives presents a profound challenge. The average American child now spends more than seven hours a day with digital media, often beginning in infancy, despite medical recommendations against screen exposure before the age of 2.

This is not merely a matter of how children spend their time but of how their very development is shaped. Digital media fundamentally alters the developmental equation, offering experiences that are structurally different from the embodied, multisensory play that has nurtured human development throughout our evolutionary history.

During early childhood, critical developmental windows open briefly, allowing essential capabilities, such as hand-eye coordination, to form. During these sensitive periods, physical interaction with the real world sparks neural connections, underpinning the visuomotor skills necessary for tasks such as catching a ball, buttoning a shirt, or even making an expressive face. Without practice through play and exploration, these foundational skills may never properly develop, robbing children of their evolutionary inheritance. Later in life, struggling with basic coordination can have a profound impact on self-confidence, quality of life, and employability. As screens increasingly substitute for hands-on play, we risk presiding over the mass-scale erosion of essential human competencies. The stakes for our children's development are sky-high. Balancing screen entertainment with ample time for physically interactive, imaginative play is crucial.

When a child watches a screen, they engage primarily through vision and hearing, while the rest of their sensory system remains understimulated. The tactile exploration that helps wire the sensorimotor cortex, the vestibular movement that organizes the proprioceptive system, the social mirroring that activates mirror neurons—all are diminished or absent in screen interaction. Critical neural connections may never form during sensitive periods when the brain is particularly receptive to specific types of embodied experiences.

Even interactive digital experiences lack the full sensory engagement of physical play. A child playing a tablet game utilizes fine motor skills in limited patterns, rather than the varied gross and fine motor movements required for activities such as climbing, building, and manipulating physical objects. The immediate cause-and-effect of digital interactions—press a button, get an instant response—differs qualitatively from the variable feedback loops of the natural world and human relationships.

Additionally, in the context of modern childhoods, the pervasive influence of screen time presents a unique challenge to developing minds and their understanding of social contexts. Excessive screen time can foster an unrealistic view of life, particularly when used as a substitute for interactive play. Movies, video games, and other digital narratives are often formulaic, crafting a world that adheres to specific, repetitive paradigms. This constant exposure can condition children to view life through a constrained lens, akin to living within a "matrix" that limits their perception of reality and possibility. Such conditioning risks encumbering their ability to navigate the nuanced, unpredictable nature of real-world social interactions and relationships. It underscores the importance of mindful media consumption and the need for parents and educators to foster environments that promote active, engaged play over passive screen viewing. This balance is crucial for supporting the holistic development of children, enabling them to explore and understand the complexity of life beyond the screen.

Most significantly for essential development, digital media typically offers prepared content that enters through the senses rather than emerging from within. The child becomes a consumer rather than a creator, receiving predigested experiences rather than generating authentic expressions of their inner life. This passive relationship to experience runs counter to the active engagement through which essence naturally manifests.

For essential curiosity in particular, digital media presents complex challenges. While screens can provide access to information that might kindle interest, the format often frames knowledge as content to consume rather than mysteries to explore. The algorithmic nature of digital platforms tends to deliver more of what the child has already encountered rather than inviting the unexpected discoveries that nourish authentic curiosity.

Sir Ken Robinson's observation that our education system is "predicated on the idea of academic ability" finds a parallel in much educational technology, which often prioritizes quantifiable learning outcomes over the open-ended exploration where essence flows most freely. The "right answer" orientation of many educational apps and games can inadvertently reinforce the very paradigm that diminishes essential curiosity.

The consequence is not just a developmental delay in observable milestones but a subtle constriction of the child's relationship with essence. The capacity for sustained attention, for tolerating boredom as a gateway to creativity, for generating play from within rather than requiring external stimulation—these are not merely skills but conduits through which essence flows. When weakened by excessive screen engagement, these capacities may not develop adequately, leaving children less able to access and express their essential nature even when screens are absent.

This doesn't make technology inherently harmful. Digital tools will be part of our children's world and can serve valuable purposes when thoughtfully integrated. But it does suggest a fundamental imbalance in contemporary childhood that requires conscious intervention from parents committed to nurturing their child's connection to essence. The goal is not to eliminate technology but to reestablish embodied, creative play as the primary medium through which children develop and express themselves, such as:

- **Supporting Essence Through Creative Play:** As parents, our task is not to direct or structure play—essence flows most freely through spontaneous, child-initiated activity—but to create conditions where authentic play can flourish. This involves both practical arrangements of the physical environment and subtle attunement to the quality of our presence during play interactions.

- **Creating Space for Unstructured Play:** The contemporary tendency to fill children's schedules with organized activities leaves little room for the meandering exploration where essence often emerges most clearly. Children need significant blocks of uninterrupted time to immerse themselves in deep play states. This may mean deliberately protecting space in the family calendar and resisting the cultural pressure to constantly enrich or accelerate development through structured programming.

- **Providing Open-Ended Materials:** The simplest play materials often provide the best support for essential expression. Basic elements like blocks, fabric, clay, water, and natural materials invite the child to impose their meaning rather than respond to predetermined functions. A stick can become a wand, a spoon, a sword, or a bridge, allowing the child's inner life to find external form. In contrast, highly specialized toys with fixed purposes often limit creative expression and the flow of essence.

- **Cultivating Your Playfulness:** Children learn what play is not through instruction but through participation with more experienced players. When parents access their playful essence—their capacity for joy, curiosity, imagination, and presence—they create an energetic field that supports the child's essence expression. This doesn't mean performing playfulness as a parental duty, but genuinely reconnecting with the playful essence that exists within each adult, however deeply buried beneath responsibilities and conditioning.

- **Honoring Questions Without Answers:** Essential curiosity thrives when questions are valued regardless of whether they have ready answers. When children ask profound questions about existence, death, time, or consciousness, our receptivity to exploring these mysteries together, without rushing to provide simplistic explanations, honors their essential connection to the deeper dimensions of reality. As Robinson observes, the educational hierarchy that places mathematics and languages at the top while relegating arts to the bottom reflects a system designed to produce "university professors" rather than fully-realized human beings. Countering this hierarchy in the home environment means valuing philosophical inquiry, artistic expression, and embodied exploration alongside conventional academic knowledge.

- **Resisting Intervention and Direction:** The parental impulse to improve or direct educational play requires conscious moderation. When we interrupt a child's play to suggest improvements or redirect toward learning objectives, we subtly communicate that their spontaneous activity is insufficient. Essence flows most freely when children feel their play is inherently valid, not a means to an adult-defined end. This restraint becomes particularly important when it comes to children's direct exploration of truth. The tendency to mediate, soften, or redirect their forthright questions about challenging topics (like death, sexuality, or social inequities) often stems from adult discomfort rather than the child's need for protection. When we can meet their authentic curiosity with presence rather than deflection, we affirm the essence that seeks direct engagement with reality.
- **Honoring Play as Valuable in Itself:** Play is not valuable merely as preparation for future roles but as present expression of the child's authentic being. When we grant play the same respect we give to adult work and relationships—protecting it from unnecessary interruption, creating conducive environments for it, speaking of it with appreciation rather than condescension—we help maintain the child's connection to the essential qualities that manifest through play.

Through these approaches, parents can counter the cultural devaluation of play and support their child's continued access to the essence that naturally expresses through playful engagement. We create sanctuaries where the pressures of acceleration and achievement temporarily recede, allowing the child's essential nature to breathe freely even as development proceeds.

**Creative Force of Reality**

Our conventional understanding of imagination pales in comparison to its true essence. Imagination is not merely a mental faculty for entertaining fanciful possibilities or escaping reality; it is the creative force through which reality itself manifests. The arising appearance of beingness as manifestation flows through divine, cosmic, or quantum imagination. Reducing it to a mental process or emotional daydreaming reveals the profound degree of our separation from essence.

This more profound understanding of imagination sheds light on the spiritual significance of children's play, particularly the symbolic and pretend play that emerges around the second year of life. When a child transforms a block into a spaceship or a blanket into a magical cloak, they are not just exercising cognitive flexibility; they are participating directly in the fundamental creative process of existence itself.

From a developmental perspective, symbolic play represents a significant cognitive achievement. Piaget identified it as the beginning of representational thought, the capacity to mentally hold images separate from direct perception. Vygotsky viewed it as the first step toward abstraction, which eventually enables conceptual thinking. The child who pretends a banana is a telephone demonstrates the foundation for understanding that written symbols can represent spoken words.

Yet these developmental frameworks, while valuable, largely miss the essential dimension of imaginative play. When children engage in pretend scenarios, they are not merely practicing cognitive skills but exercising the same creative capacity through which all of manifestation arises from unmanifest being. They are participating in what various wisdom traditions have recognized as the fundamental nature of existence itself, the continuous emergence of form from formlessness, the play of consciousness with its infinite possibilities.

This imaginative capacity appears with such universality and spontaneity precisely because it reflects the deepest nature of reality. Children do not need to be taught to transform objects symbolically or to create imaginative worlds. This emerges naturally as an expression of their essence. The ubiquity of pretend play across cultures and throughout history reveals its rootedness not in cultural transmission but in the essential structure of consciousness itself.

When we understand imagination in this light, we approach children's pretend play with profound reverence. The child absorbed in an imaginary world is not merely entertaining themselves or practicing for adult roles, but engaging directly with the creative dimension of consciousness. Their play reflects the same dynamic through which galaxies form and dissolve, through which all manifestation arises and returns to source.

The implications for parenting are significant. Rather than viewing imagination as a charming but ultimately inconsequential aspect of childhood, we recognize it as a direct connection to the creative source of all being. We create environments that honor and protect this capacity, resisting the cultural tendency to channel imagination into purely productive or rational directions. We become more cautious about interrupting children's imaginative flow with our adult agendas and expectations.

Most importantly, we recognize that by supporting our children's imaginative play, we are not merely fostering cognitive development, but also protecting their connection to the creative dimension of existence itself. As this connection becomes increasingly veiled in most adults through conditioning and conceptual overlay, children's unmediated imaginative capacity offers a window into what we have lost and what we might, through their example, begin to rediscover.

Parents can support this dimension of play not by teaching pretending as a skill but by honoring the natural emergence of imagination and creating space for its expression. This involves:

- **Respecting the Integrity of Imaginary Worlds:** When a child is absorbed in pretend play, they inhabit a coherent reality with its logic and meaning. Entering this world requires sensitivity to its terms rather than imposing adult rationality. The parent who dismissively says, "That's not a rocket, it's just a box," not only misses an opportunity to connect with their child but inadvertently reinforces the very split between imagination and reality that obscures our essential nature.

- **Participating Without Dominating:** Adults can join children's pretend scenarios as fellow players rather than directors. This requires temporarily suspending adult agendas and allowing the play to unfold according to its internal logic, even when that logic seems chaotic or incomprehensible from an adult perspective.

- **Providing Time and Space for Extended Imaginative Play:** Complex pretend scenarios often develop over extended periods, with narratives evolving and characters developing. Protecting playtime from unnecessary interruptions allows these imaginative worlds to deepen, creating richer opportunities for both developmental growth and essence expression.

Through these approaches, parents can honor imagination not merely as a cognitive function, but as a direct connection to the creative dimension of being itself—the essential process through which all manifestation continuously emerges from the unmanifest source.

**Soul's Play**

What essence seeks through play is not merely development but expression, the soul's natural desire to manifest its qualities through form and action. As parents, we serve this expression not by shaping it toward predetermined outcomes but by creating conditions where it can emerge authentically from within.

Life isn't so much about learning as it is about discovery. The soul's relationship to reality is one of curiosity and revelation. This understanding fundamentally shifts how we approach childhood play, from seeing it as educational preparation to recognizing it as the soul's direct engagement with existence. The child's body and mind serve as vehicles for the extension and expression of the soul into this dimension of being. Through play, essence finds a pathway into form, allowing the invisible to become visible, the potential to become manifest.

We might consider ourselves gardeners tending the soil in which the seed of our child's essence grows. We cannot determine what flower will bloom or when it will open, but we can provide the conditions—light, water, space, protection—that allow the inherent pattern within the seed to unfold according to its nature.

This requires a fundamental trust in the child's intrinsic wisdom and developmental trajectory. When we observe a child deeply engaged in play that appears purposeless or repetitive, we might ask not "What is this accomplishing?" but "What essential quality is finding expression here?" The toddler repeatedly filling and emptying a bucket, the preschooler enacting the same dramatic scenario with minor variations, and the school-age child absorbed in arranging collections in precise patterns may all be manifesting forms of essential work that the rational mind cannot readily categorize.

When we recognize the body-mind as a vehicle for soul extension rather than merely a biological organism to be trained, our approach to play undergoes a transformation. We become less concerned with what skills are being developed and more attuned to how essence is finding expression. The question shifts from "What is my child learning?" to "How is my child's soul discovering and revealing itself through this play?" This perspective honors the mystery at the heart of existence—that we are not merely physical beings learning to navigate a material world but spiritual beings having a human experience, using play as a primary language of discovery.

The rituals of play, from the infant's peekaboo to the adolescent's role-playing games, create containers through which essence can flow in forms appropriate to each stage of development. These containers both structure experience, making it comprehensible, and open space for the unpredictable emergence of authentic being.

As parents, our role is to honor these rituals without either dismissing them as mere entertainment or instrumentalizing them as educational tools. We provide materials, create space, offer our presence, and then step back to allow the mystery of our child's unique essence to express itself through the universal language of play.

In doing so, we acknowledge that play is not separate from the real work of development but central to it, not a diversion from growth but the very means through which the most profound development occurs. Each moment of authentic play represents not just a step toward future competencies but a present manifestation of the child's essential being in its fullest expression.

Sir Ken Robinson's clarion call for educational revolution applies equally within the family context: "I believe this passionately: that we don't grow into creativity, we grow out of it. Or rather, we get educated out of it." His observation that "the whole system of public education around the world is a protracted process of university entrance" reminds us to be cautious about importing similarly narrow values into our home environments. When we find ourselves prioritizing academic skills over artistic expression, "useful" activities over seemingly purposeless play, or correct answers over open-ended exploration, we may be unconsciously replicating the very educational paradigm that "stigmatizes mistakes" and educates children "out of their creative capacities."

> ***What if stepping back was the most generous thing a parent could do?***
> ***We should not abandon or neglect, but offer space,***
> ***trust the child's inner rhythm, and let their essence surprise us.***

In the child's absorption in play, we glimpse not just who they are becoming, but who they most fundamentally are, beyond personality and conditioning, in the immediate truth of essence manifesting through form. If we receive it with attention and reverence, this glimpse can reawaken our connection to the essential play of being that adult life so often obscures.

The child at play thus becomes not merely a being to be developed but a teacher of the very essence we seek to rediscover. Through the simple act of witnessing our children's unselfconscious immersion in play, we may find our way back to the authentic expression that is our birthright and our deepest nature. As Robinson reminds us, we must "see our creative capacities for the richness they are, and see our children for the hope that they are." By nurturing their unmediated curiosity, boundless creativity, and joyful presence, we cultivate their future and contribute to the continued evolution of human consciousness.

**Play as Sacred Practice**

When we understand play as the soul's expression rather than merely a developmental tool, it takes on a sacred dimension. The time and space we create for play becomes not just beneficial but essential, a sanctuary where essence can flow freely, even as personality structures develop and socialization proceeds.

This perspective transforms how we approach the rituals of play in family life. The blanket fort in the living room becomes not merely an amusement but a temple of imagination where the boundaries between worlds grow thin. The collection of stones arranged and rearranged on a child's windowsill represents not merely an organizing impulse but a meditation on the nature of matter and form. The elaborate pretend scenario enacted day after day becomes a spiritual practice through which the child engages with archetypal forces and existential themes.

Parents who recognize this sacred dimension approach play not with condescension but with reverence. They create protected times and spaces where play can unfold without unnecessary interruption. They offer their presence not as supervisors but as fellow pilgrims in the mystery of being. They recognize that in witnessing their child's pure absorption in play, they stand on holy ground.

This reverence extends to respecting the child's lead in play. As Almaas's Diamond Approach teaches, essence flows most freely when allowed to emerge authentically rather than being directed by externally imposed agendas. Parents support this emergence not by controlling the content or direction of play but by removing obstacles to its natural unfolding.

The obstacle most commonly encountered in contemporary family life is simple scarcity of time and space for unstructured play. In a culture obsessed with productivity and achievement, protecting the sanctity of "non-productive" time requires conscious resistance to prevailing norms. Parents who understand play as sacred practice deliberately create margin in family schedules, regarding open time not as a vacancy to be filled but as fertile ground where essence can emerge.

Another obstacle lies in adult discomfort with apparent disorder or chaos. The developmental theorists reviewed earlier help us understand that what may appear chaotic to adult perception often represents sophisticated organizing principles at work in the child's experience. A room transformed into a complex pretend landscape, with furniture repurposed and objects scattered in seemingly random patterns, may reflect an intricate inner order invisible to the adult eye. Parents who can tolerate this apparent disorder, maintaining basic safety while suspending judgment about "mess," create space for essence to express through forms that transcend conventional organization.

Perhaps the most significant obstacle, however, is the adult's disconnection from the playful dimension of essence. When parents have lost touch with their capacity for imaginative engagement, embodied joy, and present-moment absorption, they may unconsciously communicate that these qualities are childish rather than essential. Reconnecting with our playful essence, allowing ourselves to be "reeducated" by our children's example, may be the most profound gift we can offer both them and ourselves.

As the psychologist Bruno Bettelheim observed, "The child intuitively comprehends that although these stories are unreal, they are not untrue..." Children naturally operate at the intersection of imagination and reality, recognizing that symbolic truth often runs deeper than literal fact. Their play embodies this understanding, moving fluidly between worlds with a wisdom that adults frequently lose amid the fragmentation of modern consciousness.

By honoring the rituals of play as sacred practice, we help preserve this wisdom not as a phase to be outgrown but as a fundamental way of engaging with reality that remains accessible throughout life. We create family cultures where essence can continue flowing through play, even as necessary development proceeds, where joy, creativity, wonder, and presence are valued as expressions of our deepest nature, rather than childish inclinations to be abandoned in favor of productivity and rationality.

**Dance Between Structure and Freedom**

The relationship between play and development creates a fundamental paradox: the same activities that build the structures that will eventually obscure essence also provide channels through which essence can flow freely. This paradox necessitates a delicate balance between structure and freedom in our approach to children's play.

Too much structure—adult-directed activities, educational agendas, predetermined outcomes—constrains the spontaneous emergence of essence. Play becomes instrumentalized as a means to developmental ends rather than honored as an authentic expression of being. The child learns that value lies not in their inherent nature but in acquiring skills and meeting external expectations.

Conversely, too little structure—absence of boundaries, lack of consistent rhythms, unlimited options—can create anxiety rather than freedom. Without the containing function of appropriate limits, play may become scattered or frenetic rather than deeply absorptive. The child's essence needs both freedom of expression and the security of reliable boundaries within which to unfold.

Parents navigate this balance not through rigid formulas but through attunement to their specific child in specific contexts. The art of supporting play lies in discerning when to step back and when to step in; when to expand possibilities and when to provide containment; when to follow the child's lead and when to offer guidance.

This dance between structure and freedom reflects the broader relationship between development and essence illustrated in our graph. As personality structures necessarily strengthen (the ascending line), conscious connection to essence typically diminishes (the descending line). Yet through conscious parenting approaches, we can moderate the steepness of this divergence, fostering development that remains more permeable to essence.

The rituals of play offer perhaps our most powerful tool in this endeavor. By creating family cultures that value play not as a developmental stage to be outgrown but as a fundamental mode of being to be preserved, we help maintain our children's connection to their essential nature even as they navigate the necessary journey of socialization and personality development.

## The Continuing Dance

As we conclude our exploration of play, we return to its fundamental paradox: it simultaneously builds the structures that will eventually obscure essence and provides channels through which essence can continue to flow, even as these structures develop. This paradox reflects the broader relationship between development and essence, which forms the central theme of our book.

The challenge for parents lies not in resolving this paradox but in dancing with it, supporting their child's necessary development while creating conditions where essence can continue flowing with maximum freedom. By understanding play not merely as a means to developmental ends but as a direct expression of the soul's engagement with existence, parents approach this dance with greater awareness and intention.

The rituals of play, from the infant's peekaboo to the adolescent's complex social games, create containers where essence and development can potentially remain in dialogue rather than opposition. Within these containers, children explore the physical world, navigate social relationships, process emotional experiences, and construct cognitive understanding, all while potentially maintaining connection to the essential qualities that animate these activities from within.

In the temple of childhood, play stands as the primary altar where essence freely expresses itself. By honoring the sanctity of this expression, we help preserve our children's connection to their deepest nature. The dance between essence and development continues, with play providing both the music and the dance floor where this intricate choreography unfolds. Each parent finds their way of participating in this dance, guided by attunement to their child's unique expression and commitment to nurturing the spark that makes them not just a developing organism, but a soul extending into form through the miracle of embodied existence.

# Chapter 13
## Preserving the Spark

*Every child comes with the message that God is not yet discouraged of humanity.*
—Rabindranath Tagore

The phrase "preserving the spark" might suggest a deliberate effort, a set of strategies to protect something fragile. However, essence isn't delicate, and our most profound parenting doesn't come from doing but from being.

**Understanding Essence in Practical Parenting**

Essence-aware parenting isn't about adding more tasks to your already full plate or mastering new techniques. It's about showing up fully, with your whole being, in the ordinary moments that make up family life.

When your toddler melts down in the grocery store, it's not how cleverly you manage the situation that matters but your willingness to be present with both their overwhelm and your discomfort without abandoning either of you.

When your child creates something unexpected, essence flows not through your calculated praise but through your genuine curiosity and delight in witnessing their expression.

When bedtime feels endless and your patience wears thin, essence emerges not from perfect responses but from your honesty about your limits while maintaining connection despite frustration.

The most practical approach to essence isn't a strategy but a presence. This presence doesn't require special training or esoteric knowledge; it simply requires the courage to meet what is happening rather than forcing what you think should happen. A few simple truths guide this path:

- **You don't need to fix everything.** Often, what children need most isn't our solutions but our company as they navigate their experiences. When we rush to solve problems, we may inadvertently communicate that their feelings are too much or that they are incapable. Simply being with them in their struggles, without rescuing or abandoning them, creates a space where their essence can continue to flow through difficulty.

- **What you can't be with controls you.** When certain feelings or behaviors in our children trigger reactive patterns in us, we lose access to our essence and respond from conditioning instead. The willingness to feel our discomfort without an immediate reaction creates the freedom to respond from a place of presence rather than a pattern.
- **Essence recognizes essence.** When we're connected to our essential nature, we naturally recognize and respond to essence in our children. This mutual recognition doesn't require techniques or strategies; it happens naturally when we're present and undefended.

This understanding transforms parenting from a series of problems to solve into a continuously unfolding relationship between beings. Our children don't need us to have all the answers; they need us to be authentic companions in the mystery of growing.

## Creating Environments That Support Essence

The spaces we create and inhabit with our children aren't just physical arrangements but fields of relationship that either support or hinder essential connection. These environments emerge not primarily from design decisions but from the quality of presence we bring to our daily lives, such as:

- **Presence over Perfection:** An immaculate playroom where a parent hovers anxiously about mess offers less essential support than a simple space where relaxed attention allows exploration. The most beautiful nursery can't compensate for a parent who is too exhausted or preoccupied to be fully present. Rather than striving for the perfect environment, focus on bringing your genuine presence to the environment you have.
- **Spaciousness in Time:** Perhaps nothing supports essence more than unhurried time. When we're constantly rushing from one activity to the next, essence gets squeezed out in favor of efficiency. Creating pockets of unscheduled time allows both you and your child to shift from doing to being, where essence naturally emerges. This doesn't require dramatic schedule changes. Even ten minutes of fully present, unagendized time can create an opening for essence to flow.
- **Embracing the Ordinary:** Essence doesn't wait for special occasions or extraordinary circumstances; it flows through the most mundane moments when we're fully present. Washing dishes together, walking to the mailbox, and folding laundry—these everyday activities become opportunities for

connection when approached with presence rather than as tasks to be completed. The bath time that becomes a moment of delight, the meal preparation that turns into an exploration of textures and tastes—these ordinary moments often provide the richest connection to essences.

- **Allowing Natural Rhythms:** Children naturally move between periods of activity and rest, connection and solitude, structure and freedom. When we impose rigid schedules that fight against these natural rhythms, we often create unnecessary friction that obscures essence. Noticing and respecting your child's natural patterns—when they naturally wake and tire, when they seek connection or need space—allows for smoother flows that support connection to essence.

- **Making Space for Wonder:** Wonder emerges not from elaborate activities but from the quality of attention we bring to ordinary experience. A parent who can pause to really look at the snail a toddler discovers, who can share genuine fascination with how water spirals down a drain, who can marvel at the changing shapes of clouds—this parent creates a field where wonder flourishes naturally. This doesn't require special knowledge or educational agendas, just the willingness to notice and be moved by the world alongside your child.

These environmental supports for essence don't depend on perfect conditions or special resources. They emerge from our relationship with essence, our willingness to drop from busy doing into simple being, even briefly, throughout the day. As we create these openings in our experience, we naturally create environments where our children's essence can continue flowing freely.

## Discipline, Boundaries, and Essence

Few aspects of parenting challenge essence more directly than setting and maintaining appropriate boundaries. When children push limits or express themselves in ways that create problems, our essential connection is often tested most severely. This is where boundaries must arise, not from reactivity but from presence, and not from control but from clarity. Consider the following expressions of essence-based boundary-setting:

- **Beyond Strategies to Presence:** Effective boundaries emerge not primarily from clever techniques but from our grounded presence. A parent who is firmly rooted in their being, who can hold their center amid a child's storm, provides containment that feels secure rather than controlling. This presence-based boundary-setting doesn't require raised voices or elaborate consequences; it flows from the parent's embodied knowing of where they stand.

- **The Boundary of Being With:** Perhaps the most powerful boundary we can offer our children is our willingness to stay emotionally present with their feelings while limiting problematic behaviors. "I won't let you hit, and I'll stay with you while you're angry" creates a container that honors both the essential feeling and the necessary limit. This boundary of being-with allows emotion to move through rather than becoming stuck or suppressed.
- **Curiosity Instead of Certainty:** When challenging behaviors emerge, our first reaction is often to figure out how to stop them. Essence-awareness discipline begins instead with genuine curiosity: What might be happening here? What need is being expressed through this behavior? What's being called for in this moment? This curiosity isn't a technique to achieve compliance, but rather an authentic interest in understanding what's unfolding.
- **The Soul's Discipline:** Beyond rules and consequences lies what might be called the soul's discipline, the natural guidance that emerges when we respond from essence rather than conditioning. This discipline doesn't follow formulas or strategies but arises freshly in each situation from our deepest knowing. Sometimes it's firm, sometimes gentle; sometimes structured, sometimes flowing but always attuned to what this unique moment calls for.
- **Repair after Rupture:** The path of essence-aware parenting isn't about avoiding all conflict or maintaining perfect harmony. It's about developing the capacity to reconnect after inevitable disconnections. When we lose access to our essence and react from conditioning, as all parents sometimes do, the practice isn't self-judgment but honest repair. "I spoke harshly earlier. I was frustrated, but I'd like a chance to try again more calmly." This modeling of repair teaches more than any lecture on proper behavior ever could.

The essence-aware approach to discipline doesn't promise easier parenting or perfectly behaved children. It offers something more valuable: the possibility of maintaining connection through challenges, of teaching through relationship rather than control, and of helping children develop inner guidance that emerges from their essence rather than simply complying with external demands.

**Journey of Parental Growth Alongside the Child**

The most profound support for our child's connection to essence comes not from what we do for them, but from our journey of reconnection to essence. As we discover or rediscover aspects of our essential nature that may have become obscured, we naturally create an environment where our child's essence can continue flowing freely. This inward journey reveals itself in several ways:

- **The Child as Teacher:** Children often express essential qualities with a directness and purity that adults have forgotten. The delight a toddler takes in splashing puddles, the complete absorption a child brings to building with blocks, the spontaneous compassion shown to a hurt friend—these moments offer living reminders of essential qualities we too possess but may have lost touch with. By allowing ourselves to be touched and taught by our children's essential expressions, we rediscover these qualities in ourselves.

- **Meeting Our Patterns:** Nothing reveals our conditioning more clearly than parenting. When our child's behavior triggers our reactivity—perhaps their defiance evokes our control issues, their exuberance awakens our discomfort with expression, or their neediness touches our fear of dependency—we face a choice: react from a pattern or respond from presence. Each time we pause in this moment of activation, feeling our discomfort without being driven by it, we create an opening for essence to flow where conditioning previously dominated.

- **Being with What Is:** Perhaps the most fundamental practice of essence-awareness parenting is simply being with what is—the beautiful and the difficult, the connecting and the challenging, the flowing and the stuck moments that constitute family life. This being-with doesn't mean passive acceptance of harmful situations but a willingness to meet reality directly rather than constantly wishing things were different. When we fight against what is, we contract around our resistance, blocking the flow of essence. When we meet what is with open presence, we create space for essence to inform even the most difficult circumstances.

- **Growing Through Imperfection:** The path of reconnecting to essence doesn't demand perfection. In fact, our imperfections often provide the most direct openings for growth. The moments when we lose patience, miss our child's needs, and react rather than respond—these apparent failures, when met with honesty rather than denial, become invitations to a deeper connection with essence. It's not our perfection but our humanity that ultimately creates the most supportive environment for our child's essence to flourish.

- **The Mutual Discovery:** At its heart, essence-aware parenting involves a mutual discovery where parent and child continually reveal essence to each other through their ordinary interactions. The child who says "Look at me!" isn't just seeking approval; they are inviting a shared presence. The parent who truly looks, who allows themselves to be touched by their child's being, receives as much as they give in this exchange. This mutuality transforms parenting from a one-way responsibility into a shared journey of growth and development.

This journey doesn't follow a linear path of constant progress. It unfolds through cycles of connection and disconnection, presence and absence, essence flow and conditioning. What sustains the journey isn't technique or discipline, but a fundamental commitment to showing up—to meeting each moment, each challenge, and each joy—as fully as we can, and beginning again whenever we lose our way.

## Finding Balance Between Autonomy and Connection

The dance between autonomy and connection unfolds naturally throughout childhood, with each phase bringing its essential challenges and opportunities. Rather than managing this process, essence-aware parents attune to its natural rhythm, supporting without controlling its unfolding. This attunement takes shape in several key recognitions:

- **The Wisdom of Development:** Each developmental phase has its wisdom and purpose. The toddler asserting "no" and "mine" isn't being difficult, but discovering essential Will and Autonomy. The child who alternates between clingy dependence and fierce independence isn't confused; they are navigating the natural tension between connection and separation. By trusting the developmental process rather than fighting against it, we allow essence to flow through each phase in its own way.
- **Being with Ambivalence**: The path toward healthy autonomy rarely proceeds linearly. More often, it involves ambivalence, wanting independence one moment and closeness the next, asserting boundaries, then seeking reassurance. This ambivalence doesn't indicate a problem but a natural integration process as children learn to hold both autonomy and

connection simultaneously. Our willingness to be with this ambivalence without needing to resolve it in either direction supports the awareness of essence through these fluctuations.

- **The Security That Supports Exploration:** When children feel secure in connection, they naturally move toward appropriate autonomy. This security doesn't come from clinging or controlling, but from reliable presence that allows both closeness and distance as needed. A parent who can be emotionally available without being intrusive creates the conditions where independence can develop without defensive separation. This security emerges not from techniques but from our comfort with both connection and autonomy, our ability to be close without clinging and separate without abandoning.
- **Respecting the Child's Rhythm:** Each child has their own timing and rhythm in the autonomy-connection dance. Some individuals move more quickly toward independence, while others hold on to connection; some process transitions easily, while others require more time and support during changes. Essence-aware parenting involves attuning to your specific child's rhythm rather than imposing developmental expectations based on external timelines. This attunement doesn't require expert knowledge but simply close attention to your child's unique being.
- **Being with Power Struggles:** The assertion of autonomy inevitably creates moments of clash—the toddler who refuses to leave the park, the preschooler who insists on wearing shorts in winter. Rather than viewing these as problems to solve with clever strategies, essence-aware parents recognize them as natural expressions of emerging Will. By maintaining our center while acknowledging the legitimacy of our child's perspective, we create space where both necessary boundaries and genuine autonomy can be honored without power struggles becoming battlegrounds of will.

This balance between autonomy and connection isn't achieved through formulas or techniques but through our willingness to be present with its natural unfolding—supporting without controlling, guiding without suppressing, connecting without clinging. As we find this balance within ourselves, we naturally support its emergence in our children.

### Increasing Independence and Sense of Self

As children grow, they develop an increasingly defined sense of self with unique preferences, capabilities, and perspectives. This necessary development can either remain in living relationship with essence or create rigid structures that obscure it, depending mainly on how we respond to our child's emerging selfhood. This responsiveness begins with a shift in orientation:

- **Beyond Labels to Presence:** When children begin defining themselves—"I'm good at climbing," "I'm shy," "I like dinosaurs"—they're making sense of their experience through emerging self-concepts. Rather than either reinforcing or challenging these labels, essence-aware parents bring curious presence to the experience beneath the label. "You're enjoying climbing today," acknowledges the present experience without fixing it as an identity. This presence allows self-understanding to develop without hardening into limiting definitions.
- **The Family Ecosystem and Personality Development:** The family environment has a profound influence on how a child's sense of self develops. In our book, *The Enneagram World of the Child*, we explore how the family ecosystem, particularly parental personality patterns, impacts the developing child's relationship with their essence and personality development. The Enneagram offers a valuable lens not for typing children (which would prematurely fix their fluid identity) but for understanding the patterns adults bring to parenting.

When parents gain insight into their personality structures—the habitual attention patterns, core motivations, and defensive strategies of their Enneagram (personality) type—they can become more conscious of how these patterns influence their children's development. A Type One parent's focus on improvement might inadvertently communicate that natural expression isn't good enough. A Type Two's emphasis on relationship might subtly discourage independence. The child might interpret a Type Five's need for space as a form of emotional distance.

Understanding these dynamics doesn't require labeling children with personality types. Instead, it invites parents to become more aware of the "water their family swims in"—the implicit messages, emotional tones, and relational patterns that create the environment in which the child's sense of self naturally forms. This awareness creates possibilities for more conscious parenting that supports healthy development while maintaining essential connection. This approach includes:

- **Being with Comparison:** Around age four, children become increasingly aware of how they compare to others. This developmental shift isn't a problem to solve but a natural expansion of social awareness. When children express comparison ("She's better at drawing than me."), essence-aware parents neither dismiss the observation nor reinforce its evaluative component. Instead, they bring presence to the experience: "You're noticing differences in how people draw. Each person has their way of seeing and creating." This presence allows children to notice differences without defining worth through comparison.

- **Supporting Authentic Expression:** As children develop stronger preferences and perspectives, they may face social pressure to conform or perform. Essence-aware parents support authenticity not by fighting against these social realities but by creating spaces where genuine expression is welcomed and valued. A child who knows they can be fully themselves at home develops resilience that helps them navigate social expectations without losing touch with their essential nature.
- **Being with the Child Who Is:** Perhaps most fundamentally, essence-aware parenting involves meeting the child who is, not the child we imagine or wish for. When we project our unfulfilled dreams, fears, or expectations onto our children, we create distortions that obscure both their essence and our own. The practice of continually returning to the actual child before us, with their unique temperament, gifts, challenges, and timing, creates the foundation for authentic development that remains connected to essence.
- **The Gift of Being Seen:** Nothing supports the integration of developing selfhood with continuing connection to essence more powerfully than the experience of being truly seen. When we recognize not just our child's behaviors or achievements but their essential being, when our eyes light up at their simple presence before any doing, we affirm that their worth isn't tied to performance or conformity. This recognition doesn't require special insight or understanding; it simply requires the willingness to set aside our agendas and preconceptions long enough to meet the being before us.

As children grow toward increasing independence, our role shifts but doesn't diminish. We remain essential witnesses to their unfolding, creating through our presence a field where development can proceed naturally without unnecessary obscuration of essence. This witnessing isn't a technique to master but a way of being with our children that honors both their growing autonomy and their continuing essence.

**When Parenting Challenges Our Essential Connection**

Parenting brings some of life's greatest joys and deepest fulfillments. It also brings us face-to-face with our limitations in ways few other experiences can. These challenging moments—when we feel overwhelmed, inadequate, frustrated, or lost—aren't failures of essence-aware parenting but powerful invitations into deeper truth. These invitations often take the form of:

- **Meeting Frustration:** The parent who has patiently explained the same thing for what feels like the hundredth time, who has tried every approach they can think of, and who reaches the edge of their capacity, this parent stands at a powerful threshold. When we meet frustration not as an enemy to overcome but as a messenger pointing to our current limits, something profound can shift. The simple acknowledgment "I'm feeling really frustrated right now" opens up space where there was only constriction before. This truth-telling doesn't solve the situation but creates breathing room where new possibilities can emerge.

- **Embracing Not-Knowing:** Modern parenting culture bombards us with expert advice, proven techniques, and confident pronouncements about the "right way" to raise children. Yet every parent eventually faces moments when none of this knowledge helps, when we simply don't know what to do or how to proceed. These moments of acknowledged ignorance, rather than failures, are opportunities to drop from the realm of information into the wisdom of presence. When we can say honestly, "I don't know what to do here" without shame or panic, we open to a deeper knowing that transcends techniques and strategies.

- **The Gift of Helplessness:** Perhaps no feeling is more uncomfortable for parents than helplessness—those moments when our child suffers and we cannot fix it, when circumstances overwhelm our resources, when our best efforts make no visible difference. Yet paradoxically, these moments of acknowledged helplessness often become powerful turning points. When we stop fighting against our limitations and simply acknowledge "I can't solve this right now," something shifts. This surrender isn't resignation but a recognition of a truth that often creates space for unexpected grace to enter.

- **When Our Way Meets Reality:** We all carry images of the parents we want to be—patient, wise, consistent, kind. When reality repeatedly fails to match these images—when we lose our temper despite our best intentions, when we make mistakes we promised ourselves we wouldn't make—we face a crucial choice. We can double down on our ideal image, creating increasing tension between aspiration and reality, or we can meet the truth of our humanity with compassion. This compassionate truth-telling doesn't lower standards but creates authentic ground from which real growth can occur.

- **Curiosity as the Way Through:** When parenting brings us to our knees, when we've reached the end of our knowledge, patience, or capacity, curiosity offers a way forward. Not the analytical curiosity that seeks explanations or solutions, but the open curiosity that wonders: "What's really happening here?" "What am I not seeing?" "What might this difficulty be inviting me into? "This curiosity doesn't seek quick answers but creates space where fixed perspectives can soften and new understanding can emerge.
- **Presence as the Ultimate Resource:** Beneath all the specific challenges of parenting lies a universal truth: presence is our deepest resource and most reliable guide. Not a perfect, untroubled presence that never experiences difficulty, but an honest, embodied presence that can acknowledge challenges without being defined by them. This presence doesn't solve all problems or prevent all pain, but it provides solid ground from which we can meet whatever arises with as much openness, truth, and compassion as we can access in this moment.

These challenging moments in parenting, rather than obstacles to essential connection, often become its most direct pathways. When we're stripped of our strategies and certainties, when we stand vulnerable in our not-knowing, we frequently discover a deeper ground of being that has been here all along. From this ground, we find resources we didn't know we had and capacities that transcend our familiar limitations. This isn't a dramatic transformation but a quiet recognition of what has always been true: essence flows not despite our humanity, but through it, not beyond our limitations, but within them, not after our struggles, but in their very midst.

**The Unending Invitation**

The preservation of the spark ultimately doesn't depend on perfect parenting or special knowledge. It emerges from our willingness to be present, to meet each moment with as much awareness and authenticity as we can bring, and to begin again whenever we lose our way. Through this presence—imperfect, human, and real—we create the conditions where our children's essence can continue illuminating their development, and where our essence can guide us through the profound journey of parenting.

Parenting is not primarily a task to master but a relationship to inhabit; not a problem to solve but a mystery to live. The child before us, this particular being with their unique temperament, gifts, challenges, and timing, brings exactly what is needed to call forth our growth and awakening. As we meet them with increasing presence and decreasing agenda, both their essence and ours find space to flow more freely through the ordinary moments that make up family life.

The journey never ends and is never perfected. It unfolds day by day, moment by moment, through cycles of connection and disconnection, presence and absence, essence flow and conditioning. What sustains this journey isn't technique or discipline but a fundamental commitment to showing up, to meeting each moment, each challenge, each joy as fully as we can, and beginning again whenever we lose our way.

In the end, the most valuable gift we offer our children isn't perfect guidance or ideal conditions but our honest presence, our willingness to be with them as they are, to let them be with us as we are and to discover together the mystery and wonder of being fully alive. This gift requires no special training or esoteric knowledge, just the courage to meet what is happening rather than forcing what we think should happen.

The spark preserves itself when given space to breathe. Our task is to keep clearing away what obscures it—our expectations, our agendas, our certainties—and to recognize it when it appears in the ordinary miracle of our child's unfolding life. This recognition doesn't depend on special circumstances or dramatic revelations but on the quality of attention we bring to everyday moments. In the child's laughter, in their tears, in their questions and discoveries, in their struggles and triumphs, essence continually reveals itself to those willing to see.

The invitation is always now. The door is always here. The spark is always present, waiting only for our recognition to illuminate the profound journey we share with our children.

# SECTION 3: The Developmental Lens

## Chapter 14
## Birth to 6 Months

**The Infant's Sensory Experience**

From the moment of birth, infants are immersed in a world of sensory experiences. Unlike adults, who filter sensory information through layers of conceptual understanding, newborns encounter the world directly, without the mediating influence of language or categorization.

Their vision, though initially limited to about 8-12 inches—roughly the distance to a caregiver's face during feeding—gradually sharpens. High-contrast patterns and human faces particularly captivate them. Hearing is well-developed at birth, with newborns showing a preference for human voices, especially the familiar voices of their primary caregivers. Touch provides essential comfort and regulation, with skin-to-skin contact proving particularly soothing and supportive for developing infants.

The infant's experience is primarily one of sensation without clear differentiation between self and other. As Winnicott describes, the newborn exists as an "unintegrated matrix" with no defined self-other boundary. This state of being represents what Almaas refers to as an "undifferentiated field of conscious awareness" where essence flows freely, unobstructed by personality structures that will later develop.

**Developmental Theories Applied to the Earliest Stage**

During these first 6 months, each of our developmental theorists offers crucial insights into the infant's experience and needs:

- **Piaget's Sensorimotor Stage:** During these first 6 months, infants progress from reflexive activity to more intentional behaviors, primarily learning through sensory experiences and motor actions as part of the initial substages of sensorimotor development. Toward the end of this period, around 4 to 5 months, the crucial cognitive milestone of object permanence begins to develop.

- **Bowlby's Attachment Theory:** During the initial 6 months, infants are in the pre-attachment phase, forming foundational bonds with their primary caregivers. Consistent, responsive care that meets their innate seeking behaviors (such as crying and cooing) is crucial for establishing the groundwork for secure attachment and building a sense of security.
- **Erikson's Trust vs. Mistrust:** The first psychosocial crisis, Trust vs. Mistrust, is pivotal during the initial 6 months. Consistent and nurturing care helps infants develop a fundamental sense of trust in their caregivers and the world, a foundation that is essential for all subsequent development.
- **Mahler's Autistic and Symbiotic Phases:** According to Mahler, the earliest weeks fall into the "normal autism" phase, with infants primarily focused on internal sensations. This is followed by the "symbiotic phase" (approximately 1-5 months), during which infants start to develop awareness of the caregiver, albeit as an extension of themselves rather than a distinct individual.

## Foundation of Trust

Despite their diverse theoretical orientations, our nine developmental theorists converge remarkably on the **critical importance of trust during the first 6 months of life.** This convergence illuminates something profound about the infant's world and needs during this period:

### Bowlby's Attachment Theory:

- Emphasizes that the foundation for secure attachment begins forming immediately after birth
- The infant's pre-attachment behaviors (crying, smiling, grasping) are designed to maintain proximity to caregivers
- Responsive caregiving during this period begins establishing the infant's internal working model that the world is safe and caregivers are reliable

### Erikson's Trust vs. Mistrust:

- Identifies the first psychosocial crisis as trust versus mistrust
- Consistent, predictable, and warm caregiving helps the infant develop basic trust in the world
- This trust becomes the foundation upon which all future psychosocial development builds

**Winnicott's Holding Environment:**

- Describes the "good enough mother" who provides a supportive physical and psychological environment

- The infant experiences a sense of being "held" both physically and emotionally

- This holding environment creates continuity of being for the infant, facilitating the emergence of the true self

**Mahler's Autistic and Symbiotic Phases:**

- Describes the first few weeks as a period of "normal autism," where the infant is primarily absorbed in internal sensations

- This transitions into the "symbiotic phase" from approximately 1-5 months, where the infant begins to develop awareness of the caregiver but experiences them as an extension of themselves

- Both phases rely on consistent caregiving that meets the infant's needs

**Piaget's Sensorimotor Stage:**

- During the first substage of the sensorimotor period, infants learn primarily through reflexes and sensory experiences

- They begin to develop basic trust in the predictability of their own bodies and the environment

- This predictability is essential for cognitive development to progress

**Significance for the Child's World**

This convergence tells us something profound about the infant's experience during this period:

- **The infant lives in a world where trust is existential, not conceptual.** For the newborn, trust is not a belief but an embodied experience of having needs met, discomfort relieved, and connection provided.

- **The infant's entire reality is relationship-dependent.** They cannot regulate their physiological or emotional states and depend entirely on caregivers to fulfill this function.

- **The foundation being built is preverbal and preconceptual.** The trust or mistrust developed during this stage operates at a bodily, sensory level that will influence all future development.

- **Consistency matters more than perfection.** All theorists emphasize that it is the pattern of responsive care, rather than flawless care, that establishes trust.

The convergence of these theories around trust reveals that during the first 6 months, the infant's primary developmental task is establishing a fundamental sense of security in existence itself. This transcends particular developmental domains (cognitive, social, emotional) and forms the bedrock upon which all future growth depends.

## Developmental Milestones Through a Combined Lens

When we integrate insights from our developmental theorists, we can appreciate the remarkable progression that occurs during the first 6 months:

### Birth to 2 Months:

- Reflexive responses dominate (Piaget)
- Focus on internal sensations in "normal autism" phase (Mahler)
- Pre-attachment behaviors emerge (Bowlby)
- The beginnings of trust formation through consistent caregiving (Erikson)
- Reliance on the "holding environment" (Winnicott)

### 2 to 4 Months:

- Transition to the "symbiotic phase" where the infant begins to recognize caregivers (Mahler)
- Social smiling emerges, a significant attachment behavior (Bowlby)
- Primary circular reactions develop as babies repeat actions that produce interesting results (Piaget)
- Early vocalizations and turn-taking in "conversations" (Vygotsky)
- Increasing responsiveness to social engagement (Bandura)

**4 to 6 Months:**

- Secondary circular reactions develop as babies begin intentionally repeating actions that affect their environment (Piaget)

- More distinct attachment behaviors form as infants show a preference for primary caregivers (Bowlby)

- Increasing emotional attunement between infant and caregiver (Winnicott)

- Beginnings of object permanence (Piaget)

- More deliberate social engagement and responsiveness (Vygotsky, Bandura)

**Trust, Security, and the Holding Environment**

Winnicott's concept of the "holding environment" proves particularly valuable for understanding the infant's needs during this phase. This environment encompasses both physical holding and the psychological containment provided by attentive caregiving. The caregiver who attunes to the infant's needs, providing comfort, nutrition, and appropriate stimulation, creates what Winnicott termed a "good enough" holding environment.

This holding environment does more than meet physical needs; it provides the psychological security necessary for healthy development. When an infant's distress signals are consistently met with sensitive responsiveness, they directly experience what Almaas calls "basic trust, a non-conceptual, preverbal confidence in the fundamental goodness and support of reality itself.

This basic trust differs from conventional trust in its focus on specific outcomes or individuals. It represents a deeper, more essential orientation toward existence, an implicit sense that being itself is benevolent and supportive. An infant operating from basic trust exhibits an unquestioned sense of safety, which manifests in their relaxed body, easy engagement with the environment, and capacity to be soothed after distress.

**Dominance of Merging Gold Essence**

From the perspective of essence, the first 6 months are characterized by what Almaas terms "Merging Gold Essence," a quality of essence characterized by profound togetherness and contentment. This quality manifests as a state of complete peace, where the boundaries between the infant and caregiver temporarily dissolve, creating a harmonious experience of oneness.

Parents can recognize Merging Gold Essence in their infant as a state of blissful contentment, often occurring during feeding, gentle holding, or quiet alertness. The infant appears to melt into the caregiver, perfectly relaxed and at ease. Their facial expressions soften, their bodies relax, and they emanate a quality of peaceful presence.

This merging essence can be experienced as a golden, honey-like substance that melts boundaries and relaxes one into the sweet goodness of being. It represents the infant's natural capacity to surrender entirely to the moment, experiencing the world without separation or resistance.

Parents might observe this essential expression following what developmental psychologists call the "charge-discharge cycle." When an infant transitions from a state of distress to one of regulation, such as from crying to calm after being fed or comforted, there is often a noticeable "melting" quality as their nervous system settles. This represents the activation of the parasympathetic nervous system, allowing essence to flow more freely.

**Recognition and Support of Merging Essence in Infants**

For parents, recognizing and supporting Merging Gold Essence involves creating opportunities for unrushed, attuned connection. Skin-to-skin contact, gentle holding, soft singing, or simply being fully present with the infant can invite this quality to emerge. Parents who themselves relax into these moments, allowing their boundaries to soften during connection, can deepen the infant's experience of merging essence.

**Myth of Perfect Parenting**

The collective wisdom from developmental psychology offers a clear message on "perfect parenting," "The quest for perfection in parenting is a myth and an unattainable ideal." Instead, these theorists emphasize the importance of responsive, sensitive, and understanding parenting practices that adapt to the child's needs.

Winnicott's concept of the "good enough" mother (or primary caregiver) celebrates the imperfections of parenting. It acknowledges that when repaired, minor failures in responsiveness can contribute to the child's resilience and understanding of a nuanced world.

For parents caught in the pursuit of perfect parenting, working on understanding and, if necessary, moderating the demands of their superego can be incredibly liberating. Exploring the origins of one's ideals enables a more compassionate approach to parenting, where mistakes are viewed as natural and learning opportunities rather than failures.

**Parental Practices**

For parents navigating these first 6 months, several practices can support both development and essential connection:

- **Responsive Caregiving:** Responding promptly and sensitively to your infant's needs builds trust and security. This doesn't mean perfect caregiving, but rather an attentive presence that acknowledges and addresses distress.

- **Creating Rhythm and Continuity:** Establishing gentle routines provides predictability that helps infants regulate their states and develop a sense of security in the flow of daily life.

- **Physical Closeness:** Frequent holding, skin-to-skin contact, and gentle touch support physical development and connection to essence.

- **Attuned Stimulation:** Offering sensory experiences tailored to your infant's current state—active play during alert periods, soothing during periods of fatigue—supports cognitive development while respecting their unique essence.

- **Mindful Presence:** Spending time simply being with your infant, noticing their breathing, expressions, and movements without an agenda, creates space for connection to essence.

- **Self-Reflection:** Journaling about your observations and experiences with your infant can deepen your awareness of both their development and essential expressions.

**Self-Reflection Questions for Parents**

- **Reflecting on Responses and Environment:** How do you and your infant adapt to and interact with different environments and routines? Reflect on how your infant responds to various settings and what actions or routines provide comfort. Reflect on your feelings during these interactions and any adjustments you've made to accommodate your infant's needs and preferences.

- **Communication and Development Insights:** In what ways have you observed your infant's communication evolving, and how have you responded? Discuss any changes in cooing, eye contact, or reactions to different caregivers, and share your thoughts and feelings about your infant's milestones and development.

- **Balancing Personal Time and Caregiving:** How do you balance the need for personal time with the demands of caring for your infant? Reflect on the challenges you've faced, such as adjusting to your infant's sleep patterns, and the strategies you've employed to maintain your well-being alongside your caregiving responsibilities.

- **Incorporating Theoretical Insights into Parenting:** How do you incorporate insights from developmental theorists into your daily interactions with your infant? Reflect on how this knowledge has influenced your parenting style and any adjustments you've made based on new information or feedback.

- **Exploring Your Parenting Influences:** How have your early attachments, caregiving experiences, and the parenting models you were exposed to shaped your expectations and practices as a parent? Identify any preconceived notions about parenting and how these have been challenged or reinforced.

- **Self-care and Support Systems:** Reflect on your self-care practices and their effectiveness in helping you cope with stress and fatigue. How comfortable are you with seeking support when needed, and how has reaching out for help impacted your parenting journey?

The first 6 months lay a crucial foundation for all future development. By understanding both the developmental needs and the essential qualities of this stage, parents can support their infants in forming secure attachment, developing basic trust, and maintaining connection with their essential nature. This integrated approach honors both the necessary developmental processes and the profound essence that each infant brings into the world.

# Chapter 15
# 6 to 12 Months

The period from 6 to 12 months marks a dramatic transformation in a child's development. During this time, infants evolve from relatively stationary beings who can sit independently to increasingly mobile explorers on the verge of their first steps. This six-month window encompasses profound physical, cognitive, social, and emotional changes that establish the foundation for the child's growing independence and sense of self.

**From Merging Gold to Essential Strength**

Around 6 months, infants enter what Margaret Mahler termed the "differentiation subphase" of the separation-individuation process. Having previously experienced themselves as merged with their primary caregiver during the symbiotic phase, they now begin to recognize the distinction between self and other. This heightened awareness coincides with increased physical capabilities—sitting unassisted, reaching with precision, and eventually crawling—that enable greater exploration of the environment.

From A.H. Almaas's Diamond Approach perspective, this period marks a crucial transition in the infant's experience of essence. The Merging Gold Essence, which dominated the earliest months, characterized by a honey-like, boundary-dissolving quality of complete oneness, gradually begins to wane over the next six months. As this happens, Essential Strength emerges with increasing prominence to support the developmental task of separation and individuation.

According to Almaas, Essential Strength is characterized by its red, fiery quality, a vital, expansive energy that supports autonomy, boundary formation, and the assertion of self. This essential quality manifests as aliveness, vitality, and the inner power to establish and maintain boundaries. The timing of this transition is no coincidence. As the developmental task shifts from fusion to differentiation, the essential qualities naturally shift to support this new challenge.

**What parents should know:** During this period, your infant is undergoing a profound transition not just in their physical and cognitive development but in their experience of essence. The sweet merging quality that characterized early infancy gradually gives way to the fiery vitality of Essential Strength. This shift supports their emerging need to define themselves as separate beings while maintaining their sense of aliveness and presence. By recognizing and honoring both these essential qualities —supporting connection while also encouraging healthy separation —you help your child navigate this critical transition.

**What to look for:** Notice how your baby's quality of presence shifts between different states. The merging quality remains, particularly during quiet moments of connection, feeding, or comfort—a honey-like melting into oneness. But increasingly, especially in the second half of this period, you'll observe moments of vibrant, expansive energy—a red, fiery quality that emerges as they assert independence, explore boundaries, and discover their separate self. These qualities have distinct feels that become recognizable with practice.

**Development of Mobility and Emerging Independence**

The acquisition of mobility is perhaps the most significant achievement of the 6-12 month period. Most infants progress from sitting independently to crawling. By the end of this period, many are pulling to stand and cruising along furniture, with some taking their first independent steps. This newfound mobility transforms the infant's relationship with both the physical environment and the social world.

Our developmental theorists offer complementary perspectives on this crucial stage:

- From **Piaget's cognitive perspective**, the infant's newfound mobility during these months is crucial for constructing knowledge within the sensorimotor stage. Active experimentation with objects, such as knocking over blocks or dropping food, allows them to discover properties and understand cause-and-effect relationships through direct manipulation.
- Building on **Erikson's concept of basic trust** (established in earlier months), the mastery of motor skills during this period reinforces the infant's confidence in a predictable world. These successful experiences of mobility and exploration set the stage for the next psychosocial challenge: budding autonomy.
- Within **Mahler's separation-individuation framework**, mobility is key to the differentiation subphase, marking the start of psychological birth. The ability to physically move away from and return to caregivers facilitates the emergence of a distinct sense of individuality.
- **Almaas's essential perspective** adds a vital dimension by recognizing that as Merging Gold Essence gradually diminishes during this period, Essential

Strength naturally rises to support the developmental tasks. Strength's fiery, red energy provides the vitality and expansiveness needed for mobility, boundary formation, and the assertion of an independent self.

- **Bowlby's attachment theory** highlights this period for establishing secure attachment patterns that foster exploration. The caregiver serves as a "secure base," enabling the infant to venture out and discover, with periodic returns for "emotional refueling" through contact.

**What parents should know:** Your child's increasing mobility isn't just a physical achievement but an expression of a profound shift in their essential experience and psychological development. The diminishing of Merging Gold and the rise of Essential Strength are a natural and necessary transition that supports their developmental journey toward greater independence. By understanding this shift, you can more consciously support both qualities, creating spaces for connection that allow moments of merging to continue while also supporting the vital, expansive energy of Strength that fuels their growing mobility.

**What to look for:** Observe how your child uses mobility to both explore independence and maintain connection. Notice their "checking back" behavior as they venture away to explore—the visual references to make sure you're still there, the periodic returns for physical contact or reassurance. These patterns reflect the delicate balance between their growing independence (supported by Essential Strength) and their continued need for connection (reflecting the remaining Merging Gold quality).

**The Beginnings of Object Permanence**

The development of object permanence continues between 6 and 12 months, as infants gradually come to understand that objects exist even when they are out of sight. This period sees specific advancements in this cognitive milestone:

- **Early stages (6-8 months):** Infants begin showing interest in finding partially hidden objects

- **Middle development (8-10 months):** They actively search for completely hidden objects, but may only look where they last saw the object

- **Later development (10-12 months):** They become more sophisticated in their search strategies, though full object permanence continues to develop into the next developmental period

The development of object permanence parallels and supports the transition from Merging Gold to Essential Strength. When infants lack object permanence, the experience of oneness with the caregiver is more total. "Out of sight" truly means "out of existence." As object permanence begins to develop during these six months, the infant gains the emerging capacity to maintain mental representations of caregivers even during brief separations, which supports the growing psychological differentiation facilitated by Essential Strength.

The cognitive development of object permanence during these months has profound emotional implications. As infants grasp that caregivers exist even when unseen, their heightened awareness of separation often triggers separation anxiety (typically emerging around 8-10 months). This anxiety, rather than a regression, signifies cognitive advancement. They now understand what (or whom) they are missing.

**What parents should know:** Your child's emerging understanding of object permanence is closely tied to their essential developmental milestones and emotional growth. As they begin to grasp that you continue to exist when not visible, they also become more aware of separation, which can trigger anxiety. This seemingly contradictory development—becoming upset about separation just as they're becoming more independent—makes perfect sense when we understand that their cognitive advances heighten their awareness of separation. By providing consistent and predictable separations and reunions, you help your child build confidence that relationships can continue even through temporary absences.

**What to look for:** Notice your child's increasing interest in finding hidden objects—their delight in peek-a-boo games, their persistence in searching for toys that roll under furniture, their growing awareness of your movements in and out of rooms. Also observe the emergence of separation anxiety—distress when you leave, even briefly, and joy upon reunion. These behaviors reflect their developing understanding that things (and people) continue to exist when not visible.

**Emergence of Intentional Communication**

During the second half of this period, infants begin to communicate with increasing intentionality and sophistication. While actual language is still developing, most babies in this age range develop several significant communicative milestones:

- **Canonical babbling** (repetitive consonant-vowel combinations like "ba-ba-ba") typically emerges around 6-7 months

- **Gesture use** (pointing, showing, giving) often appears between 9-12 months
- **First words** may emerge toward the end of this period, with many babies saying "mama," "dada," or other simple words with meaning by 12 months

From a theoretical perspective, Vygotsky would emphasize how these early communication efforts are embedded in social interaction. The infant learns that sounds and gestures can affect others' behavior, laying the groundwork for understanding language as a social tool. Piaget would note how these developments reflect the infant's growing ability to use symbols (sounds or gestures) to represent objects and desires.

From Almaas's essence perspective, this emerging communication is supported by the increasing presence of Essential Strength, which provides the energetic foundation for self-expression and the assertion of needs and interests. The infant's growing ability to communicate intentionally reflects their developing sense of themselves as separate beings with distinct desires and perspectives, a development directly supported by Essential Strength's red, fiery quality.

**What parents should know:** Your responsiveness to your child's early communication efforts supports language development and reinforces their emerging sense of agency and effectiveness. When you recognize and respond to their gestures, babbling, and early words, you communicate that their expressions matter, strengthening their communication skills and essential sense of self. This responsive interaction creates a positive feedback loop that encourages further communication attempts.

**What to look for:** Notice the increasing intentionality in your child's communication. Watch for moments when they expect a response to their sounds or gestures—the eye contact accompanying their babbling, the persistence when you don't immediately understand their intent, the satisfaction when successful communication occurs. These behaviors reflect their growing understanding of themselves as communicative beings.

### Supporting the Integration of Essential Strength

As Essential Strength emerges more prominently during this period, parents can support its healthy integration through various approaches.

**Supporting Essential Strength**

- Provide physical challenges appropriate to your child's developmental level, offering opportunities for crawling, pulling up, and early walking attempts

- Create safe spaces for exploration that allow for the expression of vitality and independence without unnecessary restriction

- Acknowledge and mirror back the strength you observe: "You're working so hard to climb up on that sofa!"

- Accept and validate your child's growing need for autonomy and boundary formation

- Provide clear, consistent boundaries while allowing freedom within those boundaries

**Supporting the Transition from Merging Gold**

- Recognize that while Merging Gold naturally diminishes during this period, it doesn't disappear entirely

- Create quiet moments of connection that allow for the melting, boundary-dissolving quality to be experienced

- Honor your child's periodic need to "refuel" through close contact that temporarily restores a sense of oneness

- Understand that the diminishment of Merging Gold is not a loss but a natural transition that makes space for growing autonomy

**What parents should know:** The transition from Merging Gold to Essential Strength isn't an either/or situation, but a gradual shift in predominance that occurs over the course of these six months. Both qualities remain available to your child, though in changing proportions. By supporting both aspects of your child's essential experience, you help them integrate the seemingly opposing needs for connection and separation. This integration lays the foundation for healthy emotional development, preventing some of the intense frustration that can emerge when Essential Strength lacks appropriate channels for expression.

**What to look for:** Observe the rhythmic alternation between different essential qualities in your child's daily activities. Notice how they might express vibrant, expansive energy during exploration, then seek moments of quiet connection where the melting quality of Merging Gold can briefly reemerge. This natural rhythm reflects the healthy balance between growing autonomy and continued connection that characterizes optimal development during this period.

## How Exploration Needs Holding

During this dynamic six-month period, our developmental theorists converge around a central theme: the delicate balance between exploration and attachment. This convergence takes on new depth when we integrate Almaas's understanding of the transition from Merging Gold to Essential Strength.

## Developmental Models Illuminate the Emergence of Self

As the infant nears their second birthday, something remarkable unfolds. Each developmental lens—psychological, cognitive, somatic, and spiritual—converges around a single truth: the self is emerging, not as a fixed identity, but as a living process.

- Bowlby shows us that children venture further not because they've outgrown dependence but because the connection thread is securely woven.

- Mahler describes this as rapprochement, a dance of distancing and return, rich with emotional nuance.

- Piaget's infant no longer reacts reflexively but manipulates the world with purpose and strategy.

- Erikson names the crisis: autonomy versus shame. The child doesn't just want to do; they want to do alone.

- Almaas reveals this phase as a shift in essence, from the early infancy oceanic merging to the fiery emergence of Essential Strength and Essential Will.

All these maps agree on this: something distinct, determined, and divine is pressing forward. It does so not by abandoning connection but by learning how to carry it within.

## Significance for the Child's World

This theoretical convergence helps us understand why the 6-12 month period is critical for development. During these months, infants establish patterns of exploration and connection that will influence their approach to the world for years to come. The emergence of mobility coincides perfectly with the rise of Essential Strength, providing both the physical capability and the essential energy for exploration and boundary formation.

**What parents should know:** Your child navigates a delicate balance between growing independence and continued connection, and a corresponding shift in essential qualities supports this balance. By understanding how Merging Gold naturally diminishes as Essential Strength emerges more prominently, you can more consciously support both aspects of your child's experience. Your responsive presence creates the secure base from which exploration can occur, while your acceptance of their growing independence validates their emerging sense of self.

**What to look for:** Notice how your child moves between exploration and connection throughout the day. Observe the influence of Essential Strength in their increasingly deliberate movements and explorations, as well as the moments when they return to you for emotional refueling. This rhythmic pattern reflects the healthy integration of independence and connection that characterizes optimal development during this period.

**Self-Reflection Questions for Parents**

- **Mobility and Independence:** How do you respond emotionally when your child moves away from you to explore? Do you notice any anxiety, pride, or other feelings arising, and how might these influence your interactions?

- **Essential Transition:** How do you observe the gradual shift from Merging Gold to Essential Strength in your child? What moments still reveal the melting, golden quality of early infancy, and when do you most clearly see the fiery, red energy of Strength?

- **Balance and Integration:** How do you support your child in integrating these seemingly opposing needs for connection and separation? What practices or routines have you found that honor both aspects of their essential experience?

- **Communication Development:** How do you respond to your child's emerging communication efforts? How do you encourage and support their early attempts to express themselves?

- **Your Essential Comfort:** Which essential quality do you find yourself more comfortable with—the close connection of Merging Gold or the fiery independence of Essential Strength? How might this preference influence your parenting approach?

- **Creating Safe Exploration:** How have you adapted your home environment to support your child's increasing mobility while maintaining appropriate safety boundaries? In what ways does your space encourage healthy exploration?

By integrating understanding of developmental needs with awareness of the essential transition from Merging Gold to Essential Strength, parents can more consciously support their children through the critical 6 to 12-month period. This balanced approach fosters healthy separation-individuation while maintaining the close connection that provides security and emotional nourishment, laying the groundwork for integrated development in the months and years ahead.

# Chapter 16
## 12 to 18 Months

**Shift from Expansive Exploration to Focused Will**

Between 12 and 18 months, your child undergoes a remarkable transformation. They're no longer babies but not yet full-fledged toddlers. This period is marked by exciting firsts—walking, talking, engaging in symbolic play, and developing growing independence. But underneath the surface, something more profound is unfolding. Your child is developing a stronger sense of self and beginning to encounter the limits of their independence.

This chapter explores that inner journey, not just the milestones you can see, but the essential qualities that support them. As we progress through the material, we'll clarify key developmental terms and explain their meanings in plain language.

- The **practicing subphase**, a concept from developmental theorist Margaret Mahler, refers to the stage when a toddler becomes more mobile and seems energized by their independence. You might notice your child running, climbing, and exploring with little concern for where you are.
- The **rapprochement subphase** usually begins toward the end of these six months. It refers to the growing awareness that, while they are a separate person, they still need you. This creates a confusing push-pull dynamic, where one wants independence yet longs for connection.
- From the Diamond Approach, we draw on the idea of *Essential Strength* and *Essential Will*. Essential Strength supports the child's push into independence. It's energetic, fiery, and expansive. Essential Will, which begins to emerge as strength wanes, is quieter but more focused. It helps the child hold their ground with steadiness and intention.

**Practicing Subphase and the Transition from Strength to Will**

By 12 months, most children are crawling confidently, cruising along furniture, or even beginning to walk. As walking takes hold, their world expands dramatically. Suddenly, everything is within reach. Movement becomes a joy in itself—repetitive, energetic, and full of curiosity. Mahler described this stage as a "love affair with the world." Children in this phase often appear bold, fearless, and exuberant.

The essential quality of strength supports this period. Essential Strength isn't about muscle; it's the inner aliveness that says, *I can*. It fuels the child's drive to explore, to try again, to take a risk. It helps form boundaries, not in a defensive way but through confident action.

But as the child continues to develop, this expansive energy begins to shift. The boundary has now been formed. What's needed next is a quality that supports keeping that boundary intact, not through motion but through inner resolve. This is where Essential Will begins to emerge.

Essential Will is the quiet, grounded force that says, *This matters to me*. It's not resistance for the sake of resistance. It's an early form of inner orientation, involving the choice to stay with and return to what feels real and important.

**What parents should know:** During these six months, you may feel like your child is growing up in fast-forward. Their energy may seem boundless at first—climbing, running, laughing with delight. This is Essential Strength at work. But as their focus deepens and their desire to assert their own choices strengthens, you'll begin to see Essential Will taking shape. Support this transition not by controlling it, but by recognizing it for what it is: the unfolding of their authentic self.

**What to look for:** Early in this phase, look for energy that is outward, joyful, and exploratory. Later, watch for signs of concentration, insistence, and preference. When your child repeats a task over and over or refuses to be redirected from something they care about, you may be seeing Essential Will in action, not defiance, but alignment.

### Theoretical Perspectives on Development

This six-month window is one of the richest intersections of multiple developmental domains—motor, emotional, cognitive, and essential. Each theory highlights a different aspect of this transformation, yet they all point to a child moving from expansive exploration toward a grounded sense of selfhood.

- **Mahler's Model:** Mahler identifies the *practicing subphase* (roughly 10 to 16 months) as a time when toddlers experience joyful independence. They appear to be absorbed in the outer world and less concerned about staying connected to their caregiver. As they near 16 to 18 months, however, the *rapprochement subphase* begins. The child begins to grasp the implications of being a separate individual and feels both the freedom and the vulnerability

that come with that realization. This marks a return to seeking closeness, but now with greater self-awareness.
- **Piaget's Cognitive Framework:** According to Piaget, this period falls within *substage 5 of the sensorimotor stage*, often referred to as "tertiary circular reactions." Children begin experimenting intentionally, dropping toys to see what happens and trying out variations on actions to achieve certain effects. This is no longer just repetition but discovery. Mental representations are beginning to form, allowing the child to "think" through actions in a rudimentary way.
- **Erikson's Psychosocial Model:** In Erikson's terms, the child is transitioning from the stage of *trust vs. mistrust* toward *autonomy vs. shame and doubt*. Having developed some basic sense of trust, the toddler now tests their ability to act independently. Success strengthens self-esteem. Failure, or punishment, can breed early feelings of shame or hesitation about asserting themselves.
- **The Diamond Approach:** From the Diamond Approach, this is the period when Essential Will begins to replace Essential Strength. In early months, Strength energizes the child's outward movement, boundary-testing, and embodied confidence. As their sense of self becomes more differentiated, what's needed isn't more expansion, but more consolidation. Essential Will provides the quiet inner backbone, the unwavering sense that *I exist* and *this matters*.

**What This Convergence Reveals**

Across all frameworks, we observe a consistent shift: from unbridled joy in exploration to a more nuanced understanding of limits, preferences, and individuality. The child begins to recognize that they are not all-powerful. They can't reach everything. They need help. They also care deeply about things and want to hold their ground. Essential Will helps them do both: honor their individuality and navigate their limitations.

**What parents should know:** You don't have to memorize each theory. What matters is recognizing the common thread: your child is no longer simply discovering the world; they're discovering themselves. Their demands, their focus, even their frustrations are signs of a profound internal shift. They are learning not just what they can do, but who they are becoming.

**What to look for:** Notice the mix of experimentation and preference. A child who drops a spoon five times isn't being difficult; they're testing reality. A child who insists on putting on their shoes may be slow, but they're practicing autonomy. These behaviors aren't random; they're signs of internal structure emerging. And beneath that structure is Will.

**Navigating the Transition Toward Rapprochement**

As children approach their 18th month, a new level of complexity emerges. The fearless exploration that marked earlier months begins to shift. The child starts to look back more often. They want to do things on their own, yet suddenly need you close. They assert independence, then collapse into your arms. Welcome to the beginning of the rapprochement subphase.

*Rapprochement* simply means coming back together. In Mahler's model, this stage arises when the child, having established some independence, now realizes just how separate they are. With this realization comes vulnerability. They are no longer just explorers of the world; they are explorers who know they can get lost. They begin to experience the tension between *I can do it myself* and *I still need you*.

This emotional push-pull can be bewildering. One moment, your child is proudly carrying their cup across the room; the next, they're furious that you won't do it for them. They want help, but on their terms. They want autonomy but with constant reassurance. This isn't defiance. It's the soul growing into itself, feeling the boundaries that come with being separate and learning how to hold them.

From the perspective of Essence, this is the perfect moment for Essential Will to emerge. The fiery red energy of Essential Strength, which supported the boundary-forming phase, is no longer what's needed. The child isn't just pushing out; they are now trying to *hold* their ground, to remain themselves even in the face of frustration, failure, or fear.

Essential Will provides the inner stability to weather the emotional volatility of this phase. It allows the child to experience need without collapse, preference without rigidity, and separation without loss of self. It helps them say, *'Yes, I want you close,'* and *'Yes, I need to do this my way,'* without falling apart in the middle.

**What parents should know:** Your child is not regressing. They are not confused. They are integrating. Their ambivalence—wanting you near and far, needing help and rejecting it—is part of learning how to be a self in relation to others. They are building the foundation of future intimacy: the ability to be close without losing themselves.

**What to look for:** Watch for contradictory behaviors: refusing your help while crying when you walk away; insisting on doing something alone, then falling apart when it doesn't work; declaring "no" to something they clearly want. These are not inconsistencies; they are the lived experience of becoming a separate person. And beneath the tears or resistance, Essential Will is beginning to organize the self around a growing sense of what matters.

## Supporting the Transition from Strength to Will

This period requires a lot from parents, not just patience but also a different perspective. You're not just managing behavior; you're witnessing the emergence of essential qualities that will shape your child's capacity for authenticity, autonomy, and inner orientation. The shift from Essential Strength to Essential Will isn't a flip of a switch; it's a gradual integration. And your attunement can make a real difference.

## Supporting the Waning of Essential Strength

Early in this period, your child may still feel like a fireball of energy. They climb everything. They laugh as they run away. They say "no" with glee. This is not misbehavior; it's Strength completing its arc. Instead of extinguishing that energy, channel it.

- Create safe spaces for exploration and movement
- Acknowledge the vitality behind their efforts: "You're really going for it today!"
- Set boundaries without shaming the energy: "It's not safe to climb that, but I see how strong you feel."

Even as Essential Strength begins to wane, it's still part of your child's toolkit. It supported the formation of boundaries, and some of that exuberance may still appear when they test those boundaries again.

## Supporting the Emergence of Essential Will

As Will begins to rise, you'll notice more intention. The energy becomes less about running and more about staying, whether with a task, a preference, or a choice. What they want becomes clearer. What they don't want becomes immovable.

- Offer simple choices: "Would you like the red cup or the blue one?"
- Respect preferences when possible, even if small: "You like the blue bowl for cereal."
- Recognize authentic determination: "You're really sticking with that puzzle."
- Distinguish between Essential Will and reactive stubbornness. One is rooted, the other is explosive.
- Allow time for persistence. Rushing undermines Will.

You're helping your child not just *do* things, but *own* them, from the inside out. This is the foundation of self-respect.

**Supporting the Entry into Rapprochement**

As they begin to sense the reality of separateness, your child will show increased vulnerability. This is not failure. This is the softening that follows individuation.

- Stay physically and emotionally available, even as they push you away.
- Reflect their experience: "You want to do it yourself, and it's also hard."
- Hold space for ambivalence: "You wanted help, but now you're mad I helped."
- Create predictable routines for security.
- Accept emotional reversals as part of integration.

This is not a stage to "solve" but one to accompany.

**What parents should know:** You don't need to manage the transition. You need to witness it, name it, and support it. The growing clarity in your child's eyes is matched by the complexity in their heart. Essential Will is there to hold that complexity, and your presence is there to hold them.

**What to look for:** Look beyond the surface of behavior. See the quality of energy: Is it expansive or focused? Is it chaotic or persistent? Is your child scattered or determined? These nuances reveal which essential quality is driving the moment. Your job is not to prefer one over the other but to recognize both as necessary steps in the unfolding of personhood.

**Language, Communication, and the Power of Will**

Between 12 and 18 months, language begins to bloom, and with it, the soul finds a new way to express presence. Communication is not just functional. It is revelatory. As words emerge, so does the self.

**Receptive Language Expands Rapidly:** Even if your child only speaks a few words, they likely understand dozens. Simple instructions, gestures, and emotional tone all register deeply. Their internal world is richer than what they can yet express.

**Expressive Vocabulary Takes Off:** From a handful of words at 12 months to sometimes over fifty by eighteen months, children begin naming what they want, what they see, and, most importantly, what matters to them.

**Gestures Become More Intentional:** Pointing, reaching, pulling you toward something are not just actions. They're declarations of preference. These gestures are often your child's most explicit early expressions of Essential Will.

**Symbolic Play Emerges:** Using a spoon as a telephone or feeding a doll shows that the child can represent one thing as another. This capacity for symbolism represents a leap in consciousness, demonstrating their ability to hold something in mind that isn't present. It foreshadows the kind of thinking that enables imagination, empathy, and a sense of narrative identity.

From the Diamond Approach perspective, the rise of language and symbolism aligns beautifully with the emergence of Essential Will. Language allows the child to say not just "no" but "mine," "more," "again," and "help." These aren't just demands; they're affirmations of existence. They say, "I am here. I have preferences. I matter."

**What parents should know:** When your child asserts with words, especially the small, emphatic ones like "no" or "mine," they are practicing a sacred skill: claiming inner authority. Rather than seeing these moments as power struggles, recognize them as opportunities to cultivate presence. Will needs a voice. When that voice is allowed (within reasonable limits), the child learns not just to speak but to speak *from themselves*.

**What to look for:** Pay attention to the quality behind their communication. When a child insists "no" with quiet steadiness, it is different from an explosive, reactive tantrum. That steadiness is Will speaking. When they return to the same word, request, or idea repeatedly, they are using language to stabilize their sense of self. That is the deeper purpose behind their emerging speech: not just naming the world, but anchoring themselves within it.

### Self Emerges: Mirrors, Mine, and Meaning

Between 12 and 18 months, something profound begins to take shape; your child starts to recognize themselves as a separate being. Not just physically separate but emotionally and psychologically distinct. This dawning selfhood is one of the significant thresholds of development.

- **Mirror Recognition Appears:** Around this age, most children begin to recognize themselves in a mirror. This might start with curiosity, then laughter, and eventually the unmistakable sign: touching their nose while looking at their reflection. This is not just cute; it's consciousness recognizing itself.
- **Possessiveness Emerges:** Words like "mine" begin to appear. While often dismissed as selfishness, these declarations are actually affirmations of boundaries. The child is saying, "I have a self, and it is not you." The object is less important than the recognition it supports.
- **Self-conscious Emotions Arise:** Emotions like embarrassment, pride, and even shame may begin to surface. These require a level of self-awareness that goes beyond basic feelings. Your child is not just *feeling* something; they are feeling themselves *being seen*.
- **The "Me" Moment:** For many parents, there is a singular, unforgettable moment when their child refers to themselves by name or uses "me" or "I" for the first time. That moment is the birth cry of the personal self. And it is sacred.

From Mahler's perspective, this self-recognition is the precursor to the rapprochement subphase. The child now knows they are separate and begins to understand what that means. They want to be close but not merged. They want to be held but not controlled.

From the Diamond Approach, the emergence of the personal self creates the need for Essential Will. Strength was about pushing outward; Will is about staying inwardly true. With growing self-awareness comes vulnerability, and Will offers the inner backbone to stand in that awareness without collapsing.

**What parents should know:** These new capacities—mirror recognition, possessiveness, pride—are not signs of ego in the negative sense. They are signs that the soul is incarnating more fully. Your child is becoming a person and needs Will to support this personhood from within. By honoring their growing awareness while offering steady boundaries, you help their Essential Will grow alongside their sense of self.

**What to look for:** Watch for minor signs: the pause before they say "me," the proud look after accomplishing a task, the moment of retreat after being praised. These moments are filled with inner meaning. They show your child navigating the tension of being seen, being separate, and wanting to remain connected, all at once. Essential Will helps them hold that complexity with integrity.

### Self-reflection Questions for Parents

This phase of development doesn't just ask something of your child; it asks something of you. As their essential qualities shift, your reactions, preferences, and conditioning are stirred. These questions invite you to reflect, not to analyze, but to become more conscious of how you're meeting your child's unfolding essence.

- **Strength and Will:** Where do you notice the fiery, expansive energy of Essential Strength still alive in your child? Where do you see the focused, grounded energy of Essential Will beginning to emerge? How do you relate differently to each?

- **Your Personal Resonance:** Which essential quality feels more familiar or comfortable to you, Strength or Will? Do you celebrate vitality more easily than determination? Or do you prefer quiet persistence to wild energy? How might this shape your responses to your child?

- **Authenticity Versus Stubbornness:** How do you tell the difference between an authentic expression of Will and reactive stubbornness? When your child says "no" or resists, do you listen for what's behind it?

- **Language and Preference:** When your child expresses preferences through words or gestures, how do you respond? Do you hear their deeper will or react to the demand? In what ways can you support their voice without giving in to every request?

- **Holding Contradiction:** How do you respond when your child pushes you away one moment and clings the next? Can you hold both their independence and their need for connection without needing to resolve the contradiction?

- **Environment as Support:** What aspects of your home and routine support Essential Strength—movement, play, risk-taking? What supports Essential Will—focus, choice, stillness? Is there space for both?

- **The Mirror Moment:** Have you witnessed your child recognize themselves in a mirror or begin using "me" or "mine"? How did it feel to see that moment? How do you support the emergence of self without overidentifying with it?

- **Rapprochement Readiness:** Are you beginning to notice the signs of the rapprochement subphase—emotional reversals, new clinginess, protest mixed with desire for help? How do you interpret these shifts? Can you meet them with curiosity rather than frustration?

These questions are not meant to produce answers. They are invitations to deepen your perception. The more you can see the essential qualities moving through your child, and through yourself, the more gracefully you can accompany them in their becoming.

## Chapter 17
## 18 to 24 Months

The period from 18 to 24 months marks a profound transition in early childhood development as toddlers enter what Margaret Mahler termed the "rapprochement subphase" of separation-individuation. During these six months, children navigate an increasingly complex emotional landscape as their growing awareness of separateness coincides with deeper recognition of their limitations and dependencies. This period also witnesses significant advances in language, cognitive capabilities, and self-awareness, all of which are supported by the continued development of Essential Will. At the same time, the overall connection to essence begins to decline significantly.

### Rapprochement Crisis and the Shift Toward Ego Dominance

The rapprochement subphase of Mahler's separation-individuation process typically begins around eighteen months, marking a new developmental challenge for toddlers. Having experienced the exhilarating independence of the practicing phase, they now face a developmental paradox: they desire independence but simultaneously become more aware of their separateness and vulnerability, leading to renewed needs for emotional connection with caregivers.

Mahler described this as the "rapprochement crisis," a period characterized by seemingly contradictory behaviors. The toddler might insist on autonomy one moment, then dissolve into tears of frustration or cling to the parent the next. They may refuse help with tasks they cannot yet master, assert "no" even to things they actually want, or vacillate between pushing parents away and seeking close connection.

From the Diamond Approach perspective, this developmental challenge aligns with a significant shift shown on our graph: as personality structures strengthen, conscious connection to essence further diminishes. Specifically, while Essential Will remains relatively accessible to support autonomy, Merging Essence has receded, and the establishment of the ego-self means that other essential qualities also become less consciously available.

While Essential Will remains relatively accessible during this period to support autonomy and boundary formation, the Merging Essence has already slipped into the background. Now, the foundational structures of the ego-self are sufficiently established, and all essential qualities begin to be less consciously available. The toddler's experience increasingly becomes dominated by the ego-self and reactivity to arising events rather than direct, unmediated connection to essence.

**What parents should know:** The sometimes perplexing behaviors your child displays during this period reflect not just the rapprochement crisis but also a significant shift in the relationship between essence and personality. As your child develops a more defined sense of separate selfhood, their experience naturally becomes more filtered through emerging personality structures rather than directly connected to essence. This is a normal, necessary developmental process, not something to prevent but to navigate with awareness. By recognizing this transition, you can support your child through the emotional challenges of rapprochement while also helping maintain as much conscious connection to essence as possible within this natural developmental trajectory.

**What to look for:** You may notice your child's experience becoming more dominated by reactivity and less by the spontaneous flow of essential qualities. Whereas their joy, strength, or will previously had a direct, unmediated quality, these experiences may now appear more filtered through defensive or adaptive personality structures. This shift manifests in their increased sensitivity to perceived threats to autonomy, their more complex emotional reactions, and their growing concern with how others perceive them. These changes reflect the natural process of ego development described in our graph, where essence increasingly moves into the background as personality structures strengthen.

### Ego as Defense and Adaptation

This developmental stage highlights the relevance of Freud's model of ego development, particularly its crucial functions in defending against anxiety and adapting to environmental demands:

- **Ego as a defense** against anxiety and overwhelming internal or external stimuli
- **Ego as adaptation** to environmental demands and social expectations

During the 18- to 24-month period, both of these functions become increasingly prominent as the toddler navigates the emotional challenges of the rapprochement stage. The growing awareness of separateness creates new vulnerabilities and anxieties that require defensive structures to manage. Simultaneously, increasing social expectations surrounding behaviors such as toilet training, sharing, and impulse control necessitate adaptive mechanisms to function effectively within the family and broader social environment.

From Freud's perspective, this period involves the continuing development of the ego as a mediator between the child's internal drives (the id) and the constraints of reality (eventually internalized as the superego). The ego's growing strength enables more sophisticated management of impulses but also initiates the process of alienation from direct experience that Almaas identifies as contributing to the disconnection of essence.

**What parents should know:** Your child's developing ego serves essential functions for their psychological survival and social adaptation. The defensive and adaptive structures that emerge during this period help them navigate the complex emotional terrain of increasing self-awareness and social expectations. From Almaas's perspective, this development invariably involves some disconnection from direct experience of essence, as illustrated in our graph. However, the quality of parental response during this period can significantly influence how permeable these developing structures remain to essence. By recognizing both the necessity of ego development and the value of connection to essence, you can support healthy personality formation that remains as open as possible to essential qualities.

**What to look for:** Notice the emergence of more complex defensive and adaptive strategies in your child's behavior. These might include psychological defenses such as denial ("I didn't do it" when they did), projection (attributing their feelings to others), or identification (adopting parental attitudes or behaviors as their own). You may also observe increasingly sophisticated social adaptations as they learn to modify behavior based on different contexts or expectations. These developments reflect the ego's growing capacity for defense and adaptation, and while necessary, they also contribute to the diminishing direct connection to essence shown in our graph.

### Conflict Between Will and Emerging Ego Structures

Essential Will, the innate capacity for authentic inner determination, faces particular challenges during this period as emerging ego structures gain precedence in the child's experience.

As ego structures strengthen, this authentic Will increasingly becomes overlaid with and sometimes confused with willfulness, which is a product not of essence but of ego defenses. Willfulness typically emerges from frustration when authentic needs or expressions meet consistent resistance or suppression. Unlike Essential Will, which has a grounded, centered quality aligned with the child's genuine needs, willfulness has a rigid, reactive quality disconnected from authentic needs and oriented toward opposition or control.

This distinction becomes particularly important during the rapprochement phase, when the toddler's authentic Will is attempting to maintain boundaries and autonomy amid the emotional complexity of increased dependency awareness. When this authentic expression is consistently thwarted or misunderstood as mere defiance, Will becomes distorted into willfulness, a defensive reaction rather than an essential quality.

**What parents should know:** During this period, your child is navigating a delicate balance between expressing authentic Essential Will and developing defensive willfulness as ego structures strengthen. This is reflected in our graph as essential qualities begin to slip into the background while ego structures become more dominant. Your ability to distinguish between these qualities—supporting the authentic Will while not reinforcing defensive willfulness—significantly impacts how this essential quality integrates with the development of personality structures. By recognizing and mirroring the essential quality when it appears ("I see how determined you are to figure this out yourself"), while setting appropriate limits on its defensive distortions, you help maintain the connection between personality and essence even as they naturally begin to diverge.

**What to look for:** Pay close attention to the qualitative difference between your child's expressions of authentic Will versus defensive willfulness. Essential Will has a grounded, steady quality focused on authentic needs and preferences, whereas willfulness has a rigid, reactive quality focused on opposition or control. By learning to discern this difference, you can respond in ways that support the integration of authentic Will with developing personality structures rather than reinforcing its defensive distortions.

### Language Development and Ego Consolidation

Explosive language growth between 18 and 24 months is critically vital for ongoing ego consolidation. From the handful of words typical at 18 months, most children progress to using hundreds of words and forming simple sentences by age 2. This language development both reflects and facilitates the strengthening of personality structures shown in our graph.

Language provides the tools for symbolic representation of experience, allowing the child to create narratives about themselves and their place in the world. The development of personal pronouns—particularly "I," "me," and "mine"—linguistically reinforces the child's growing sense of separate selfhood. This linguistic development supports the ego's function as both defense and adaptation, providing more sophisticated ways to articulate needs, negotiate boundaries, and conform to social expectations.

Language has a paradoxical relationship with essence. On one hand, it can provide tools to recognize and articulate essential experiences, potentially supporting conscious connection. On the other hand, the symbolic, conceptual nature of language inherently creates distance from direct, unmediated experience, contributing to the diminishing connection to essence shown in our graph.

**What parents should know:** Your child's rapidly expanding linguistic capabilities directly support the strengthening of ego. Language allows for more complex self-representation, social negotiation, and conceptual understanding, all vital aspects of healthy personality development. However, this same development contributes to the natural movement of essence into the background of conscious awareness. By being mindful of how you use language with your child, choosing words that acknowledge essential qualities rather than reinforcing limiting self-concepts, you can support healthy ego development while maintaining as much essential connection as possible within this natural developmental trajectory.

**What to look for:** Notice how your child increasingly uses language to describe and define themselves ("I big," "Mine do it"), to negotiate social interactions ("My turn," "No want"), and to make sense of experiences ("Daddy gone work"). These linguistic developments reflect the strengthening of ego structures. Also, pay attention to how language can sometimes create distance from direct experience, and how naming an emotion or experience can sometimes diminish its immediate, felt quality. This observation helps illuminate how language, while necessary and valuable, contributes to the natural movement of essence into the background as conceptual understanding strengthens.

## Beginnings of the "Holes" in Essence

A.H. Almaas's concept of "holes" in the fabric of being becomes increasingly relevant during this period. As our graph illustrates, essence begins to slip into the background as personality structures strengthen. Almaas describes this process as creating "holes" in the fabric of being, places where essential qualities have been lost to conscious awareness and replaced by personality structures designed to compensate for their absence.

During the 18 to 24-month period, several factors contribute to the formation of these holes:

- **Conditional responses to essential qualities:** When children receive approval only for specific expressions of essence while others are ignored or discouraged, they learn to suppress the less accepted qualities, creating holes where those qualities become unconscious.

- **Misattunement to essential needs:** When caregivers consistently misinterpret or fail to recognize the child's essential needs, the child loses contact with the authenticity of those needs, creating holes in awareness.

- **Environmental limitations:** When the environment cannot support the full expression of essence (inevitable to some degree in any family or culture), children adapt by losing conscious connection to qualities that have no space for expression.

- **Traumatic experiences:** When children encounter overwhelming experiences that they cannot integrate, they may protect themselves by disconnecting from the essential qualities most affected by the trauma.

These holes don't mean essence disappears; it remains the ground of being. They do, though, represent places where conscious connection to essence is lost and replaced by compensatory personality structures. These structures attempt to fulfill the functions of the lost essential qualities, but do so in more limited and rigid ways.

**What parents should know:** The natural developmental process of personality formation invariably involves some diminishment of conscious connection to essence. However, the specific patterns of which essential qualities remain more accessible and which become "holes" are significantly influenced by your responses to your child's essential expressions. By maintaining awareness of the full range of essential qualities and supporting their appropriate expression, you can help minimize unnecessary holes while supporting necessary personality development. This doesn't mean preventing all holes, which would be both impossible and undesirable for functioning in society, but rather supporting as many essential connections as possible within the natural developmental process.

**What to look for:** Observe which essential qualities your child expresses freely and which seem to be diminishing or becoming distorted. You might notice that qualities that were previously expressed directly now appear mainly through compensatory behaviors. For example, direct joy being replaced by people-pleasing, authentic strength being replaced by controlling behaviors, or essential value being replaced by achievement orientation. These patterns reveal the beginnings of the holes that Almaas describes, where essential qualities slip into the background and are replaced by compensatory personality structures.

**Minimizing Unnecessary Loss of Essence**

While our graph indicates that some diminishment of conscious connection to one's essence is a natural and necessary part of development, parents can significantly influence how steep this decline becomes. Several approaches can support healthy personality development while minimizing unnecessary essence disconnection:

- **Recognize and mirror essential qualities:** When you observe essential qualities expressing through your child's behavior—the focused determination of Will, the spontaneous delight of Joy, the grounded presence of Strength—name and acknowledge these qualities: "I see how determined you are to figure this out" or "Your joy is just bubbling up right now." This mirroring helps maintain conscious connection to essence even as personality structures develop.

- **Distinguish between essence and personality:** Learn to recognize the qualitative difference between essential expressions and their personality substitutes. Essential Will has a grounded, centered quality, while willfulness has a rigid, reactive quality. Essential Joy has a spontaneous, effervescent quality, while performed happiness has a mechanical, approval-seeking quality. By responding differently to these expressions, you can support essential connection while not reinforcing personality substitutes.

- **Create space for authentic expression:** Provide regular opportunities for your child to express themselves authentically, without unnecessary constraints or expectations. This might include unstructured play time, creative activities without predetermined outcomes, or regular periods of undivided attention where you follow their lead.

- **Examine your essential connection:** Your ability to support your child's essential connection is directly related to yours. By becoming more aware of your essential qualities and the holes in your experience, you can respond more consciously to your child's expressions and avoid projecting your patterns onto them.

- **Balance necessary socialization with honoring essence:** Socialization is necessary and valuable, but can be approached in ways that honor essence rather than suppressing it. When teaching social expectations, focus on the impact of behaviors rather than compliance for its own sake, and look for ways to channel essential qualities appropriately rather than suppressing them entirely.

**What parents should know:** Strengthening personality structures and diminishing connection to essence represent a natural developmental process, not a failure of parenting. Your role is not to prevent this divergence entirely, which would be both impossible and undesirable; instead, it is to support healthy personality development while minimizing unnecessary disconnection from one's essence. By maintaining awareness of essence and creating environments that honor authentic expression, you can help your child develop a personality structure that remains as permeable as possible to essence.

**What to look for:** Notice the quality of your child's presence in different contexts and activities. In which situations do they appear most authentically themselves, with essential qualities flowing freely? In which situations do they seem more constrained, mechanical, or reactive? These observations can help you identify environments and interactions that support connection to essence, allowing you to create more such opportunities within the necessary framework of social development.

### Navigating the "Terrible Twos"

The behaviors commonly associated with the "terrible twos," such as tantrums, defiance, and rapidly shifting emotions, take on new meaning when understood through the lens of our graph. These behaviors often reflect the child's struggle to integrate essential qualities with strengthening ego structures amid the emotional complexity of rapprochement.

A tantrum, for example, might be understood as:

- A manifestation of Essential Will attempting to maintain autonomy as ego structures increasingly mediate experience

- A reaction to the frustration of navigating between essential impulses and growing social expectations

- An emotional response to the anxiety created by increasing awareness of separateness and limitation

- A temporary overwhelming of the still-developing ego's capacity for emotional regulation

With this understanding, parents can approach challenging behaviors with greater awareness and effectiveness:

- **Recognize the developmental necessity:** These behaviors reflect critical developmental processes, both the rapprochement crisis and the increasing dominance of ego structures. This recognition helps prevent unnecessary power struggles or shame around normal developmental challenges.

- **Maintain your connection to essence:** Your capacity to remain connected to your essential qualities during challenging moments creates a field that helps your child reconnect with their essence after emotional upheavals.

- **Set necessary limits with compassion:** Limits are crucial for both safety and social functioning, but can be provided in ways that acknowledge and respect the essential qualities being expressed through challenging behaviors.

- **Support emotional regulation:** Help your child develop the ego capacity for emotional regulation while maintaining connection to the essential qualities underlying their feelings. This might include providing language for emotions, offering physical comfort during distress, and modeling regulated responses to challenging situations.

- **Create repair after disconnection:** After moments of conflict or disconnection, create opportunities for repair through reconnection, acknowledging both the challenging feelings and the essential qualities that may have been attempting to express through challenging behaviors.

**What parents should know:** The challenging behaviors of the "terrible twos" often reflect a natural part of the developmental process. As ego structures strengthen and connection to essence diminishes, children struggle to integrate these aspects of their experience amid the emotional complexity of growing self-awareness. By recognizing this developmental context, you can respond with greater patience and effectiveness, supporting both healthy ego development and maximum possible connection to essence during this challenging transition.

**What to look for:** Notice the quality of your child's challenging behaviors and the contexts in which they typically arise. Do tantrums occur most often during transitions, when competing with siblings, or when facing limitations? Do defiant behaviors emerge more around self-care activities, social expectations, or parental instructions? These patterns reveal your child's specific challenges in integrating essential qualities with strengthening ego structures in different contexts, allowing you to provide more targeted support.

For parents navigating this complex developmental period, several reflective practices can deepen understanding and effectiveness:

- **Reflect on your essence-personality balance:** Where do you fall on our graph in your development? Which essential qualities remain accessible to you, and where do you experience "holes" filled by personality structures? This self-awareness helps you recognize and support essential qualities in your child while being mindful of your patterns and projections.

- **Notice your reactions to ego development:** Do you find yourself resisting or overemphasizing your child's growing ego structures? Some parents, particularly those with spiritual inclinations, may unconsciously resist normal ego development out of concern for the disconnection of their essence. Others, particularly those focused on social success, may overemphasize ego development without sufficient attention to connection to essence. Becoming aware of your biases helps you support balanced development.

- **Examine your comfort with different essential qualities:** Which essential qualities do you easily recognize and support in your child and which do you find more challenging? Parents often have different relationships with qualities like Strength, Will, or Joy based on their developmental experiences. This awareness helps you provide more balanced support across the full range of essential qualities.

- **Create regular essence-honoring rituals:** Establish regular activities or interactions specifically designed to honor and support connection to essence. These might include unstructured nature time, creative expression without predetermined outcomes, or special one-on-one time where you follow your child's authentic interests and expressions.

- **Seek support for your essence reconnection:** Your capacity to support your child's connection to essence depends significantly on your own. Consider practices or therapies specifically designed to help adults reconnect with essential qualities, such as mindfulness, certain forms of therapy, or spiritual practices aligned with your values.

**What parents should know:** Your relationship with essence and personality directly impacts how you support your child through the developmental transition shown in our graph. By becoming more conscious of your patterns, triggers, and comfort zones, you can adjust your responses to better support your child's essential development. This reflective work isn't self-indulgent but a practical tool for becoming a more effective parent during this pivotal developmental period.

**What to look for in yourself:** Notice your emotional reactions to different aspects of your child's development. What brings anxiety, frustration, or judgment? What brings joy, pride, or connection? These reactions often reveal your relationship with different aspects of the essence-personality balance. By bringing awareness to these patterns, you can work toward responses that support your child's optimal development rather than reactions based on your unconscious patterns.

By approaching the 18 to 24-month period with an integrated understanding of the shifting balance between essence and personality, parents can navigate this challenging phase with greater awareness and effectiveness. The "terrible twos" become not merely a difficult period to endure but a crucial developmental transition that requires support with consciousness and care.

# Chapter 18
# 24 to 30 Months

The period from 24 to 30 months represents a critical juncture in early childhood development. Having navigated the intense emotional complexity of the rapprochement phase, toddlers now enter what Margaret Mahler identified as the "consolidation of individuality and the beginnings of emotional object constancy" subphase. During these six months, children work to integrate their experiences of both separateness and connection, developing a more stable sense of self that persists across changing states and circumstances. This period also witnesses continued advances in language, cognitive capabilities, and social understanding, all occurring against the backdrop of increasingly dominant personality structures and diminishing conscious connection to essence.

## Consolidation of Ego and Continued Loss of Essence

As our graph of essence and personality development illustrates, the period from 24 to 30 months continues the trajectory of strengthening personality structures (the ascending line) while conscious connection to essence (the descending line) further diminishes. This doesn't mean essence disappears; it remains the foundation of being. But, it does become increasingly veiled behind the growing structures of identity and conditioning.

During this period of consolidation, several significant ego developments occur:

- **Stabilization of self-representation:** The child develops a more cohesive and enduring sense of self that persists across changing circumstances and emotional states.

- **Internalization of parental expectations:** External rules and standards increasingly become internalized as the foundations of the superego begin to form.

- **Growing capacity for symbolic thinking:** The child increasingly uses symbols (language, pretend play, mental images) to represent and organize experience.

- **Expanded self-awareness:** Consciousness of themselves as objects of others' attention and evaluation grows more sophisticated.

From a psychoanalytic perspective, ego development significantly advances during this period. The ego's capacity to mediate between id impulses and external reality strengthens, and it begins to incorporate standards foundational to the later superego. Consequently, defensive mechanisms such as denial and projection become more sophisticated in managing anxiety.

From Almaas's Diamond Approach perspective, this consolidation of ego structures coincides with the continued diminishment of conscious connection to essence. As children develop more stable self-concepts and internalize parental and societal expectations, their direct access to essential qualities becomes increasingly filtered through these personality structures. The "holes" in connection to essence that began forming in earlier stages deepen and become more established as specific personality patterns develop to compensate for the loss of direct experience of essence.

**What parents should know:** The consolidation of ego structures during this period is both necessary and valuable for your child's development. A stable sense of self provides the foundation for healthy functioning in the world. However, as our graph illustrates, this development typically comes at the cost of some diminishment in conscious connection to essence. By understanding this natural process, you can support healthy ego development while also creating conditions that help maintain as much connection to essence as possible. The goal isn't to prevent ego development but to foster a personality structure that remains relatively permeable to essence.

**What to look for:** Notice how your child's sense of self becomes more stable and consistent across different contexts and emotional states. Observe their growing capacity to hold themselves to standards even when unsupervised, indicating the beginnings of superego formation. Pay attention to the increasing complexity of their pretend play and symbolic thinking, reflecting the ego's growing capacity to manipulate representations of reality. These developments indicate healthy ego consolidation. Simultaneously, be aware of which essential qualities remain readily accessible to your child and which seem to be fading from conscious awareness, becoming "holes" that are filled by compensatory personality structures.

## Formation of "Holes" and Compensatory Personality Structures

Almaas's concept of "holes," or the absence of essential qualities replaced by compensatory personality structures, becomes particularly pronounced during the 24- to 30-month period as children adapt to environmental limitations.

For example, a child whose natural expression of Essential Joy is consistently met with admonishments to "settle down" or "be serious" may gradually lose conscious connection to this quality. The resulting "hole," the felt absence of joy, becomes filled with compensatory personality structures, perhaps manifesting as a "good child" who is quiet and serious, or as exaggerated, performance-oriented excitement that mimics but lacks the authentic quality of Essential Joy.

Similarly, a child whose Essential Will is routinely overridden or punished may lose connection to this aspect of essence. The resulting hole might be filled with either excessive compliance (abandoning Will) or rigid defiance (a reaction formation that mimics but differs from true Will).

These compensatory structures are not inherently problematic; they represent the child's creative adaptation to their environment and enable them to function within family and social systems. However, they do create patterns that ultimately limit full access to the child's essential nature and potential.

**What parents should know:** The formation of holes in connection with essence is to some degree inevitable. No environment can perfectly support the expression of all essential qualities at all times. However, your awareness of this process can help minimize unnecessary holes and support the development of more flexible, less rigid compensatory structures. By recognizing which essential qualities tend to be less welcomed or supported in your family system, you can make conscious efforts to create space for their appropriate expression, helping your child maintain connection to a fuller range of their essential nature.

**What to look for:** Observe which essential qualities your child expresses freely and which seem to be diminishing or becoming distorted. You might notice that qualities that were previously expressed directly now appear mainly through compensatory behaviors. For example, direct joy being replaced by people-pleasing, authentic strength being replaced by controlling behaviors, or essential value being replaced by achievement orientation. These patterns reveal the specific holes forming in your child's connection to essence and the compensatory structures developing to fill them.

### Specific Qualities Most Affected During This Period

While all essential qualities can be impacted during this developmental stage, certain qualities appear particularly vulnerable to diminishment during the 24 to 30-month period:

**Essential Joy:** As children enter more structured environments and face increased expectations for "appropriate" behavior, their natural exuberance and spontaneous joy may be constrained. Cultural messages about "growing up" and "being serious" can further dampen conscious connection to this quality.

**Essential Autonomy:** As children's desires and actions increasingly impact others, they face necessary limits on their autonomy. However, environments that are overly controlling, that shame independence, or that foster excessive dependence can diminish connection to this essential quality.

**Essential Value:** Children in this age range become increasingly aware of evaluation and comparison. When their worth becomes contingent on performance, appearance, or behavior, their connection to Essential Value—the inherent sense of worth that is not dependent on external validation—may diminish.

**Essential Strength:** As gender socialization intensifies during these years, expressions of Strength may be channeled into narrow, gender-specific forms or discouraged entirely (particularly for girls), potentially diminishing connection to this quality.

**Essential Compassion:** The natural empathy and compassion of young children may become constrained by messages about who is "deserving" of care or by family patterns that discourage emotional openness.

**What parents should know:** Different essential qualities face different challenges in any given family or cultural context. By becoming aware of which qualities tend to be less supported or more constrained in your specific environment, you can make conscious efforts to provide appropriate channels for their expression. This doesn't mean allowing unlimited or inappropriate expressions, but instead, finding age-appropriate ways for these qualities to be recognized and integrated into your child's developing personality.

**What to look for:** Notice which essential qualities your child seems to express most freely and which appear to be diminishing or becoming distorted. Pay attention to your comfort or discomfort with different qualities. Parents often unconsciously support qualities they value while constraining those that trigger their pain. These observations can help you identify areas where additional support or acceptance might help maintain your child's connection to their full essential nature.

**Signs of Essence Loss and Preservation**

Parents can observe both the diminishment of and continued connection to essence in their toddler through various behaviors and qualities of presence.

**Signs of Disconnection from Essence:**

- Excessive self-consciousness or self-monitoring
- Frequent seeking of approval or validation
- Performance-oriented behavior that lacks spontaneity
- Rigid adherence to routines or rules without understanding their purpose
- Diminished creativity or spontaneity in play
- Heightened comparison with others
- The emergence of a "false self" presentation that differs markedly from the child's private behavior

**Signs of Continuing Connection with Essence:**

- Moments of complete absorption in activities without self-consciousness
- Spontaneous expressions of wonder, curiosity, and delight
- Authentic emotional expression that moves through rather than getting stuck
- Creativity and imaginative play that has a quality of freshness and originality
- Natural compassion and empathy that arise without prompting
- Periods of contentment and ease in simply being

It's important to note that most children will exhibit both sets of signs, moving in and out of essential connection throughout the day. The goal is not to eliminate all personality development, which would be neither possible nor desirable, but to support continued access to essence alongside healthy personality formation.

**What parents should know:** The relationship between essence and personality is not an either/or proposition but a continuum of connection and veiling. Your child will naturally move between greater and lesser connections of essence depending on the context, emotional state, and the specific activity. By recognizing both the signs of connection and disconnection, you can better support your child's overall development, creating more opportunities for essential connection while not becoming alarmed by normal personality development. This balanced perspective helps you avoid both the over-pathologizing of normal development and the failure to recognize concerning patterns of essence disconnection.

**What to look for:** Observe the quality of your child's presence in different activities and contexts. When do they seem most authentically themselves, with essential qualities flowing freely? When do they seem more constricted, performance-oriented, or externally focused? These observations can help you identify environments and interactions that support connection to essence, allowing you to create more such opportunities within the necessary framework of social development.

## Language Explosion and Its Impact on Essence

During the 24 to 30-month period, most children experience remarkable advances in language development. Many enter this period with basic sentence structure and exit with the ability to engage in complex conversations, ask sophisticated questions, and use language to reason about causes, intentions, and possibilities. This language explosion creates both challenges and opportunities for essential connection.

**Challenges to Essential Connection:**

- Language introduces abstraction and conceptualization that can distance children from direct, immediate experience.

- Self-descriptive language ("I am brave," "I am smart," "I am bad at this") can solidify limiting self-concepts.

- Language enables comparison and evaluation that may diminish connection to inherent value.

- Internal dialogue can create a running commentary that interferes with present-moment awareness.

**Opportunities for Essence Support:**

- Language allows children to articulate and process experiences, potentially deepening their understanding of essential qualities.

- Naming essential qualities when observed can help children maintain awareness of them ("I notice how focused and determined you are right now").

- Stories and narratives can provide metaphors and representations of essential qualities.

- Language enables more complex sharing of inner experience between parent and child.

From Almaas's perspective, language has a paradoxical relationship with essence. While it can create distance from direct experience through conceptualization, it can also provide tools for recognizing and maintaining conscious connection to essential qualities. The impact of language on connection to essence largely depends on how it is used, whether to reinforce limiting self-concepts or to acknowledge and articulate essential experiences.

**What parents should know:** Your child's rapidly expanding language capabilities create both challenges and opportunities for essential connection. By being mindful of how you use language and how you respond to your child's verbal expressions, you can help maintain connection to essence even as conceptual understanding develops. Particularly important is the language you use to describe your child to themselves—labels and characterizations that define identity ("You're so shy," "You're our little athlete") tend to solidify self-concepts that can obscure essence, while descriptive language that acknowledges qualities in specific contexts ("You're feeling cautious in this new situation," "You really enjoyed running fast today") supports more flexible self-understanding that remains permeable to essence.

**What to look for:** Notice how your child uses language to describe themselves and their experiences. Pay attention to emerging patterns of self-labeling or self-limitation that are revealed through language. Also, observe moments when language seems to enhance rather than diminish connection to essence, such as when your child finds words for profound experiences or when naming a quality helps them recognize and integrate it. These observations can help you support language development that maintains a connection to essence rather than obscuring it.

**Practices for Nurturing Essence During Ego Consolidation**

While our graph indicates that some diminishment of conscious connection to one's essence is a natural and necessary part of development, parents can significantly influence how steep this decline becomes. Several approaches can support healthy personality development while minimizing unnecessary essence disconnection during this period of ego consolidation:

- **Create balance between structure and freedom:** Provide clear boundaries and expectations while also allowing ample space for exploration, creativity, and authentic self-expression. This balance helps develop a healthy ego that remains relatively permeable to essence.

- **Use essence-honoring language:** Choose words that acknowledge essence qualities rather than reinforcing limiting self-concepts. "I notice how joyful you are while dancing" maintains connection to the essential quality, while "You're such a good dancer" emphasizes performance and evaluation.

- **Support integration of feeling and thinking:** Help your child maintain connection between emotional experience and cognitive understanding, preventing the split between intellect and emotion that often contributes to essence disconnection. Simple practices like naming feelings while acknowledging their validity support this integration.

- **Provide mirroring of essence:** When you observe essential qualities expressed through your child's activities, reflect these qualities back: "I notice how focused and determined you are with that puzzle." This mirroring helps maintain conscious awareness of essence even as personality develops.

- **Create spaciousness in daily life:** Overscheduling and constant stimulation can interfere with connection to essence. Create regular periods of unstructured time where your child can simply be, without pressure to perform or achieve specific outcomes.

- **Honor all emotions:** When emotions are selectively validated based on cultural or family preferences, children lose connection to aspects of their essential experience. By accepting the full range of emotions while providing guidance on appropriate expression, you help maintain connection to essence across different feeling states.

- **Model connection to essence:** Your own relationship with essence directly influences your child's development. By maintaining your own connection to essence and authentically sharing your experience, you provide a powerful model for integrated development.

**What parents should know:** The integration of healthy ego development with continued connection to essence requires conscious attention but not extraordinary intervention. Small, consistent choices in how you interact with your child—the language you use, the balance you strike between structure and freedom, the emotions you validate, the space you create for being rather than just doing—collectively support an optimal developmental trajectory. These choices won't prevent the natural divergence between personality development and connection to essence. Still, they can moderate its steepness, helping your child develop a personality structure that remains more permeable to essence.

**What to look for:** Pay attention to contexts and activities where your child seems most authentically themselves, with essential qualities flowing freely. Notice what characterizes these situations—perhaps less time pressure, less evaluation, more creative freedom, or more supportive connection. These observations can help you create more such opportunities within the necessary framework of social development and ego consolidation.

**Personality Formation and Essence Diminishment**

The dynamics illustrated by our graph—personality formation strengthening as connection to essence diminishes—take on additional significance when considering the accelerated superego development characteristic of the 24 to 30-month period. This pattern continues as ego consolidation advances and connection to essence further diminishes, although not at the same rate for all essential qualities or in all contexts.

It's essential to recognize that this pattern is not a developmental failure, but rather a natural aspect of human growth. A stable personality structure is necessary for functioning in the physical and social world; without it, navigating complex human environments would be impossible. The challenge is not to prevent personality development but to foster structures that remain as permeable as possible to essence.

From Almaas's Diamond Approach perspective, the relationship between personality and essence is ultimately one of potential integration rather than permanent opposition. While early development typically involves some obscuring of essence behind personality structures, later development can include the rediscovery and reintegration of essence with a mature personality. The foundation for this later integration is laid in early childhood through parenting approaches that support both healthy personality development and maximum possible connection to essence.

**What parents should know:** Our graph represents a natural, necessary developmental process, not something to be prevented. Your role is to support healthy personality development while creating conditions that maintain as much connection to essence as possible. The quality of this early development significantly influences your child's later capacity to reintegrate essence with personality, a concept referred to in some spiritual traditions as "awakening" or "self-realization." By understanding this developmental pattern, you can approach parenting with awareness of both immediate developmental needs and long-term potential for essence integration.

**What to look for:** Notice the specific patterns of essence veiling and personality formation in your child. Which essential qualities remain more accessible? Which seem to be fading from conscious awareness? What personality patterns are emerging to compensate for diminished connection to essence? These observations can help you provide targeted support for maintaining connection to specific essential qualities while ensuring healthy ego development.

**Self-Reflection Questions for Parents**

- **Ego Development and Essence Balance:** How do you feel about the natural process of ego consolidation and diminishing connection to essence shown in our graph? Do you find yourself either resisting normal ego development or overly emphasizing it at the expense of connection to essence?

- **Your Essence-Personality Balance:** Where do you fall on our graph in your development? Which essential qualities remain accessible to you, and where do you experience "holes" filled by personality structures? How might your patterns influence your parenting approach?

- **Family Environmental Factors:** Which essential qualities are well-supported in your family environment and which tend to be constrained or discouraged? How might you create more space for the full range of essential qualities to be expressed appropriately?

- **Language and Self-Concept:** How do you typically describe your child to themselves? Do you use language that reinforces fixed identity labels or language that acknowledges qualities in specific contexts? How might you shift your language to better support connection to essence?

- **Structure and Freedom Balance:** How do you balance necessary structure and expectations with freedom for authentic self-expression? Where might you need to provide more structure, and where might more freedom be beneficial?

- **Recognizing Essence vs. Personality:** How effectively can you distinguish between your child's expressions of essence and their personality patterns? What helps you recognize the qualitative difference between these modes of being?

By reflecting on these questions, parents can become more conscious of how they are navigating the natural developmental process illustrated in our graph. This awareness supports more intentional choices that foster healthy ego development while maintaining maximum possible connection to essence during this critical period of consolidation.

The period from 24 to 30 months represents both a challenge and an opportunity, as children consolidate their ego structures while essence continues its natural movement into the background of conscious awareness. By understanding this developmental pattern and its manifestation in your specific child, you can provide support that honors both the necessity of healthy personality development and the value of continued connection to essence, laying the foundation for optimal development in the years ahead.

# Chapter 19
# 30 to 36 Months

Between 30 and 36 months, as toddlers transition to early childhood, the separation-individuation process culminates in a critical juncture for the development of the superego. Building on the autonomy established through earlier "no" phases, the internalization of parental standards and prohibitions now intensifies dramatically, alongside advances in language, play, and social understanding. This chapter focuses on the accelerated formation of the superego and its impact on the child's developing personality and sense of self.

**Superego Formation in High Gear**

As children approach their third birthday, they reach a pivotal stage in the development of their superego. The groundwork laid during earlier phases of separation-individuation now accelerates into what could be described as superego formation in "high gear." The autonomy and boundary issues that emerged through the toddler's persistent "no" phase now evolve into a more complex internalization of rules, standards, and prohibitions.

From a psychoanalytic perspective, this period is particularly significant for three key aspects of superego development:

- **Internalization of parental prohibitions:** External rules increasingly become inner standards that guide behavior even in the absence of supervision.

- **Development of self-evaluation:** Children begin judging their actions against these internalized standards, experiencing pride or shame independently of external feedback.

- **Identification with authority figures:** Children incorporate aspects of parental figures into their developing self-concept, often adopting similar tones, phrases, and attitudes.

This accelerated superego development creates a new internal dynamic as the child begins to experience the tension between impulses (id), practical realities (ego), and moral standards (emerging superego). The "no" that was previously directed outward as an assertion of autonomy now becomes partially directed inward as self-prohibition.

**What parents should know:** The intensification of superego development during this period represents a necessary developmental process that supports your child's growing capacity for self-regulation and moral reasoning. However, the quality of this superego formation significantly influences your child's future relationship with authority, rules, and their impulses. Harsh, arbitrary, or inconsistent limit-setting during this sensitive period can lead to an overly rigid or punitive superego, while a complete lack of limits fails to support necessary structure. By providing clear, consistent, and compassionate boundaries that are explained rather than merely enforced, you help foster a balanced superego that guides without crushing the child's essential nature.

**What to look for:** Notice how your child begins to police their behavior, sometimes literally stopping themselves mid-action while saying "no" or "don't" to themselves. Observe their growing concern with rules and their tendency to enforce these rules on others, often with the same tone and words you use. Pay attention to expressions of shame or pride that occur even without external feedback, indicating internalization of standards. These behaviors reflect the superego formation that is now in high gear, with significant implications for your child's developing relationship with rules, authority, and their impulses.

**Parental Dynamics and Superego Quality**

During this critical phase of superego formation, parental responses to autonomy and boundary-testing behaviors have a profound influence on the quality of the developing superego. The frustration that often accompanies this period can lead to parenting patterns that significantly impact superego development:

> **Impatience and arbitrary enforcement of rules:** When parents become overwhelmed by constant boundary-testing, they may resort to arbitrary enforcement ("Because I said so") rather than providing explanations that help children understand the purpose behind limits. This pattern tends to create a superego that operates on rigid authority rather than understanding.
>
> **"Might makes right" approaches:** Power-based discipline, which relies primarily on the parent's greater size and authority, teaches children that rules are determined by power rather than principle. This can lead to a

superego that is either excessively submissive to authority or rebellious against it, depending on the child's temperament.

**"Do as I say, not as I do" inconsistencies:** When parents hold children to standards they don't follow themselves, they create confusion about the legitimacy of rules. This inconsistency can lead to a superego that is either selectively applied or fundamentally mistrusted.

These parental dynamics are especially impactful during the 30-36-month period because the child's superego formation is in high gear, rapidly incorporating experiences into enduring structures that will influence self-regulation and moral reasoning for years to come.

**What parents should know:** The frustration that often accompanies this period of intense boundary-testing and rule negotiation is entirely normal. However, how you manage this frustration significantly impacts the quality of your child's developing superego. By being aware of patterns such as arbitrary enforcement, power-based discipline, or "do as I say, not as I do" inconsistencies, you can make more conscious choices about the messages you convey about rules and authority. This awareness doesn't mean perfect parenting, which isn't possible or necessary, but rather a willingness to repair after moments when frustration leads to less-than-optimal responses.

**What to look for in yourself:** Notice your triggers during boundary-testing situations. Do you find yourself resorting to power-based responses when tired or stressed? Do you sometimes enforce rules arbitrarily simply because you lack the energy for explanation? Are there areas where you hold your child to standards you don't maintain yourself? This self-awareness is not for self-judgment but for recognizing patterns that might be shaping your child's superego in unintended ways.

**Impact on Connection to Essence**

As our graph of essence and personality development illustrates, the accelerated superego formation of this period coincides with further diminishment of conscious connection to essence. This correlation is not coincidental. The internalization of rules, standards, and prohibitions that characterizes superego development directly contributes to the veiling of essence in several ways:

- **Conditionality of acceptance:** As children learn that approval depends on meeting standards, they may lose connection to Essential Value, the inherent sense of worth independent of performance or behavior

- **Suppression of "unacceptable" qualities:** When certain essential qualities (like anger, exuberance, or assertiveness) are consistently deemed inappropriate, children learn to suppress these aspects, creating holes in their connection to essence

- **Self-monitoring instead of direct experience:** The emerging capacity for self-evaluation shifts awareness from direct experience to observation and judgment of that experience, creating distance from the immediacy characteristic of connection to essence

- **Identification with rules rather than being:** As children incorporate parental standards into their self-concept, they may begin identifying more with these rules and roles than with their essential nature

At this stage, the superego functions as a substitute for objective consciousness. Because young children are not yet capable of perceiving reality with the clarity and discernment of later development, the superego temporarily fills this role by providing an internalized structure of rules and prohibitions. While necessary, this substitution means that children relate to themselves more through standards and judgments than through direct recognition of truth. The quality of this substitute—harsh and rigid, or compassionate and value-based—shapes how much essence remains accessible during this transition.

This impact on essential connection is particularly pronounced when superego development is characterized by harshness, arbitrariness, or excessive rigidity. When rules and standards are presented as absolute commands rather than as guidelines supporting wellbeing and relationship, they tend to create more opaque barriers to essence.

**What parents should know:** The development of a moral compass through superego formation is a valuable and necessary aspect of your child's growth. However, how this process unfolds significantly influences the relationship between personality structures and connection to essence. By providing guidance that explains rather than merely commands, that connects rules to values rather than just authority, and that maintains unconditional acceptance of the child's being even while addressing behavior, you can support healthy superego development that remains relatively permeable to essence.

**What to look for:** Notice how your child's relationship with rules affects their spontaneity, joy, and authenticity. Do they seem excessively concerned with "being good" at the expense of genuine expression? Have they begun hiding certain feelings or needs that they've learned are "bad" or unacceptable? Or, conversely, do they demonstrate healthy integration of guidelines while retaining their essential spark? These observations reveal how superego development is interacting with the connection to the essence of your specific child.

## Birth to 36 Month Trajectory of Superego Formation

Looking back across the entire birth-to-36-month period provides a valuable perspective on the trajectory of superego development. This development follows a clear progression that culminates in the "high gear" formation of the 30-to-36-month period:

> **0-12 Months**: During infancy, the foundations for later superego development are established through consistent and responsive caregiving that fosters basic trust. While no true superego exists yet, the quality of early attachment relationships creates the emotional template for how external guidance will be received and integrated.

> **12-24 Months**: With increasing mobility and the emergence of the "no" phase, toddlers begin actively testing boundaries and experiencing the limits set by caregivers. This period represents the earliest phase of superego development, during which children begin to recognize prohibited actions, although they still require external enforcement of these limits.

> **24-30 Months**: As language and cognitive capacities expand, children begin showing early signs of rule internalization, occasionally stopping themselves or expressing awareness of expectations. The superego is beginning to form but remains highly dependent on external reinforcement.

> **30-36 Months**: The culmination of this trajectory arrives as children develop the cognitive and emotional capacity for significant internalization. The superego shifts into "high gear," with children not only following rules but enforcing them on themselves and others, experiencing pride or shame based on adherence to standards, and incorporating parental attitudes toward behavior into their self-concept.

This trajectory reveals that while superego development is ongoing throughout early childhood, the 30 to 36-month period represents a particularly critical window during which internalization accelerates dramatically. The standards, approaches, and emotional tone that characterize limit-setting during this period have a profoundly lasting influence.

**What parents should know:** Understanding this developmental trajectory helps you provide age-appropriate guidance that evolves as your child's capacities grow. The shift from external regulation in earlier stages to the internalization characteristic of the 30 to 36-month period represents a significant developmental achievement. By recognizing this milestone, you can consciously support healthy superego development, which provides the necessary structure while avoiding excessive rigidity or shame-based moral development.

**What to look for:** Observe how your child's relationship with rules has evolved over the entire birth to 36-month period. Notice the progression from needing external limits to showing awareness of expectations to actively internalizing and enforcing standards. This perspective helps you appreciate the developmental achievement that superego formation represents while being mindful of how your guidance approaches might need to adapt to support healthy internalization.

### Navigating Discipline During Superego Formation

The 30 to 36-month period, with its accelerated superego development, presents both challenges and opportunities for practical discipline approaches. Several strategies can support healthy superego formation while minimizing unnecessary essence disconnection:

- **Connect rules to relationships and values:** When children understand how guidelines support wellbeing and connection rather than merely representing authority, they develop a superego oriented toward values rather than just obedience. "We use gentle hands because hurting others damages friendship and trust" creates a different internalization than "No hitting because I said so."

- **Maintain unconditional acceptance:** Clearly distinguish between behavior and being, helping children understand that while specific actions are unacceptable, they are always valued and loved. This distinction supports the development of the superego without compromising the essential connection to Value.

- **Model repair after mistakes:** When you make parenting missteps, as all parents inevitably do, model taking responsibility and making amends. This teaches that moral standards apply to everyone and that repair is always possible, fostering a more compassionate superego.

- **Explain developmental limitations:** Help children understand that certain expectations exist because of their developmental stage rather than as a reflection of inherent badness. "Small bodies need help staying safe around roads" creates a different internalization than "You're too little to be trusted."

- **Use natural and logical consequences:** When possible, allow children to experience the natural results of their choices rather than arbitrary punishments. This helps them develop a superego based on understanding rather than fear.

- **Support emotional integration:** Create space for all feelings while guiding expression. "All feelings are okay, but not all actions are okay" helps prevent the superego from suppressing emotional experience.

- **Notice and appreciate self-regulation:** When children show developing self-control or consideration, acknowledge these moments. "You remembered to use a quiet voice in the library" reinforces internalization more effectively than only addressing mistakes.

**What parents should know:** The discipline approaches you use during this critical window of superego development have a lasting influence on your child's relationship with rules, authority, and their impulses. By being intentional about fostering understanding rather than just compliance, you help develop a superego that guides without crushing your child's essential nature. This doesn't mean avoiding all limits, which would leave your child without necessary structure, but rather providing boundaries in ways that support integration rather than opposition between essence and personality.

**What to look for:** Notice how your child responds to different approaches to guidance. Do they seem to internalize understanding when you explain the "why" behind limits, or do they primarily focus on avoiding punishment? Do they show emerging capacity to regulate behavior based on values and consideration rather than just rules? These responses provide valuable feedback about how your discipline approaches are influencing superego development.

**Gender Socialization and Superego Formation**

During the 30 to 36-month period, gender socialization often intensifies as children develop stronger gender identification and greater awareness of gender-based expectations. This socialization interacts significantly with superego development, as children internalize different standards and prohibitions based on gender:

- Girls may internalize stronger prohibitions against anger expression and assertiveness, developing a superego that more harshly judges these qualities.

- Boys may develop stricter superego constraints against vulnerability and emotional expression, judging these as weaknesses.

- Children of all genders may internalize different standards for appearance, achievement, caretaking, and independence based on gender expectations.

From a developmental perspective, some gender-based identification is normal as children work to understand social categories and establish their identity within these categories. However, when gender socialization creates dramatically different superego demands for different genders, it can unnecessarily restrict development and essential connection.

**What parents should know:** The intersection of gender socialization and superego development during this period has significant implications for your child's relationship with their impulses, feelings, and expressions. By being aware of gender-based double standards and striving to establish more consistent expectations regardless of gender, you can foster superego development that remains more balanced and adaptable. This doesn't mean preventing all gender identification, but rather being mindful of how gendered expectations might be creating unnecessary restrictions in superego formation.

**What to look for:** Notice whether you or others in your child's life hold different standards for behavior based on gender. Do you have different tolerances for physical exuberance, emotional expression, or independence depending on whether a child is a boy or a girl? Are certain essential qualities more strongly discouraged based on gender? These patterns reveal how gender socialization may be influencing superego development in ways that could unnecessarily restrict your child's full expression.

## Supporting Healthy Superego Development

While our graph indicates that some diminishment of conscious connection to essence is a natural and necessary part of development, parents can significantly influence the quality of superego formation and its impact on connection to essence. Several approaches can support healthy superego development while minimizing unnecessary essence veiling:

- **Focus on understanding rather than just obedience:** When children comprehend the reasons behind limits, they develop a superego based on values rather than just authority. This understanding-based superego tends to be more flexible and less opposed to essence.

- **Balance structure with acceptance:** Clear, consistent boundaries provide the necessary structure for healthy development, while unconditional acceptance of the child's being supports continued connection to essence. This balance helps integrate superego development with essence rather than setting them in opposition.

- **Acknowledge the full range of feelings:** Create space for all emotions while guiding expression. This prevents the superego from developing prohibitions against certain feelings, which would create holes in the essential connection.

- **Model integrated authority:** Demonstrate that setting and following guidelines comes from wisdom rather than just power. This helps children develop a superego that guides them from an understanding rather than a dominating perspective, rooted in fear.

- **Support self-reflection rather than self-judgment:** Help children develop awareness of impacts rather than global self-evaluation. "How did that make your friend feel?" fosters a different superego quality than "That was a bad thing to do."

- **Create repair rituals:** Establish clear ways to make amends after mistakes, helping children understand that repair is always possible. This prevents the development of a harsh, punitive superego that creates shame-based barriers to essence.

- **Balance rule-following with critical thinking:** Even while teaching important standards, encourage age-appropriate questioning and understanding. This helps develop a superego that remains open to growth and adjustment rather than becoming rigidly fixed.

**What parents should know:** The development of the superego during this period is both necessary and valuable for your child's functioning in increasingly complex social environments. However, the quality of this superego formation significantly influences how permeable personality structures remain to essence. By supporting understanding-based rather than fear-based internalization, you help your child develop a superego that guides without creating unnecessary barriers to essential connection. This balanced approach recognizes both the value of moral development and the importance of maintaining connection to essential qualities.

**What to look for:** Notice the emotional tone of your child's emerging self-regulation. Does it have a harsh, judgmental quality or a more balanced, understanding-oriented nature? Pay attention to how they respond to mistakes—with shame and hiding or with acknowledgment and repair. These patterns reveal the quality of superego development and its relationship with connection to essence, helping you identify areas where additional support might be beneficial.

**Superego Development and Veiling Essence**

The superego represents a particularly potent aspect of personality structure that can create significant barriers to essence if developed in ways that emphasize rigid judgment rather than understanding-based guidance.

Internalization accelerates during this period as superego formation shifts into "high gear," with children rapidly internalizing standards, prohibitions, and expectations. This internalization process necessarily involves some veiling of essence as children learn to regulate behavior according to standards rather than responding directly from essential qualities.

However, the steepness of this divergence—how quickly and completely essence becomes veiled behind personality structures—depends significantly on the quality of superego formation. When the developing superego is harsh, rigid, and based primarily on authority and fear, it tends to create more opaque barriers to essence. When it develops with understanding, compassion, and a value-oriented approach, it can fulfill its necessary functions while remaining more permeable to essential qualities.

**What parents should know:** Our graph represents a natural, necessary developmental process, not something to be prevented entirely. The superego provides crucial structure for functioning in social environments and developing moral reasoning. Your role is not to prevent superego formation but to support its development in ways that fulfill these necessary functions while remaining as permeable as possible to essence. By understanding how different approaches to guidance and limit-setting influence the quality of superego formation, you can make more conscious choices that support optimal development.

**What to look for:** Notice how your child's internalization of standards influences their spontaneity, joy, and authenticity. Does their emerging conscience seem to guide without crushing their essential nature, or does it appear to create rigid restrictions that significantly diminish their connection to essence? These observations reveal how superego development specifically influences the general pattern shown in our graph, helping you identify adjustments that might better support the integration of necessary structure with continued connection to essence.

### Self-Reflection Questions for Parents

- **Your Superego:** How would you characterize your superego? Is it harsh and judgmental, balanced and guiding, or perhaps inconsistent in its influence? How might your relationship with internal standards and authority be influencing your approaches to guidance and limit-setting?

- **Frustration and Boundaries:** How do you typically respond when feeling frustrated by your child's boundary-testing behaviors? Do you notice patterns of arbitrary enforcement, power-based approaches, or "do as I say, not as I do" inconsistencies during these moments?

- **Gender and Standards:** Do you find yourself holding different standards for behavior based on your child's gender? Are certain essential qualities more accepted or discouraged depending on whether a child is a boy or a girl? How might these differences influence the development of the superego?

- **Rules and Understanding:** What balance do you strike between expecting compliance with rules and fostering understanding of reasons? How often do you explain the "why" behind limits versus simply enforcing them?

- **Repair after Mistakes:** How do you handle situations where you've responded to your child in ways that don't align with your parenting intentions? What repair practices help restore connection while modeling accountability?

- **Values and Guidance:** What core values inform your approaches to guidance and limit-setting? How explicitly do you connect rules and expectations to these underlying values when communicating with your child?

By reflecting on these questions, parents can become more conscious of how they are influencing superego development during this critical period. This awareness supports more intentional choices that foster healthy moral development while maintaining maximum possible connection to essence.

The period from 30 to 36 months, with superego formation in high gear, represents both a challenge and an opportunity for parents. By understanding the profound influence of this developmental window on both personality formation and connection to essence, you can provide guidance that supports necessary structure while preserving the essential spark that makes your child uniquely themselves. This balanced approach lays the foundation for a lifelong relationship with both inner guidance and authentic essence that will serve them well in the years ahead.

# SECTION 4: Essential Qualities

Before we explore the specific essential qualities that flow through your child's development, it's crucial to understand the fundamental relationship between essence and personality. This dynamic shapes every moment of your child's unfolding life.

As explored in Chapter 9, Essence is your and your child's true nature—an actual, palpable presence that is independent of conditioning, roles, or learned behaviors. It is not merely a state of mind or a beautiful idea about human potential but an actual, palpable presence that can be directly experienced. When your infant gazes at you with complete openness, when your toddler erupts in spontaneous laughter, when your preschooler becomes absorbed in wonder at a butterfly—these moments reveal essence expressing itself through the developing personality.

This essential nature manifests through various qualities, such as the golden sweetness of merging love, the red fire of strength, the focused determination of will, and the effervescent delight of joy. Each quality has its distinctive feel, color, and texture, which become recognizable to parents who learn to perceive beyond behavior to the deeper currents of being that animate their child's actions.

Yet, essence faces an inevitable challenge as development proceeds. The very process that enables your child to function effectively in the world—the formation of personality structures, self-concepts, and adaptive strategies—also tends to veil their direct awareness of these essential qualities. This isn't a developmental failure but a natural consequence of becoming a separate, functioning individual. As your child learns to navigate relationships, meet social expectations, and develop a coherent sense of self, their spontaneous connection to essence gradually dims, often disappearing from conscious awareness entirely within the first few years of life.

This process occurs so naturally that most of us forget we ever experienced life differently. By the time personality development is complete, we have become so completely identified with our learned patterns, defensive strategies, and self-concepts that we believe this constructed self is who we truly are. The personality, while necessary for functioning in a complex world, becomes like a thick coat that keeps us warm but also separates us from direct contact with the essential aliveness that remains our deepest nature.

Understanding this relationship helps parents approach their child's development with both realism and hope. Some veiling of essence is inevitable and even necessary. Your child needs to develop the psychological structures that enable effective functioning in society. Yet, how this process unfolds makes an enormous difference. When parents recognize and support essential qualities even as personality develops, they help ensure that these structures remain permeable to the child's deeper nature rather than becoming opaque barriers against it.

The following chapters explore the specific essential qualities that emerge most prominently during early childhood development, how they naturally evolve and sometimes become obscured, and how conscious parenting can support their continued accessibility even as necessary personality development proceeds. By understanding what lives beneath the surface of your child's behavior, you become capable of nurturing not just their adaptation to the world but their connection to the essential aliveness that makes that adaptation meaningful.

## Chapter 20
## Merging Gold Essence

*Merging Love has a sweetness and wholeness, a richness, a sense of appreciation, and can feel almost syrupy like honey.* —A.H. Almaas

### The Golden Honey of Being

Before language, before the sense of "I" and "other," before the complex negotiations of relationship, there exists a quality of being so fundamental that it shapes our most profound understanding of love, connection, and unity. This is Merging Gold Essence, a luminous, honey-like presence that dissolves boundaries, revealing the felt experience of oneness.

This essential quality represents one of the purest expressions of what A.H. Almaas calls our "true nature, " the fundamental being that exists independent of conditioning, learned behaviors, or adaptive strategies. Unlike the personality structures that will gradually develop to help your child navigate the complexities of social life, Merging Gold Essence is present from birth as an intrinsic aspect of your child's being. Infants don't need to learn how to experience this golden unity; they arrive already embodying it, offering parents a direct window into the essential nature that will increasingly become veiled as development proceeds.

Merging Gold Essence is not an emotion or a psychological state, though it profoundly affects both. It is a quality of True Nature, a self-existing consciousness that manifests as the sweetest, most tender form of love imaginable. When this quality is present, the ordinary boundaries that define "self" and "other" begin to soften and melt like honey warmed by the sun.

Parents often experience this quality most vividly in those precious moments of complete attunement with their infant—during quiet nursing sessions when time seems to stop, in the peaceful aftermath of comforting a distressed baby, or in those magical periods when parent and child seem to breathe as one. These aren't just beautiful bonding experiences; they are actual manifestations of Merging Gold Essence flowing through the parent-child relationship.

**First Unity**

From the perspective of child development, Merging Gold Essence dominates the earliest months of life. During what researchers call the "symbiotic phase," roughly from 1 to 5 months, infant and caregiver exist in a state that Almaas refers to as "Dual Unity." This isn't simply psychological fusion but an actual manifestation of the merging quality of being itself.

The newborn arrives from a state of undifferentiated essence into a world where Merging Gold Essence provides the bridge between the oceanic consciousness of the womb and the gradual emergence of individual awareness. This golden, honey-like quality allows the infant to experience profound connection and nourishment while still maintaining their essential being.

In these early months, the boundary between infant and caregiver is genuinely permeable. The baby's nervous system entrains with the caregiver's, their breathing synchronizes, and their heart rates coordinate. This isn't just biological co-regulation; it's Merging Gold Essence, creating an actual field of unified being within which both parent and child rest.

Watch a mother nursing her month-old baby in those quiet moments when all struggle has ceased. Notice how both beings seem to melt into a single, peaceful presence. The mother's face softens, her breathing deepens, and a quality of luminous stillness surrounds them both. The baby's body relaxes completely, not just from satiation but from the deep satisfaction of existing within this merged field of being. This is Merging Gold Essence in its purest manifestation.

**Phenomenology of Golden Sweetness**

Merging Gold Essence has distinctive qualities that parents can learn to recognize both in themselves and their children:

- **Honey-Like Sweetness:** The most characteristic quality is a sweet sensation, as if consciousness has become honey. This sweetness has substance; it's not just a pleasant feeling but an actual quality of presence that seems to drip through awareness like golden syrup.
- **Luminous Clarity:** Despite its soft, melting quality, Merging Gold is "luminous, bright, clear, and crisp." There's no cloudiness or confusion in this state; rather, a crystalline clarity shines through the honey-like sweetness.

- **Boundary Dissolution:** When this quality arises, the usual sense of being contained within the boundaries of the body begins to soften. Parent and child may feel like "one homogeneous substance, like a pool of water," where individual identity remains, but the sense of separation dissolves.
- **Profound Peace:** Merging Gold brings what Almaas describes as "total peace and contentment, like a baby taken care of by its attuned mother." This isn't the peace of absence but the peace of complete fulfillment and care.
- **Tender Gentleness:** Everything becomes soft and gentle when this quality is present. Movements slow, voices naturally lower, and there's an instinctive protectiveness of this delicate state.
- **Nourishing Fullness:** Unlike the emptiness that sometimes accompanies mystical states, Merging Gold Essence feels deeply nourishing and fulfilling. It satisfies at the most fundamental level of being.

## Developmental Function of Merging

Merging Gold Essence serves crucial functions in early development that extend far beyond simple bonding. This quality provides the energetic foundation for several essential developmental achievements:

- **Basic Trust Formation:** Erik Erikson's concept of basic trust, the infant's fundamental sense that the world is safe and supportive, develops within the field of Merging Gold. When parent and child rest together in this unified presence, the baby absorbs a cellular-level knowing that existence itself is benevolent.
- **Nervous System Regulation:** The honey-like quality of Merging Gold directly affects the autonomic nervous system, creating profound regulation for both parent and child. This isn't just psychological comfort but actual neurological co-regulation that helps establish healthy patterns for lifelong stress management.
- **Attachment Security:** The secure attachment that John Bowlby identified as crucial for healthy development forms within experiences of Merging Gold. The child doesn't just learn that the caregiver is reliable; they experience unity with a presence that feels utterly trustworthy and nourishing.
- **Foundation for Love:** Most importantly, Merging Gold provides the child's first experience of love as a quality of being rather than just an

emotion or relationship dynamic. This establishes a template for recognizing authentic love throughout life.

**Natural Diminishment**

As our graph of essence and personality development illustrates, Merging Gold naturally diminishes as the child grows and individuates. This diminishment isn't a developmental failure but a necessary part of becoming a separate, autonomous being. The same forces that support healthy individuation—the emergence of boundaries, the development of individual identity, the capacity for independent functioning—also naturally reduce the permeability that allows Merging Gold to flow freely.

Around seven months, as Essential Strength begins to emerge more prominently to support the differentiation process, Merging Gold starts its gradual retreat into the background. This shift supports the infant's growing need to experience themselves as a separate being while maintaining enough connection to feel secure and loved.

By the toddler years, Merging Gold typically appears only in special moments, perhaps during illness when boundaries naturally soften, in the peaceful transition to sleep, or in rare instances of complete harmony during play or affection. The quality hasn't disappeared, but it's no longer the dominant mode of being.

This natural diminishment serves critical developmental functions. If Merging Gold remained dominant throughout childhood, the crucial work of separation-individuation couldn't proceed. The child needs to experience their boundaries, their individual preferences, and their capacity for autonomous action. These achievements require a certain degree of separation from the merged state.

**Longing for Return**

As Merging Gold recedes from daily experience, it leaves behind what Almaas calls "the symbiotic wish," a deep longing to return to that original state of perfect unity and nourishment. This longing becomes one of the most powerful motivating forces in human psychology, driving much of what we refer to as the search for love, connection, and meaning.

In children, this longing manifests in various ways:

- **Attachment Behaviors:** The child's seeking of physical closeness, comfort objects, and reunion after separation all contain echoes of the desire to return to the state of being merged.
- **Preference for Familiar Caregivers:** The toddler's sometimes intense preference for specific caregivers reflects not just attachment but a longing for the particular quality of merging they experienced with that person.
- **Comfort-Seeking:** The child's reaching for particular blankets, toys, or routines when distressed represents attempts to recreate the safety and nourishment of the original merged state.
- **Moments of Melting:** Even as independence grows, children continue to seek moments when they can temporarily dissolve boundaries, such as cuddling in bed in the morning, long embraces after separation, or quiet times of simple togetherness.

This longing isn't pathological or something to be outgrown. It represents the soul's deep memory of its essential nature and serves as an inner compass pointing toward authentic connection throughout life.

## Challenge of Fake Merging

As the natural capacity for Merging Gold diminishes, children (and later adults) often develop substitutes that attempt to recreate the experience through personality-level strategies. Almaas calls these attempts "fake merging," imitations that may provide temporary relief but lack the authentic nourishment of the real quality.

In children, fake merging might manifest as:

- **Emotional Enmeshment:** Becoming so identified with a parent's emotional state that the child loses track of their feelings, creating a pseudo-merged state that lacks the clarity and nourishment of actual merging.
- **Clinging Behaviors:** Desperate attempts to maintain physical closeness that stem from anxiety rather than natural affection, creating connection based on need rather than love.
- **People-Pleasing:** Adapting so completely to others' expectations that the child loses touch with their authentic responses, creating a false unity based on compliance rather than genuine connection.

- **Negative Merging**: When early experiences of merging were consistently disrupted or contained frustration and unmet needs, children may develop patterns of conflictual connection, relationships characterized by drama, intensity, and emotional entanglement that create a kind of connection but one filled with pain and confusion.

These strategies represent the personality's creative attempts to fulfill the authentic need for merging. Still, they invariably fall short of the real experience and often create additional complications in relationships and self-understanding.

## Supporting Continued Access to Merging Gold

While some diminishment of Merging Gold is natural and necessary for healthy development, parents can support their child's continued access to this quality through conscious attention and appropriate practices:

- **Create Sacred Quiet Time:** Regular periods of unhurried, unagendized time together create opportunities for boundaries to soften naturally. This might be during bedtime routines, quiet morning moments, or simply sitting together without stimulation or conversation.
- **Practice Presence Over Activity:** Merging Gold emerges more easily in states of being rather than doing. Create space for simply existing together without the pressure to accomplish, learn, or achieve anything.
- **Honor Natural Rhythms:** Pay attention to when your child seems most open to connection and melting. For many children, this occurs during transitions, such as waking up, settling down for sleep, or in the quiet aftermath of emotional storms.
- **Support Rather Than Force**: Merging Gold cannot be manufactured or demanded. It arises naturally when conditions are right, when both parent and child feel safe, unhurried, and open. Your role is to create these conditions rather than trying to produce the experience directly.
- **Maintain Your Connection:** Your child's access to Merging Gold is significantly influenced by your relationship with this quality. When you can occasionally access states of soft, boundary-dissolved presence, you create a field that naturally invites similar experiences in your child.
- **Respect the Natural Cycles:** Accept that as your child grows, experiences of Merging Gold will become less frequent and more brief. This is appropriate and healthy. The goal isn't to maintain the merged

state of early infancy but to preserve access to this quality as one color in the full spectrum of your child's essential nature.

## Merging and Codependence

One of the most important distinctions for parents to understand is the difference between healthy Merging Gold experiences and codependent patterns that can develop when the longing for merging becomes distorted.

## Healthy Merging Gold:

- Feels nourishing and peaceful for both participants
- Maintains an underlying clarity and presence
- Doesn't require the sacrifice of individual authenticity
- Emerges naturally without forcing or manipulation
- Includes respect for natural boundaries and timing
- Supports rather than undermines individual development

## Codependent Patterns:

- Often feel effortful or anxiety-producing
- Create confusion about individual needs and feelings
- Require one or both people to suppress authentic responses
- Involve strategies, manipulation, or emotional pressure
- Resist natural boundaries and developmental changes
- Ultimately inhibit rather than support growth and individuation

Understanding this distinction helps parents support their child's natural longing for connection without inadvertently creating unhealthy patterns of enmeshment or emotional fusion.

## Merging Gold in Family Life

Even as children grow and individuate, families can maintain access to the nourishing quality of Merging Gold through various practices and approaches:

- **Family Rituals:** Regular rituals that create a sense of unity and belonging, such as shared meals, bedtime routines, and seasonal celebrations, can invoke the merging quality while honoring individual differences.
- **Quiet Togetherness:** Creating regular opportunities for the family to be together without an agenda, such as reading quietly in the same room, taking peaceful walks, or sharing unstructured time, allows for natural moments of boundary softening.
- **Presence During Transitions:** The natural vulnerability that occurs during transitions, such as waking up, returning home, or preparing for bed, often creates openings for experiences of Merging Gold. By bringing full presence to these moments rather than rushing through them, parents can support their natural unfolding.
- **Comfort During Distress:** When children are hurt, sick, or emotionally upset, they often naturally return to more merged states. These moments provide opportunities to offer the nourishing presence of Merging Gold while respecting the child's growing autonomy.
- **Celebration of Unity:** Acknowledging and celebrating moments when the family feels exceptionally connected and harmonious reinforces the value of unity while supporting individual expression within that unity.

**Merging Gold Through Life**

The early experiences of Merging Gold in infancy and childhood establish a template that influences relationships and spiritual development throughout life. Children who had sufficient positive experiences of this quality tend to:

- Maintain a fundamental trust in the possibility of authentic connection
- Recognize genuine love when they encounter it
- Have access to states of peace and contentment that don't depend on external circumstances
- Feel comfortable with appropriate intimacy and vulnerability in relationships
- Possess an inner compass that can distinguish between authentic unity and its personality-level substitutes

This doesn't mean they'll live in a constant state of merging. That would interfere with healthy functioning in the world. Instead, they'll have access to this quality as one essential resource among many, able to experience both healthy separateness and appropriate unity as circumstances warrant.

For parents, understanding Merging Gold helps create realistic expectations about connection and separation throughout your child's development. The intense unity of early infancy naturally gives way to increasing individuation, but this doesn't represent a loss of love or connection. Instead, it serves as the foundation for more mature forms of love that can honor both unity and individuality.

The golden honey of Merging Gold never truly disappears; it becomes a background presence that can be accessed when needed throughout life. By supporting your child's early experiences of this quality while accepting its natural diminishment, you help ensure that the template for authentic love and connection remains available even as they grow into their unique, separate selfhood.

**Recognizing the Golden Thread**

Learning to recognize Merging Gold in your family life requires developing sensitivity to the subtle qualities of presence and connection. This essential quality often appears more as an absence of something than a presence of something, a lack of struggle, effort, or the need to maintain boundaries.

- **In Daily Life:** Notice moments when family interactions feel effortless and nourishing, when conversation flows naturally, when even silence feels comfortable and connecting. These may be expressions of Merging Gold manifesting through ordinary activities.
- **In Physical Connection:** Pay attention to the quality of physical affection in your family. Merging Gold often appears during embraces that feel particularly satisfying, during hand-holding that creates a sense of unity, or during physical comfort that feels deeply nourishing rather than just consoling.
- **In Shared Activities:** Sometimes, Merging Gold emerges during activities that naturally soften boundaries, such as listening to music together, sharing meals, enjoying nature, or engaging in creative projects where individual contributions blend into a harmonious whole.
- **In Emotional Moments:** The quality often appears during times of emotional openness, when sharing feelings, offering comfort, or celebrating together in ways that create a sense of shared heart space.

The key is learning to recognize the felt sense of this quality—the honey-like sweetness, the gentle dissolution of boundaries, the profound peace and contentment that characterize authentic experiences of Merging Gold. Once you develop familiarity with this quality, you can begin to notice when it's present and create conditions that support its natural emergence.

**Sacred Ordinary**

Perhaps the most beautiful aspect of Merging Gold is how it can transform the most ordinary moments into experiences of profound connection and meaning. The simple act of nursing a baby becomes a doorway into unity. A quiet moment cuddling before sleep becomes an experience of shared being. Even washing a child's face or combing their hair can become suffused with the golden sweetness of authentic love.

This quality reminds us that the sacred isn't separate from daily life but infuses it when we're present enough to notice. The early parent-child relationship provides one of the most accessible gateways to this recognition, offering ongoing invitations to experience the depths of being that exist within the simplest acts of care and connection.

By understanding and honoring Merging Gold Essence, parents can approach the inevitable changes of development with greater wisdom and acceptance. The intense unity of early infancy doesn't have to be lost entirely as children grow. It can be transformed into a foundation for more mature forms of love that honor both connection and individuality.

This is the gift of Merging Gold: it provides a lived experience of authentic unity that serves as a template for recognizing love throughout life. In supporting your child's early experiences of this quality, you're not just fostering secure attachment; you're helping them maintain access to one of the most precious aspects of human experience, the golden sweetness of being that connects us all.

# Chapter 21
# Essential Strength

*Strength is the source of energy that initiates action and is the means through which Being asserts itself.* —A.H. Almaas

## Presence of Strength Sensing Itself

Essential Strength, introduced in Chapter 9 as a red, fiery quality of presence linked to vitality and autonomy, is more than mere muscular power or willpower. It is the presence of strength sensing itself, manifesting in a child as an unmistakable, expansive vitality that radiates like a warming red fire.

Essential Strength differs fundamentally from the personality-based substitutes that often replace it as development proceeds. While learned behaviors like aggression, willpower, or competitive drive are responses developed through experience, Essential Strength is an intrinsic quality that exists before conditioning. As personality structures develop to help the child adapt to their environment, this authentic strength may become overlaid with imitations that attempt to fulfill the same function but lack the effortless flow and nourishing quality of the genuine article. Almaas refers to these as "false qualities."

This is the life force itself, not mere survival but the passionate, explosive energy that makes existence thrilling. When Essential Strength is present in a child, you witness something far more profound than motivation or assertion. You see the actual fire of being, the force that burns away limitations and expands into new possibilities with each breath.

Parents often recognize this quality before they have words for it. You see it in the seven-month-old who pushes slightly away from your chest to get a better look at the world—that surge of separating energy that says, "I am here, I am my being." You feel it in the toddler who declares, "I do it myself!" with such clear conviction that you know they mean it, not from stubbornness but from an authentic knowing of their capacity. You witness it in the child who, when truly seen and supported, radiates an "I can" presence that seems to come from their very core.

But most importantly, you recognize Essential Strength by its quality of passionate aliveness. When this red fire is burning, the child doesn't just exist; the child lives. Their very presence has a quality of expansive vitality that makes ordinary moments feel alive and significant. They approach life not as a series of problems to be solved but as an adventure to be lived fully.

**Fire That Burns Everything Old**

Essential Strength is fundamentally a destructive force, not destructive in the sense of causing harm, but destructive in the sense that it burns through whatever has outlived its usefulness. Like a forest fire that clears dead undergrowth to make room for new growth, Essential Strength continually destroys old forms, old patterns, old ways of being that no longer serve the child's expanding nature.

This quality appears phenomenologically as a red, fiery energy that seems to radiate outward from the child's core, particularly concentrated in the belly and spreading through the limbs. When Essential Strength is flowing, the child's entire being becomes a furnace of transformation, burning through limitations and expanding into greater possibilities.

Watch a baby around 7 to 9 months old exploring something new. Notice how their entire body becomes engaged, with movements that possess a quality of passionate involvement that extends far beyond mere motor activity. This is Essential Strength in its pure form—not trying to accomplish something, not working toward a goal, but simply expressing the natural fire of life that burns brightest when it encounters the unknown.

The child operating from Essential Strength doesn't approach challenges with anxiety or hesitation. They engage with what Almaas calls "the courage to encounter difficulties," not because they've developed bravery but because the fire of their essential nature naturally burns through obstacles. Difficulties become fuel for this fire rather than barriers against it.

**Life as Passionate Adventure**

Understanding Essential Strength requires recognizing that life, in its essence, is not about survival or security; it is about passionate engagement with the unknown. The child who maintains connection to this quality approaches existence as what it is—an ongoing adventure into mystery.

Real life is not the accumulation of experiences or the achievement of goals. Real life is the quality of aliveness itself, the felt sense of being a vital, expanding presence engaged passionately with whatever arises. When Essential Strength is flowing, the child doesn't live their life; they become life itself.

This understanding transforms our perspective on childhood development. We're not watching a small person learn to adapt to a predetermined world. We're witnessing the emergence of a unique expression of the life force, a being whose very presence contributes to the ongoing creation of reality. The child with access to Essential Strength isn't trying to become something; they are something, something vibrantly alive and endlessly creative.

The phenomenology of this aliveness has a particular quality that parents can learn to recognize. When Essential Strength is present, the child seems more substantial, more definitely here. Their presence fills space differently. There's a tangible sense of fire, of energy that appears to radiate outward, touching everything around them with vitality.

## Developmental Emergence of the Red

Essential Strength typically begins to emerge prominently around seven months, coinciding with what Margaret Mahler called the differentiation subphase of separation-individuation. This timing reveals the intimate connection between this essential quality and the monumental task of psychological birth.

During this period, the child faces the fundamental challenge of individuating from the merged unity of early infancy while maintaining their essential aliveness. They must develop the capacity to be a separate being without losing connection to the vital force that animates their existence. Essential Strength provides exactly what this process requires—the energy to burn through old forms while maintaining passionate engagement with life.

But this developmental emergence is not merely psychological; it's existential. The child is not just learning to be separate; they're learning to be a unique expression of life itself. Essential Strength provides the fire that fuels this transformation, the passionate force that enables them to become themselves without losing their essential vitality.

When you observe a baby around eight months beginning to assert their preferences more clearly, you're witnessing more than psychological development. You're seeing the emergence of a being who can maintain their connection to the life force while navigating the complexities of individual existence. The baby who makes their hunger known "in no uncertain terms," whose cry has a quality of clear demand rather than mere distress; this is Essential Strength expressing through the developing organism.

**Courage to Live Fully**

Essential Strength manifests most clearly as courage, not the false bravery that pushes through fear, but the natural fearlessness that emerges when one is aligned with the life force itself. The child expressing this quality doesn't need to muster courage; courage is what they are when they're being themselves authentically.

This courage has several distinctive characteristics:

- **The Willingness to Risk Everything:** True courage means being willing to lose all securities, all comforts, all accumulated safety in service of authentic living. The child with Essential Strength naturally takes risks because they know intuitively that real security comes from their connection to life itself, not from external protections.
- **The Capacity for Adventure:** Life is approached as an adventure into unknown territory. The child doesn't need familiar experiences or predictable outcomes to feel safe. They find their security in their capacity to meet whatever arises with full presence.
- **The Strength to Transform:** Essential Strength provides the energy needed for ongoing transformation. The child can allow old forms of themselves to die because they trust in their capacity to continually regenerate and expand.
- **The Fire That Burns Pretense:** This quality naturally burns through anything false or artificial. The child cannot maintain pretense when Essential Strength is flowing because this fire only feeds on what is real and authentic.
- **The Passion for Truth:** The courage of Essential Strength is fundamentally a passion for reality. The child wants to know what is true rather than what would be comfortable or familiar.

When parents recognize these qualities in their child, they're witnessing something profound—a being who is naturally aligned with the forces of life and growth rather than the forces of stagnation and defense.

**Environmental Challenge to the Life Force**

Essential Strength faces perhaps the most significant resistance among all the essential qualities within the family ecosystem because it directly challenges the static structures that characterize most human environments. Unlike compliance or adaptability, the life force cannot be controlled or managed; it can only be supported or suppressed.

Several environmental factors commonly interfere with the natural flow of Essential Strength:

- **Fear of the Child's Power:** When parents sense the magnitude of the life force in their child, they may become frightened. This isn't a small, manageable energy that can be channeled in safe directions. This is the actual fire of existence, and it burns everything that isn't real. Parents who haven't made peace with their life force may unconsciously suppress their child's.
- **Cultural Demands for Safety:** A culture obsessed with security, comfort, and risk-avoidance provides little support for Essential Strength. The child learns that passionate engagement with life is dangerous, that adventure is irresponsible, that the fire of their nature should be dampened for their protection.
- **Educational Systems That Deaden:** Most educational environments are designed to produce compliance rather than to fan the flames of passionate engagement. The child learns to sit still, follow directions, and achieve predetermined outcomes rather than exploring, discovering, and creating from their fire.
- **Parental Projections of Limitation:** Parents who have lost touch with their Essential Strength may project their limitations onto their child. They signal that life is primarily about survival rather than passionate engagement, that security is more critical than aliveness, that growing up means dampening the fire rather than learning to channel it.
- **Social Expectations of Conformity:** The pressure to fit in, to be like other children, and to meet social expectations can gradually extinguish the child's natural curiosity and enthusiasm. They learn that their uniqueness is a problem to be solved rather than a gift to be expressed.

When Essential Strength is consistently suppressed, the child faces a profound existential crisis: choosing between authentic living and environmental acceptance. Often, the solution is to disconnect from the life force and develop compensatory patterns that simulate strength while avoiding its risks.

**Many Faces of False Strength**

When Essential Strength cannot flow freely, it doesn't simply disappear; it becomes distorted into various forms of false strength. These compensations serve the crucial function of maintaining some connection to power and vitality while avoiding the risks that come with authentic engagement with the life force.

- **Anger as Counterfeit Fire**: Perhaps the most common distortion is the transformation of Essential Strength into anger. Anger contains some of the fire and energy of true strength, but it's reactive rather than spontaneous. Anger needs something to push against. Essential Strength simply is. The child who has lost access to their natural fire may use anger as a substitute, but this counterfeit eventually becomes exhausting and isolating.
- **Aggressive Domination:** Some children develop patterns of forcing their will upon others as a way to experience strength and power. This isn't the natural assertion of Essential Strength but a compensation for feeling fundamentally helpless and powerless. True strength doesn't need to dominate because it doesn't experience itself as separate from what it encounters.
- **Rigid Willfulness:** The child may develop inflexible patterns of stubborn resistance as a way to maintain some sense of agency. This willfulness feels hard and effortful, unlike the flowing quality of Essential Strength. The child becomes rigidly attached to specific outcomes rather than remaining open to the adventure of life.
- **Grandiose Inflation:** Some children compensate for the loss of true strength by developing fantastical notions of their capabilities. This inflation is a defense against feeling small and deficient. The child creates an imaginary version of strength to fill the hole left by the missing essential quality.
- **Identification with Weakness:** Paradoxically, one of the most profound defenses against the loss of Essential Strength is to identify completely with being weak. If the environment cannot tolerate the child's fire, they may choose to disown it entirely, building their identity around being the "gentle child" who never causes trouble.
- **Compulsive Achievement:** Other children channel their unexpressed life force into relentless achievement and performance. While this may be successful in conventional terms, it lacks the effortless flow and joy that

characterize Essential Strength. The child becomes driven rather than naturally motivated.

These distortions enable the child to maintain some connection to strength and vitality while avoiding the vulnerability that accompanies authentic strength. However, they require enormous energy to maintain and never provide the deep satisfaction that comes from genuine Essential Strength.

**Strength Hole and Its Consequences**

When Essential Strength is chronically unavailable, it creates what Almaas calls the "Strength Hole," a specific deficiency state that has its own phenomenology and developmental consequences. This isn't simply weakness but an active sense of deflation where natural vitality should be.

Children experiencing the Strength Hole may manifest:

- **Chronic Exhaustion:** A pervasive sense of being tired that doesn't respond to rest. This fatigue comes from the enormous energy required to live without access to the natural life force.
- **Pervasive "I Can't:"** A default assumption that they cannot meet life's challenges. This isn't low self-esteem but an accurate assessment of their disconnection from Essential Strength.
- **Dependence on External Energy:** Needing others to provide motivation, enthusiasm, or life force because they cannot access their. The child becomes an energy vampire, unconsciously drawing vitality from their environment.
- **Collapse under Pressure:** When faced with any significant challenge, the child deflates rather than rising to meet it. Without access to the life force, even small obstacles can feel overwhelming.
- **Terror of Aloneness:** The Strength Hole often manifests as intense fear of being without external support. The child knows at some level that they lack the inner fire needed to sustain themselves.
- **Deadness behind the Eyes:** Perhaps most tragically, the light goes out of the child's eyes. Their gaze becomes flat and mechanical, lacking the spark that characterizes natural Essential Strength.

The Strength Hole creates a particular kind of suffering because it represents disconnection from life itself. The child continues to exist but loses contact with the force that makes existence meaningful and vital.

## Distinguishing True Strength from Counterfeits

Parents must develop the ability to distinguish between Essential Strength and its various imitations. This discrimination is crucial for supporting authentic development rather than reinforcing compensatory patterns.

**Essential Strength characteristics:**

- Feels effortless and natural, like a river flowing downhill
- Arises spontaneously from present-moment engagement
- Has a quality of passionate involvement rather than grim determination
- Maintains flexibility and responsiveness to changing circumstances
- Includes natural consideration for others and realistic assessment of limitations
- Feels alive and energizing to be around
- Contains joy and playfulness even when facing difficulties
- Burns through obstacles rather than fighting against them
- Expresses the child's unique nature rather than copying others

**False Strength characteristics:**

- Requires effort and force to maintain
- Often oppositional; defining itself against something else
- Feels rigid, tense, or mechanical
- Becomes more fixed under pressure
- May sacrifice relationship or authentic values for control
- Often draining or aggressive to be around
- Lacks joy and spontaneity
- Fights against obstacles rather than flowing through them
- Mimics external models rather than expressing authentic nature

Learning this distinction allows parents to support genuine expressions of strength while guiding compensatory patterns. This requires developing sensitivity to the quality of energy rather than focusing solely on behaviors or outcomes.

**Supporting the Red in Your Child**

Understanding Essential Strength enables parents to provide conscious support for this vital quality. This support must honor the child's natural fire while providing appropriate structure and guidance.

- **Create Space for Passionate Engagement:** Look for opportunities for your child to become deeply involved in activities that genuinely interest them. Essential Strength emerges through passionate engagement, not through forced participation in predetermined activities.
- **Support Adventure within Safety:** Provide a secure base from which your child can explore and take risks. The goal is not to eliminate all dangers but to create an environment where the child can engage adventurously with life while having reliable support to return to.
- **Model Authentic Enthusiasm:** Your relationship with Essential Strength has a direct influence on your child's development. Children learn more from witnessing authentic passion than from any instruction about how to be strong.
- **Distinguish Challenge from Overwhelm:** Essential Strength grows through meeting appropriate challenges. Learn to recognize the difference between challenges that strengthen your child and demands that overwhelm their current capacity.
- **Honor Their Unique Fire:** Each child's Essential Strength has its particular flavor and expression. Support your child's authentic way of engaging with life rather than trying to mold them into predetermined patterns.
- **Address Your Relationship with Life:** If you find yourself consistently dampening your child's enthusiasm or discouraging their adventurous impulses, explore your relationship with the life force. Your unresolved fears about passionate living become environmental obstacles to your child's development.
- **Provide Realistic Feedback:** Help your child develop an accurate assessment of their capabilities and limitations without crushing their natural confidence. Essential Strength grows through realistic engagement with what is possible.

**Paradox of Strength and Vulnerability**

One of the most profound insights about Essential Strength is that it includes rather than excludes vulnerability. True strength doesn't arise from invulnerability but from the willingness to remain open and responsive even under challenging circumstances.

The child expressing Essential Strength can acknowledge their current limitations without losing their fundamental sense of capacity. They can ask for help from strength rather than weakness, admit they don't know something without feeling diminished, and face the unknown without contracting into defensive patterns.

This understanding helps parents avoid the common mistake of trying to make their child invulnerable. The goal is not to shield them from all difficulties but to support their natural capacity to meet whatever arises with full presence and an authentic response.

When Essential Strength is flowing, the child experiences what we might call passionate vulnerability, the willingness to be fully open to life, even knowing that this openness includes the possibility of pain, failure, or loss. This is the courage that makes authentic living possible.

**Expansiveness of Life**

Essential Strength is ultimately about expansion, not the expansion of the ego or the accumulation of external power, but the expansion of life itself through the unique expression of each individual. When this quality is present, the child becomes a conscious participant in the ongoing creation of reality.

This expansion has several key characteristics:

- **Beyond Personal Boundaries:** True expansion dissolves the artificial boundaries between self and other. The child discovers that their authentic strength serves not just their individual development but the vitality of the whole.
- **Continuous Regeneration:** Essential Strength provides the energy for ongoing transformation. The child can allow old forms of themselves to die because they trust in their capacity to continually regenerate and expand.
- **Creative Responsiveness:** Rather than following predetermined patterns, the child develops the capacity to respond creatively to whatever life presents. Each moment becomes an opportunity for fresh engagement.

- **Service to Life:** The ultimate expression of Essential Strength is when the child's unique fire serves the larger patterns of life and growth. Their individual development contributes to the overall evolution.
- **Fearless Engagement:** The child can engage fully with life because they know that their essential nature is indestructible. They can risk everything because they discover that their true security lies in their connection to the life force itself.

## A Life of Passionate Engagement

The early development of Essential Strength establishes the foundation for a lifetime of passionate engagement with existence. Children who maintain connection to this quality grow into adults who approach life as an ongoing adventure rather than a series of problems to be solved.

This doesn't mean they never experience fear, doubt, or difficulty; rather, they have access to an inner fire that enables them to meet whatever arises with full presence and authentic response. They become what Almaas calls "lion-hearted," capable of taking the risks that real living requires.

The child who develops Essential Strength becomes an adult who can:

- Engage passionately with their authentic interests and values
- Take creative risks without being paralyzed by fear of failure
- Transform obstacles into fuel for further growth
- Maintain their vitality even in challenging circumstances
- Inspire others through their natural enthusiasm and courage
- Serve larger purposes while remaining true to their unique nature
- Face the unknown with curiosity rather than contraction

Perhaps most importantly, they develop the capacity to live as expressions of life itself rather than merely surviving as separate individuals fighting for resources and security.

## Recognizing the Fire of Being

Learning to recognize Essential Strength in your child requires developing sensitivity to the quality of their aliveness rather than just observing their behaviors.

This fire has a distinctive feel that becomes unmistakable once you know what to look for.

- **In Early Infancy (7-12 months):** Notice the surge of energy when your baby pushes away to explore, the quality of determination in their reaching, the clear assertion of needs without apology. Most importantly, notice when their presence has a particularly vital, alive quality that fills the space around them.
- **In Toddlerhood (1-3 years):** Observe moments when your child's "No!" or "I do it!" has a quality of joyful assertion rather than reactive opposition. Notice when they approach challenges with natural confidence, when they recover quickly from setbacks, when their entire being seems to glow with vitality.
- **In Early Childhood (3-6 years):** Watch for times when your child becomes passionately absorbed in activities, when they take on challenges with enthusiasm rather than anxiety, when they express their authentic interests despite social pressure to conform.
- **The Unmistakable Quality:** Most importantly, learn to recognize the felt sense of this fire. When Essential Strength is present, the child's very presence becomes more substantial, more vivid, more alive. This isn't something you think about; it's something you feel. The space around them seems to sparkle with possibility and adventure.

When you learn to recognize and support this red, robust fire in your child, you become a guardian of one of the most precious qualities a human being can possess: the capacity to live life as a passionate adventure rather than a mere survival strategy. This is perhaps the greatest gift you can offer, not just supporting your child's development but supporting their connection to the very force that makes existence meaningful and alive.

The development of Essential Strength is ultimately about more than individual growth; it's about ensuring that the fire of life itself continues to burn brightly in the world. When children maintain their connection to this quality, they become torchbearers, carrying the flame of passionate engagement into all their future encounters with existence.

# Chapter 22
# Essential Will

*True Will is complete surrender to what is experienced in this moment. It is surrender to oneself, to life, to experience, to the truth of now.* —A.H. Almaas

## The Silver Presence of "I Will"

Essential Will appears in the developing child as a silver or white presence, a quality of being that carries the unmistakable feeling of "I will." This is not the mental decision-making of the adult mind or the reactive opposition of the wounded ego. It is something far more fundamental—the capacity to be oneself completely and to act from that authentic ground.

When Essential Will is present, the child demonstrates what we might call effortless determination. They pursue what genuinely matters to them with a quality that is both relaxed and unstoppable. There's no strain, no pushing against reality, no forcing outcomes. Instead, there's a natural confidence that flows from their direct contact with what is real and immediate.

Parents often first recognize this quality when their toddler begins to express clear preferences, typically around 16 to 24 months. However, unlike the demanding willfulness that characterizes much of childhood behavior, Essential Will has a distinctly different flavor. The child saying "I do it myself" from this place speaks not from opposition but from authentic self-direction. Their intention arises not from what they think they should want but from immediate contact with what they experience.

This quality appears phenomenologically as a silver or white presence, particularly felt in the belly and solar plexus. The child operating from Essential Will seems more substantial, more definitely present in their body. They have what we might call ontological weight, a sense of existing that doesn't depend on external validation or internal fantasy.

## Essential Will as Grounded Reality

To understand Essential Will, we must first understand what supports it: contact with concrete, physical reality precisely as it is. Essential Will cannot function in the realm of fantasy, projection, or mental construction. It requires what the Diamond

Approach calls "white purity," perception and experience free from the contamination of ideas about how things should be.

A child expressing Essential Will is fundamentally grounded. They are present to what is actually happening rather than lost in reactions to what they imagine is happening. When they want something, they want it based on immediate experience, not on stories about what they should want or what would make them feel better about themselves.

This groundedness has a particular quality that parents can learn to recognize. The child seems more solid, more definitively here. Their movements have precision, their attention has focus, and their choices emerge from clear contact with present circumstances rather than from internal pressure or external demand.

Watch an eighteen-month-old working steadily to fit shapes into a sorter. When Essential Will is present, there's no frustration when a piece doesn't fit immediately. No throwing or forcing, just clear, sustained intention that continues until completion. The child's entire being is organized around this simple, immediate task. They are not thinking about success or failure, nor are they worried about looking good or avoiding disappointment. They are simply present to what is needed in this moment.

This is what we mean by purity, not moral righteousness but the absence of mental extras. The child sees the shape, feels the opening, and responds to what is there. No fantasies about what should happen, no ideas about what it means to them if they succeed or fail. Just direct, immediate contact with reality as it is.

This purity represents essential nature expressing itself before personality structures overlay it with mental extras, defensive strategies, or compensatory patterns. As children develop the psychological structures necessary for functioning in complex social environments, this direct contact with reality often becomes mediated through self-concepts, learned behaviors, and adaptive strategies. The challenge for parents is to support the development of necessary personality structures while preserving their child's access to this essential foundation of authentic self-direction.

**Emergence of Authentic Self-Direction**

Essential Will typically begins to emerge more prominently around 16 to 24 months, precisely during what Margaret Mahler called the "rapprochement subphase" of separation-individuation. This timing is not coincidental. As the child becomes increasingly aware of their separateness and, simultaneously, conscious of their limitations and dependencies, they need an essential quality that can support authentic individuation without losing contact with reality.

The rapprochement crisis presents the child with a fundamental challenge: how to be themselves without losing connection to what supports them. The toddler wants independence but also needs relationship. They assert their preferences but also require guidance. They begin to sense their unique nature but haven't yet developed the psychological structures to maintain it consistently.

Essential Will provides the inner support that allows the child to navigate this paradox. It gives them the capacity to be themselves steadily and reliably, regardless of external pressure to conform or internal pressure to please. But this is not the rigid stubbornness of defended autonomy. Essential Will remains flexible, responsive to changing circumstances, always grounded in present reality rather than past decisions or future goals.

When a child can access Essential Will, they don't need to choose between being themselves and being in relationship. They can maintain their authentic nature while also recognizing the legitimate needs and boundaries of others. They can assert their preferences without losing empathy, pursue their interests without becoming selfish, and express their nature without becoming oppositional.

**Phenomenology of Effortless Determination**

Essential Will has distinctive characteristics that distinguish it from both passive compliance and effortful forcing:

- **Effortless Flow:** True Will feels easy and natural, not strained or forced. The child expressing this quality doesn't appear to be working hard; they continue with quiet persistence. Their actions have the quality of water flowing downhill, following the path of least resistance while maintaining clear direction.
- **Present-Moment Orientation:** The Essential Will is always focused on what is happening now rather than forcing future outcomes or fighting against current reality. The child remains responsive to changing circumstances while maintaining their essential direction.
- **Embodied Presence:** Unlike mental decision-making, Essential Will is felt throughout the body. The child seems more solid, more definitely present

in their physical form. Their movements are precise, and their attention is focused.
- **Realistic Assessment:** True Will is inherently realistic. When this quality is present, the child naturally assesses what is possible rather than being driven by fantasy or compensation. They pursue goals that emerge from an accurate perception of current circumstances.
- **Inner Confidence**: There's an implicit confidence that doesn't depend on past successes or external validation. It's the felt sense that authentic intention, grounded in reality, naturally leads to appropriate action.
- **Support for Being:** Most fundamentally, Essential Will provides the support to be oneself completely without pretense or image. When this quality is present, the child naturally expresses their authentic nature rather than performing a role designed to get approval or avoid rejection.

**Environmental Challenge to Authentic Will**

Essential Will faces particular developmental challenges because it directly supports the child's capacity for authentic self-direction, a quality that can trigger significant anxiety in parents and caregivers. Unlike compliance, which feels safe and manageable, genuine autonomy can feel threatening to adults who have lost touch with their own authentic will.

Several environmental factors commonly interfere with the natural development of Essential Will:

- **Overcontrolling Environments:** When parents need to direct or manage most aspects of the child's experience, there is little space for Essential Will to develop. The child learns that their impulses and intentions are less important than external demands, and they begin to lose contact with their inner sense of direction.
- **Premature Independence Demands:** Conversely, when children are expected to exercise will before they have adequate support—emotional, physical, or practical—they may develop compensatory patterns of false will that mask the absence of genuine will. The child learns to push and effort rather than flow from authentic intention.
- **Inconsistent Boundaries:** Essential Will develops best within clear, consistent boundaries that the child can understand and work with. When limits are arbitrary, constantly changing, or emotionally driven, the child

cannot develop confident agency within them. They become either rigidly controlling or helplessly dependent.
- **Parental Projection:** Parents who have lost touch with their Essential Will may unconsciously sabotage their child's expressions of authentic intention. This can manifest as overwhelming the child with the parent's agenda, becoming threatened by the child's growing autonomy, or demanding compliance with decisions that serve the parent's psychological needs rather than the child's developmental requirements.
- **Fantasy-Based Parenting:** When parents relate to their child through fantasies about who the child should be rather than an accurate perception of who they are, Essential Will cannot develop naturally. The child learns to perform an identity designed to match parental expectations rather than expressing their authentic nature.
- **Cultural Devaluation:** In cultures that emphasize compliance over authentic expression, or achievement over being, Essential Will may receive little support or recognition. The child learns that success means conforming to external standards rather than developing inner direction.

When Essential Will cannot flow freely, the child doesn't simply become passive; instead, they develop compensatory strategies designed to maintain some sense of agency and control. These strategies, while psychologically necessary, create the foundation for lifelong struggles with authentic self-direction.

**Formation of False Will**

When Essential Will becomes consistently unavailable, it doesn't disappear; it becomes distorted into what we call "false will" or "ego will." These distortions represent the personality's attempt to fulfill the authentic functions of Will through compensatory strategies that, while initially protective, ultimately separate the child from their natural capacity for effortless determination.

- **Willfulness and Opposition:** Perhaps the most common distortion is the development of rigid, oppositional patterns. The child who cannot access Essential Will may become willful, not from genuine intention but from defensive reaction against feeling powerless or controlled. This willfulness feels hard and effortful, requiring constant energy to maintain.
- **Effortful Striving:** False will involves pushing, trying, fighting, and forcing. Unlike the easy flow of Essential Will, these patterns feel labored and

exhausting. The child learns to achieve goals through mental effort and physical tension rather than aligning with natural intention.
- **Mental Control:** False will operates primarily from the head rather than from embodied presence. The child develops elaborate strategies for managing situations through mental manipulation rather than accessing their natural capacity for authentic action. They learn to think their way through life rather than allowing an authentic response to emerge.
- **Compensatory Achievement:** Some children develop patterns of excessive performance as a way to experience a sense of agency and effectiveness. While this compensation may be successful in conventional terms, it lacks the inner satisfaction that comes from Essential Will. The child becomes driven rather than naturally motivated.
- **Passive Resistance:** Others develop patterns of passive resistance, appearing to comply while subtly undermining or avoiding authentic engagement. This represents will turning against itself rather than expressing naturally. The child learns to maintain some sense of autonomy through covert non-cooperation.
- **Grandiose Control:** Some children develop inflated notions of their capacity to control outcomes, manifesting as unrealistic expectations or demanding behavior that attempts to force the environment to comply with their wishes. This pattern mistakes mental intention for essential will.

These distortions serve critical psychological functions, maintaining some sense of agency when authentic will is unavailable. However, they create ongoing internal conflict and rarely provide the deep satisfaction that comes from essential action. The child learns to struggle rather than flow, to effort rather than allow, to force rather than respond.

## The "Will Hole" and Its Consequences

When Essential Will is consistently blocked or unavailable, it creates what the Diamond Approach refers to as the "Will Hole," a specific deficiency state that carries its own phenomenology and developmental consequences. This is not simply the absence of willpower, but an active sense of inner emptiness where natural self-direction should be.

Children experiencing the Will Hole may manifest:
- **Chronic Indecisiveness:** Difficulty making even simple choices, not from lack of preferences but from disconnection from their inner sense of

direction. The child knows what they're supposed to want but has lost contact with their heart's desire.

- **Lack of Follow-Through:** Initiating projects or expressing intentions but failing to sustain them through to completion. Without access to Essential Will, the child cannot bridge the gap between intention and sustained action.
- **Dependence on External Direction:** Needing others to provide motivation, structure, or permission for authentic self-expression. The child becomes dependent on external will because they cannot access their own.
- **Pervasive Inadequacy:** A deep sense that they lack the inner resources to affect their circumstances or pursue their authentic interests. This is not low self-esteem but an accurate assessment of their disconnection from Essential Will.
- **Support Anxiety:** In its most profound form, the Will Hole manifests as anxiety about falling or losing support, reflecting the absence of inner support that Essential Will provides. The child may develop specific fears about their capacity to stand on their own.
- **Castration Fears:** The Will Hole can manifest as what psychoanalysis calls castration anxiety, a fear of fundamental inadequacy or powerlessness that may include actual physical sensations of emptiness in the belly or solar plexus area.

The Will Hole is particularly challenging because it directly undermines the child's capacity for authentic self-direction, creating a dependency on external support that can persist throughout life if not addressed. The child learns to look outside themselves for the motivation and direction that should naturally arise from within.

## Distinguishing Essential Will from Its Distortions

One of the most crucial skills parents can develop is the ability to distinguish between Essential Will and its various compensations. This discrimination is essential for responding appropriately to the child's expressions and supporting healthy development.

**Essential Will characteristics:**

- Feels easy and flowing, without strain or effort
- Arises from present-moment awareness rather than mental planning

- Has a quality of surrender to what is authentic rather than fighting against what is
- Feels grounded and embodied rather than mental or strategic
- Maintains connection to love and other essential qualities
- Remains realistic about what is possible
- Carries implicit confidence and inner support
- Allows flexibility and adaptation as circumstances change
- Includes natural consideration for others and realistic limitations

**False Will/Willfulness characteristics:**

- Involves pushing, efforting, or forcing outcomes
- Often oppositional, defining itself against something rather than for something
- Feels rigid, tense, or effortful in the body
- Operates primarily from mental strategies rather than embodied presence
- May sacrifice other values (relationship, integrity, joy) for control
- Often unrealistic about what can be controlled or achieved
- Carries undertones of anxiety, anger, or defensive compensation
- Becomes more rigid when challenged or thwarted
- Shows little genuine consideration for others or realistic limitations

Learning to make this distinction allows parents to support authentic expressions of Will while providing appropriate guidance around its distortions. This requires developing sensitivity to the quality of the child's intention rather than focusing solely on the content of their choices or the outcomes of their actions.

**Supporting Essential Will in Your Child**

Understanding Essential Will and its developmental challenges enables parents to provide more conscious support for this vital quality. This support must be grounded in reality rather than fantasy, focused on the child's authentic nature rather than parental projections.

- **Create Space for Authentic Choice:** Look for age-appropriate opportunities for your child to exercise genuine choice and follow through on their authentic impulses. This doesn't mean giving the child unlimited freedom, but rather providing structured opportunities for them to experience their inner direction.
- **Ground Yourself in Present Reality:** Essential Will requires contact with what is happening rather than dwelling on ideas about what should be happening. The more grounded you are in present reality, the more you can support your child's natural connection to Essential Will.
- **Respect Natural Timing:** Essential Will unfolds according to the child's inner rhythm, not external schedules or developmental timelines. Support their natural pace rather than pushing for premature independence or maintaining unnecessary dependence.
- **Provide Clear, Consistent Boundaries:** Will develops best within clear, understandable limits that children can work with. These boundaries should be based on a realistic assessment of what supports the child's development rather than arbitrary parental preferences.
- **Distinguish Support from Control:** Learn the difference between providing support that enables your child's authentic expression and control that substitutes your will for theirs. Support asks, "What do you need to pursue what genuinely matters to you?" Control decides what the child should want.
- **Model Embodied Will:** Your relationship with Essential Will directly influences your child's development. Children learn more from what they observe than from what they're told about self-direction and authentic intention.
- **Address Your Control Issues:** If you find yourself consistently overriding your child's authentic expressions of will, explore your relationship with control, power, and authentic self-direction. Your unresolved issues will become environmental obstacles to your child's development.
- **Support Realistic Assessment:** Help your child develop the capacity to assess what is possible rather than being driven by fantasy or wishful thinking. This means responding to their authentic capabilities and limitations rather than projecting what you think they should be capable of.

**Paradox of Will and Surrender**

One of the most profound insights about Essential Will is that it's a form of surrender, not to external authority, but to one's authentic nature and the truth of each moment. This paradox can be challenging for parents to understand, especially in a culture that often equates will with force and control.

True Will doesn't fight against reality; it aligns with what is authentic and possible in each moment. When a child is expressing Essential Will, they're not forcing outcomes but allowing their genuine nature to express itself through appropriate action. They remain responsive to changing circumstances while maintaining connection to their essential direction.

This understanding transforms how parents approach issues of compliance and cooperation. Rather than demanding obedience to external authority, the focus shifts to supporting the child's capacity to align with their authentic nature, which naturally includes appropriate consideration for others and realistic assessment of circumstances.

The child operating from Essential Will doesn't need to be forced to cooperate; they naturally assess what the situation calls for and respond authentically. This doesn't mean they'll always do what parents want. Instead, their responses will come from genuine consideration rather than automatic compliance or reactive opposition.

When Essential Will is present, the child can maintain their authentic self while also recognizing the legitimate needs and limitations of their environment. They can be autonomous without being selfish, self-directed without being inconsiderate, and determined without being rigid.

**Essential Will Throughout Development**

The early development of Essential Will establishes patterns that influence self-direction and authentic action throughout life. Children who maintain some connection to this quality develop into adults who can:

- Make decisions from authentic assessment rather than external pressure or internal compulsion
- Follow through on commitments that align with their genuine values and interests

- Maintain their authentic self even in challenging or demanding circumstances
- Take appropriate action without needing external motivation or permission
- Distinguish between authentic intention and compensatory striving
- Access inner support for pursuing what genuinely matters to them
- Remain flexible and responsive while maintaining essential direction

This doesn't mean they'll never experience doubt, confusion, or the need for external support. But they'll have access to an inner resource that enables authentic self-direction when needed.

For parents, understanding Essential Will helps create realistic expectations about autonomy and compliance throughout development. The goal is not perfect obedience or premature independence but the gradual development of the child's capacity for authentic self-direction within appropriate boundaries.

The child who develops Essential Will becomes an adult who can respond to life's challenges from their authentic nature rather than from defensive patterns or compensatory strategies. They develop what we might call ontological confidence, the felt sense that they exist as themselves and can act from that authentic ground.

**Recognizing the Silver Thread**

Learning to recognize Essential Will in your child requires attention to the quality of their intention and action rather than just the content. This essential quality has a distinctive feel that becomes recognizable with practice:

- **In Sustained Attention:** Notice moments when your child becomes absorbed in activities with a quality of steady, relaxed focus. There's no strain or effort, just clear, sustained intention that continues naturally.
- **In Authentic Choice:** Observe times when your child makes decisions that seem to arise from genuine preference rather than reaction to external pressure or internal compulsion. Their choices feel organic rather than forced.
- **In Embodied Presence:** Pay attention to your child's physical presence when they're operating from authentic Will. There is usually a sense of groundedness, confidence, and embodied presence that feels distinct from compensation or defense.

- **In Effortless Follow-Through:** Notice your child's capacity to pursue intentions to completion, especially when the pursuit requires sustained effort or navigating obstacles. Essential Will provides natural persistence without strain.
- **In Realistic Response:** Observe how your child responds to changing circumstances. Essential Will allows flexible adaptation while maintaining essential direction, unlike the rigid persistence of false will.

The silver thread of Essential Will may be subtle, especially as children grow and encounter increasing pressure to conform or achieve. But this quality remains available as an inner resource, providing the foundation for authentic self-direction throughout life.

When Essential Will is present, the child experiences what we might call ontological support, the felt sense that they exist as themselves and can act from that authentic ground. This is perhaps the greatest gift we can support in our children: not the capacity to get what they want, but the capacity to know what they authentically wish to and to pursue it from a place of groundedness and flow.

By understanding and supporting Essential Will, parents help ensure that their child's growing autonomy remains connected to their authentic nature rather than becoming a vehicle for compensation or rebellion. This support creates the foundation for a lifetime of authentic action, the capacity to be oneself and act from that authentic being in service of what genuinely matters.

The development of Essential Will is ultimately about supporting the child's capacity to live from their authentic nature rather than from defensive patterns or external expectations. When this capacity develops naturally, the child grows into an adult who can navigate life's complexities while remaining grounded in their essential self, able to respond to what is needed without losing contact with who they are.

# Chapter 23
# Essential Joy

*Joy is the feeling quality of the Yellow Essence... it goes with delight, playfulness, and an innocent, carefree happiness and engagement of the heart.* —A.H. Almaas

## Bubbling Spring of Being

Watch a ten-month-old baby discover their toes. Notice the complete absorption, the delighted squeals, the way their entire being seems to sparkle with discovery. This isn't happiness about something; it's the pure effervescence of joy itself, bubbling up from the very ground of their being like a spring that has never known drought.

Essential Joy appears phenomenologically as a golden, sparkling quality that seems to carbonate the child's entire presence. Unlike happiness, which typically has an object or cause, Essential Joy is causeless, a fundamental quality of being that delights in existence itself. It manifests as what feels like champagne bubbles of light dancing through consciousness, creating an atmosphere of celebration wherever it appears.

This quality reaches its natural peak during what Margaret Mahler called the "practicing subphase," roughly between 10 and 18 months, when toddlers experience what she described as a "love affair with the world." During this period, Essential Joy fuels the child's exuberant exploration of their expanding capabilities, creating the emotional foundation for healthy curiosity, learning, and engagement with life that can last a lifetime.

This golden effervescence typically begins to diminish as personality structures strengthen and social conditioning intensifies. Understanding both the nature of Essential Joy and the forces that obscure it provides parents with crucial guidance for supporting their child's lifelong capacity for authentic delight and wonder.

## Yellow Essence and the Heart's Engagement

In A.H. Almaas's understanding of essential qualities, Joy represents the feeling aspect of what he calls the "Yellow Latifa," a fundamental center of essential consciousness characterized by innocent, carefree happiness and the heart's playful engagement with reality. This isn't the emotion of joy but the essential quality from which the emotion derives, the very capacity for delight that makes happiness possible.

Essential Joy manifests as a golden, sparkling presence that seems to illuminate everything it touches. When this quality is present in a child, their very presence becomes infectious; their delight naturally evokes joy in others, their curiosity opens new possibilities for discovery, and their playfulness invites genuine engagement. This is why children operating from Essential Joy often become the center of attention, not through performing but simply by being themselves.

Essential Joy differs fundamentally from emotional happiness in several key ways:

- **Causeless Nature:** While everyday happiness typically depends on external circumstances—getting what we want and avoiding what we don't want (Freud's pleasure principle)—Essential Joy arises spontaneously from the simple fact of being alive. The baby discovering their toes isn't happy about anything specific; they're expressing the pure delight of consciousness encountering itself.
- **Self-Renewing Quality:** Emotional states typically have a beginning, peak, and decline. Essential Joy has a self-renewing quality; it bubbles up endlessly from an inexhaustible source. The toddler who experiences genuine Essential Joy doesn't get tired of being delighted; each moment offers fresh possibilities for wonder.
- **Inclusive Expansion:** While happiness can be possessive or exclusive ("I'm happy and I don't want anything to disturb it"), Essential Joy naturally includes and celebrates others. The child expressing this quality wants to share their discoveries, invite others into their delight, and expand the circle of celebration.
- **Present-Moment Orientation:** Essential Joy is always now. It doesn't depend on memories of past happiness or anticipation of future pleasure. It finds endless delight in whatever is immediately present, transforming the ordinary into the extraordinary through the quality of attention it brings.
- **Innocent Curiosity:** Perhaps most characteristically, Essential Joy expresses itself through what Almaas calls "innocent curiosity," the open-ended desire to know and explore that has no agenda beyond the sheer delight of discovery.

**Joy's Natural Season**

Essential Joy reaches its natural flowering during the practicing subphase of separation-individuation, which typically occurs between 10 and 18 months. This period, characterized by the toddler's new mobility and confident exploration, provides ideal conditions for joy to manifest freely:

- **Physical Mastery and Delight:** As toddlers develop walking, climbing, and increasingly sophisticated motor skills, they experience what can only be described as pure delight in their expanding capabilities. This isn't pride in accomplishment but the joy of embodied existence expressing itself through movement and mastery.
- **Fearless Exploration:** During this phase, toddlers often display remarkable fearlessness, approaching new situations with curiosity rather than anxiety. This fearlessness reflects their natural joy, which experiences the unknown as an invitation to discovery rather than a threat to be avoided.
- **Apparent Obliviousness:** Mahler noted that children in the practicing phase often appear temporarily oblivious to dangers and limitations, as they are so absorbed in their exploration. This "obliviousness" actually reflects their absorption in the joy of discovery. They're not ignoring reality but experiencing it as fundamentally benevolent and interesting.
- **Love Affair with the World:** The phrase Mahler used to describe this period, "love affair with the world," perfectly captures the quality of Essential Joy. The toddler relates to existence not as a problem to be solved but as a beloved to be celebrated and explored.
- **Infectious Enthusiasm:** Children in this phase naturally draw others into their enthusiasm. Their joy is so authentic and immediate that it awakens similar qualities in adults who haven't become too defended against their capacity for delight.

Parents who understand this natural season of joy can create conditions that support its fullest expression while avoiding the premature dampening that often occurs when adults become anxious about the child's fearless exploration or exuberant expression.

**Curiosity as Joy's Natural Expression**

One of the most beautiful aspects of Essential Joy is how naturally it expresses itself through curiosity. Unlike the goal-oriented investigation of the adult mind, the child's curiosity emerges from pure delight in discovery. This innocent curiosity has several distinctive characteristics:

- **Open-Ended Wonder:** The child's "why" questions don't seek specific answers but express the joy of wondering itself. "Why is the sky blue?" opens into "Why do we have eyes?" which flows into "Why do we sleep?" The joy lies not in accumulating information but in the dance of wondering.
- **Unlimited Scope:** Children's curiosity naturally extends to everything—how things work, why people behave as they do, what happens when different elements combine, what exists beyond the visible. This boundless scope reflects joy's natural tendency to celebrate all of existence.
- **Innocent Agenda:** Unlike adult curiosity, which often serves practical purposes or personal interests, children's curiosity is innocent; it seeks to know for the sheer delight of knowing. This innocent quality is what makes children such natural philosophers and scientists.
- **Embodied Investigation:** Before children can verbalize questions, they explore through taste, touch, and physical manipulation. Everything goes into the baby's mouth, not just from hunger but from the joy of knowing through direct sensory contact. This embodied curiosity reveals joy's connection to immediate, present-moment experience.
- **Fearless Inquiry:** Children's natural curiosity extends to topics that adults often find uncomfortable, such as death, sex, conflict, and difference. This fearlessness reflects joy's fundamental trust in reality; whatever exists is worthy of exploration and understanding.

When parents recognize curiosity as an expression of Essential Joy rather than as a potential nuisance or distraction, they can respond in ways that nurture rather than diminish this precious quality.

**Environmental Challenge to Joy**

Essential Joy, despite its robust and effervescent nature, faces significant environmental challenges during early development. Several factors commonly contribute to its premature diminishment:

- **Cultural Discomfort with Exuberance:** Many families and cultures find discomfort with high-energy, exuberant expressions. Children may receive messages to "calm down," "settle down," or "use your inside voice" so frequently that they learn their natural joy is problematic and needs to be suppressed.

- **Adult Anxiety about Fearlessness**: The fearless exploration that characterizes Joy-filled children often triggers anxiety in adults responsible for their safety. While appropriate boundaries are necessary, over-anxious responses can teach children that the world is dangerous and their natural enthusiasm is risky.
- **Conditional Approval for Expression:** When children receive approval for their Joy only under specific circumstances, such as performing for relatives, expressing enthusiasm about approved activities, or being happy when it's convenient for adults, they learn that authentic joy is conditional and may begin to perform happiness rather than genuinely expressing it.
- **Comparison and Competition:** As children enter social environments where they're compared to others, their natural Joy may become contaminated with performance anxiety. They may learn to express enthusiasm only when they're successful or to suppress it when others are struggling.
- **Adult Depression and Unavailability:** Children naturally want to share their joy with significant adults. When parents are consistently depressed, overwhelmed, or emotionally unavailable, children may suppress their Joy to avoid adding to adult burdens or to prevent highlighting the contrast between their aliveness and adult deadness.
- **Premature Seriousness:** Cultural messages that equate growing up with becoming serious can prematurely dampen Essential Joy. Children may learn that joy is childish and needs to be abandoned in favor of more "mature" emotional states.
- **Overstimulation and Artificial Excitement:** Paradoxically, environments that provide excessive artificial stimulation can diminish Essential Joy by creating tolerance for only high-intensity experiences. The child loses appreciation for the subtle delights that naturally evoke authentic joy.

When Essential Joy cannot flow freely, children don't simply become sad; they develop compensatory patterns designed to approximate the experience of Joy while avoiding its vulnerability.

**Formation of False Joy**

When Essential Joy becomes consistently unavailable, children develop what might be called "false joy" or "pseudo-enthusiasm," imitations that attempt to fulfill Joy's functions while protecting against the disappointment or rejection that authentic joy might encounter:

- **Performed Happiness:** Children may learn to perform enthusiasm and happiness to gain approval or avoid disappointing others. This performance leaves happiness feeling hollow and effortful, requiring constant energy to sustain. Unlike Essential Joy, which is self-renewing, performed happiness depletes the child over time.
- **Manic Excitement:** Some children develop patterns of excessive excitement as a way to approximate joy while avoiding quieter, more vulnerable forms of delight. This manic quality feels forced and frantic rather than bubbling and natural, often overwhelming others rather than including them.
- **Achievement-Based Enthusiasm:** False joy may become tied to accomplishments, acquisitions, or external validation. The child learns to feel excited about getting good grades, winning competitions, or receiving praise rather than finding delight in learning, playing, or simply being themselves.
- **Attention-Seeking Behavior:** When natural joy doesn't receive appropriate recognition, children may develop dramatic or attention-seeking patterns as a way to approximate the connection and sharing that authentic Joy naturally creates.
- **Compulsive Optimism:** Some children develop rigid patterns of forced positivity, suppressing any negative emotions while maintaining an artificial cheerfulness. This compulsive optimism lacks the authentic spontaneity and emotional range that characterizes Essential Joy.
- **Addictive Stimulation:** Children may become dependent on external sources of excitement, such as overstimulating toys, entertainment, sugar, or social drama, to approximate the aliveness that Essential Joy provides naturally from within.

These false forms of Joy serve important functions. They maintain some connection to enthusiasm and aliveness while protecting against the vulnerability of authentic delight; however, they require enormous energy to maintain and never provide the deep satisfaction that comes from Essential Joy.

## Hole of Joy and Its Consequences

When Essential Joy becomes chronically unavailable, it creates what Almaas calls the "Hole of Joy," a specific deficiency state characterized by deadness, depression, and the absence of the effervescent aliveness that should naturally characterize human consciousness.

Children experiencing the hole of joy may manifest:

- **Chronic Flatness:** A pervasive lack of enthusiasm or delight that doesn't respond to external stimulation. This isn't sadness but the absence of the sparkling quality that makes life feel alive and meaningful.
- **Depression and Hopelessness:** In its more severe forms, the hole of joy manifests as actual depression, a sense that life lacks meaning, beauty, or possibility. The child loses connection to the fundamental benevolence of existence that Joy naturally reveals.
- **Anhedonia:** The clinical term for the inability to experience pleasure, anhedonia represents the hole of joy in its most crystallized form. The child can function but finds no real satisfaction or delight in activities that should naturally bring happiness.
- **Cynicism and Skepticism:** Children with holes of joy may develop protective cynicism, viewing enthusiasm and delight as naive or foolish. This cynicism serves to justify their disconnection from Joy while protecting against the pain of longing for it.
- **Addictive Seeking:** The emptiness of the hole of joy often drives compulsive seeking for external sources of stimulation, excitement, or pleasure. The child becomes dependent on ever-increasing levels of external input to approximate the aliveness they've lost connection to internally.
- **Social Withdrawal:** Since Essential Joy naturally creates connection and sharing, its absence often leads to social isolation. The child may withdraw from relationships rather than risk revealing their inner deadness or having their lack of enthusiasm exposed.

The hole of joy creates a particular kind of suffering because it represents disconnection from the very quality that makes existence feel worthwhile and meaningful. The child continues to function but loses contact with the force that naturally celebrates and enjoys life.

## Distinguishing Essential Joy from Its Counterfeits

Parents benefit enormously from developing the ability to distinguish between Essential Joy and its various imitations. This discrimination is crucial for supporting authentic development rather than reinforcing compensatory patterns.

**Essential Joy characteristics:**

- Arises spontaneously without external cause
- Feels effortless and self-renewing
- Naturally includes and celebrates others
- Maintains a quality of innocent wonder
- Creates authentic connection and sharing
- Remains present-focused rather than goal-oriented
- Contains natural consideration and empathy
- Feels nourishing to both the child and others

**False Joy characteristics:**

- Requires external stimulation or approval to maintain
- Feels forced, performed, or effortful
- Often excludes others or creates competition
- Lacks innocence and contains hidden agendas
- May manipulate others for attention or approval
- Focused on future rewards or past successes
- May lack consideration for others' feelings
- Often feels draining or overwhelming to others

Learning this distinction allows parents to support genuine expressions of joy while providing appropriate guidance around compensatory patterns. This doesn't mean immediately attempting to eliminate all false joy, which serves important protective functions, but instead creating conditions where Essential Joy can emerge naturally.

**Supporting Essential Joy in Your Child**

Understanding Essential Joy enables parents to provide conscious support for this vital quality throughout their child's development. This support must honor Joy's natural spontaneity while providing appropriate structure and guidance.

- **Create Unstructured Play Time:** Essential Joy emerges most naturally during unstructured activities where children can follow their authentic interests without predetermined outcomes. Regular periods of free play, exploration time, and "boredom" create space for Joy to bubble up spontaneously.
- **Celebrate Discovery Over Achievement:** Focus your enthusiasm on your child's process of discovery rather than just their accomplishments. "I notice how delighted you are to figure out how that works!" supports Joy more effectively than "Good job finishing that puzzle!"
- **Share in Their Wonder:** When your child expresses curiosity or delight, join them in the experience rather than immediately trying to educate or redirect. Follow their lead into wonder before offering information or guidance.
- **Protect Fearless Exploration:** While maintaining necessary safety boundaries, avoid dampening your child's natural fearlessness and enthusiasm for exploration. Find ways to say "yes" to their adventurous spirit whenever possible.
- **Model Authentic Enthusiasm:** Your relationship with Joy and curiosity directly influences your child's development. Cultivate your capacity for wonder, delight, and innocent curiosity as a gift to both yourself and your child.
- **Respond to Curiosity with Delight:** When your child asks questions, even inconvenient or repetitive ones, try to respond with appreciation for their curious spirit rather than annoyance at the interruption. Your reception of their curiosity significantly influences its continued expression.
- **Create Joy-Supporting Rhythms:** Establish family rhythms that support the conditions where Joy naturally arises—unhurried time together, regular exposure to nature, creative activities without pressure, celebrations of small discoveries and achievements.
- **Address Your Relationship with Joy:** If you find yourself consistently dampening your child's enthusiasm or feeling uncomfortable with their

exuberance, explore your relationship with joy. Your unresolved hole of joy becomes an environmental obstacle to your child's natural expression.

**Innocent Curiosity of the Philosopher Child**

One of the most precious gifts parents can nurture is their child's natural capacity for philosophical wonder. Children are born philosophers, asking the deepest questions with innocent directness: "Why do people die?" "Where do thoughts come from?" "What makes something real?" "Why is there anything instead of nothing?"

This philosophical curiosity embodies Essential Joy in one of its most refined forms: the pure delight in pondering the nature of existence. Unlike adult philosophy, which often becomes abstract and intellectual, children's philosophical wonder remains grounded in immediate experience and innocent openness to mystery.

Supporting this capacity involves:

- **Taking Children's Questions Seriously:** Respond to profound questions with the respect they deserve rather than dismissing them as cute or providing simplistic answers that shut down further inquiry.
- **Exploring Together:** Instead of always providing answers, join your child in wondering. "That's such an interesting question. What do you think?" or "I wonder about that too. Let's explore it together."
- **Modeling Wonder:** Share your genuine questions and curiosity about existence. Children need to see that wondering is valuable throughout life, not just during childhood.
- **Creating Space for Mystery:** It's okay, even beneficial, to acknowledge that some questions don't have easy answers. "Some things remain mysterious, and wondering about them can be even more interesting than having answers."
- **Connecting Wonder to Experience:** Help children ground their philosophical curiosity in immediate experience. "When you're feeling angry, what does it feel like in your body? Where do you think that feeling comes from?"

This support for philosophical wonder not only nurtures Essential Joy but also establishes patterns of inquiry and openness that serve the child throughout their life as valuable resources for learning, growth, and spiritual development.

## Joy and the Development of Authentic Learning

Essential Joy provides the foundation for authentic learning, which emerges from genuine curiosity rather than external pressure or reward. When children maintain connection to their natural joy, they approach new information, skills, and experiences with the delight of discovery rather than the anxiety of performance.

This joy-based learning has several distinctive characteristics:

- **Intrinsic Motivation:** Children learning from joy are motivated by the inherent satisfaction of understanding and discovery rather than external rewards or approval. This intrinsic motivation proves more sustainable and satisfying than learning driven by external consequences.
- **Fearless Experimentation:** Joy-connected children approach learning challenges with natural confidence, viewing mistakes as interesting discoveries rather than failures to be avoided. This fearlessness supports deeper, more creative learning.
- **Holistic Integration:** Learning that emerges from joy naturally integrates cognitive, emotional, and physical dimensions. The child doesn't just understand intellectually; they feel the delight of comprehension throughout their being.
- **Sustained Attention:** Children can maintain remarkable focus on activities that genuinely delight them. This natural concentration, supported by joy, often exceeds what can be achieved through external motivation or discipline.
- **Creative Application:** Joy-based learning naturally leads to creative application and extension. Children spontaneously find new ways to use what they've learned, creating games, stories, and innovations that extend their understanding.
- **Social Sharing:** The natural inclusivity of Essential Joy means that children want to share their discoveries and learning with others, creating collaborative rather than competitive learning environments.

Parents can support joy-based learning by following their child's authentic interests, providing rich environments for exploration, and maintaining focus on the process of discovery rather than predetermined outcomes.

**Joy as a Lifelong Resource**

The early development of Essential Joy establishes patterns that influence the child's relationship with learning, creativity, and life satisfaction throughout their development. Children who maintain some connection to this quality develop into adults who can:

- Find genuine delight in simple experiences and everyday moments
- Approach challenges with curiosity rather than anxiety
- Maintain natural enthusiasm for learning and growth
- Create authentic connections with others through shared wonder and discovery
- Access internal sources of satisfaction that don't depend on external circumstances
- Sustain motivation through intrinsic rather than purely external rewards
- Maintain openness to mystery and the unknown throughout life

This doesn't mean they'll never experience sadness, disappointment, or other challenging emotions. However, they'll have access to an essential resource that enables them to find meaning and delight even in the most difficult circumstances.

For parents, understanding Essential Joy helps create realistic expectations about childhood emotional development. The goal is not constant happiness or the elimination of all difficult emotions, but the preservation of the child's natural capacity for authentic delight and wonder alongside their growing ability to navigate life's full emotional spectrum.

**Recognizing the Golden Sparkle**

Learning to recognize Essential Joy in your child requires attention to the quality of their enthusiasm rather than just its intensity or content. This quality has a distinctive feel that becomes unmistakable once you know what to look for:

- **In Spontaneous Discovery:** Notice moments when your child becomes completely absorbed in exploration or discovery, when their whole being seems to sparkle with delight. This isn't the excitement of getting something they want but the effervescent joy of encountering reality directly.

- **In Authentic Curiosity:** Pay attention to the quality of your child's questions and wonderings. Essential Joy manifests as innocent, open-ended curiosity that delights in wondering, rather than seeking specific answers.
- **In Natural Sharing:** Observe how your child shares their discoveries and enthusiasms. Essential Joy naturally wants to include others in its delight, creating connection through shared wonder rather than competition or performance.
- **In Present-Moment Absorption:** Notice times when your child is completely present, neither dwelling on past experiences nor anticipating future rewards but fully engaged with immediate reality.
- **In Fearless Engagement:** Watch for moments when your child approaches new experiences with natural confidence and delight rather than anxiety or cautious calculation.

The golden sparkle of Essential Joy may become less frequent as children grow and encounter increasing social conditioning, but it never disappears entirely. By learning to recognize and appreciate this quality when it appears, parents can help maintain their child's connection to one of the most precious aspects of human experience.

## Infectious Nature of Authentic Joy

One of the most beautiful characteristics of Essential Joy is its naturally infectious quality. When a child expresses authentic joy, it naturally evokes similar qualities in others, not through manipulation or performance, but through the sheer vitality and aliveness they embody.

This infectious quality reveals something profound about Essential Joy; it's not a personal possession but a quality of being that naturally wants to be shared and celebrated. The child expressing Essential Joy doesn't hoard their delight; instead, they spontaneously include others in their discoveries and enthusiasms.

Parents can observe this dynamic in their families and communities. The child who maintains connection to Essential Joy often becomes a catalyst for aliveness in others. Their curiosity reawakens adult wonder, their fearless exploration invites others into adventure, and their innocent delight reminds everyone of what's possible when we approach life with openness and trust.

This understanding changes how parents perceive their role in supporting Joy. Rather than trying to create joy in their children, parents can focus on removing obstacles to its natural expression and creating conditions where it can flow freely. Joy, like water, naturally bubbles up when not blocked. The parent's role is more about clearing obstructions than generating the flow.

**Golden Thread Through Development**

Essential Joy represents perhaps the most obviously precious of all essential qualities, the golden effervescence that makes life feel worth living and existence worth celebrating. While some diminishment of this quality is natural as children develop the structures needed to function in a complex world, conscious parenting can significantly influence how much connection to Joy is preserved and how readily it can be reaccessed throughout life.

The child who grows up with support for their Essential Joy develops what we might call "robust delight," the capacity to find genuine satisfaction and wonder in both simple pleasures and complex challenges. They learn that happiness doesn't depend primarily on external circumstances but can bubble up from their essential nature when conditions allow.

Perhaps most importantly, they develop trust in their capacity for authentic enthusiasm and curiosity. Rather than becoming dependent on external sources of excitement or stimulation, they maintain connection to the internal spring that naturally celebrates existence and delights in discovery.

For parents, supporting Essential Joy becomes both a practice in itself and a gateway to supporting all other essential qualities. Joy's natural curiosity opens pathways to truth and understanding. Its fearless enthusiasm supports the development of strength and will. It's an inclusive celebration that creates the foundation for love and compassion. Its present-moment aliveness connects to peace and stillness.

By understanding and nurturing Essential Joy, parents help ensure that their children maintain access to what may be life's most fundamental gift: the capacity to experience existence not as a problem to be solved or a burden to be endured, but as an ongoing celebration worthy of our deepest appreciation and most authentic engagement.

The golden thread of Essential Joy, when preserved through conscious parenting, becomes a resource that can sustain and inspire the child throughout their entire life journey. It provides the sparkle that makes learning delightful, relationships meaningful, challenges interesting, and simple moments precious. In a world that often teaches children to find satisfaction through external achievement and accumulation, the child who maintains connection to Essential Joy carries within them a treasure more valuable than any external success: the capacity to find genuine delight in the simple miracle of being alive.

# Chapter 24
# Value, Peace, Space, and Nourishment

*The most profound qualities of essence often flow so naturally through young children that we barely notice them—until they begin to fade.* —John Harper

## The Invisible Foundation

While our developmental graph tracks the more dramatic essential qualities that rise and fall through early childhood, these hidden qualities represent what remains constant in our essential nature even as personality develops. They don't show prominent peaks because they form part of the fundamental ground of being, so basic to the child's nature that they're easily overlooked as personality structures gradually develop to mediate the child's experience of themselves and their world. As Almaas describes, essence is "gradually lost or covered up as the personality develops over a few years until there is no awareness of it at all." Yet, these foundational qualities often remain accessible longer precisely because they're so fundamental to existence itself.

Value, Peace, Space, and Nourishment represent what we might call "ground qualities" of essence, so fundamental to the child's being that they're easily overlooked, like the air we breathe or the ground we walk on. Yet as our graph illustrates, with the general pattern of essence diminishment alongside personality development, these hidden qualities follow their subtle trajectory of veiling, often slipping away so gradually that neither parent nor child notices their absence until much later.

Understanding these qualities helps parents recognize a broader range of what can be preserved or lost during the crucial early years. While they may not require the same developmental support as the more prominent essential qualities, their gradual obscuration contributes significantly to the overall pattern of essence veiling that characterizes normal development.

## Essential Value

Every child arrives carrying an amber-colored quality of inherent preciousness, what A.H. Almaas calls Essential Value. This isn't self-esteem or confidence but something far more fundamental—the felt sense of being inherently precious, valuable, and worthwhile simply for existing.

In infancy and early toddlerhood, this quality flows naturally through the child's being. You can see it in the way a baby receives attention and care as their natural due, without embarrassment or apology. You witness it in the toddler's unselfconscious delight in their existence, their assumption that they deserve love and attention simply for being who they are.

## How Value Becomes Veiled

As personality structures strengthen, Essential Value faces particular challenges. The conditional nature of much approval—being praised for achievements, appearance, or behavior—gradually teaches the child that their worth depends on performance. The amber light of inherent value dims as it is replaced by self-esteem based on external validation.

Parents often inadvertently contribute to this veiling through well-meaning but conditional responses: "I'm so proud of you for getting an A," "You're such a good girl when you help mommy," "Look how beautiful you are in that dress." While not inherently harmful, when such conditional recognition dominates the child's experience, it subtly teaches that value comes from doing or being something specific rather than simply existing.

The superego formation that accelerates during the 30-36-month period particularly impacts value, as children internalize standards by which they judge their worth. The emerging inner critic begins evaluating whether they measure up, gradually obscuring the direct experience of inherent preciousness with concerns about adequacy and performance.

## Essential Peace

Peace represents the profound stillness and uncaused contentment that forms the natural ground of the child's being. This isn't the absence of activity or emotion but a deep, settled presence that remains even amid the child's natural exuberance and exploration.

Young children naturally access this quality during quiet moments—the contentment of a nursing infant, the settled satisfaction of a toddler absorbed in play, the easy relaxation of a child simply being without agenda. Unlike adult concepts of peace as the absence of conflict, Essential Peace in children manifests as an unspeakable contentment and inner calm that needs no external cause.

**How Peace Becomes Veiled**

The increasing pace and stimulation of modern childhood gradually fill the spaciousness where Essential Peace naturally flows. As personality structures strengthen and the mind becomes more active, the child's natural stillness gets crowded out by mental activity, planning, worrying, and the internal agitation that characterizes ego development.

The cultural equation of activity with value—the belief that children should always be "doing something productive"—leaves little room for the apparent "emptiness" in which peace naturally arises. Parents may feel uncomfortable with their child's stillness, interpreting it as boredom or depression rather than recognizing it as the natural ground of being.

Additionally, as the superego develops and children begin to monitor their experience, the simple presence of peace can be overlooked in favor of more dramatic emotional states or achievements that feel more substantial to the developing ego.

**Essential Space**

Essential Space represents the boundless, open dimension of awareness within which all the child's experience unfolds. This isn't physical space but the quality of inner spaciousness, the sense of having room to breathe, think, feel, and be without constriction.

In early childhood, this spaciousness manifests as the child's natural openness to experience, their capacity to be fully present without the mental clutter that characterizes adult consciousness. Young children live in what we might call "uncrowded awareness." Their attention flows freely, unburdened by the mental commentary and self-monitoring that will later fill this space.

**How Space Becomes Veiled**

As personality structures strengthen, one of the most significant changes is the gradual filling of this natural spaciousness with mental content. The developing ego creates increasingly complex structures—self-concepts, defensive patterns, internal narratives—that crowd the open space of awareness.

The acceleration of language development particularly impacts space, as children learn to think about their experience rather than simply experiencing it directly.

While language brings tremendous gifts, it also introduces conceptual overlays that can distance the child from the immediate spaciousness of direct experience.

Self-image formation, which intensifies as children become more socially aware, literally fills the space of awareness with concerns about how they appear to others, how they compare, and how they should be. The natural spaciousness becomes occupied by the ego's protective and adaptive structures.

## Essential Nourishment

Nourishment represents the sweet, milk-like quality that feeds the soul's growth and development. While connected to physical feeding in infancy, Essential Nourishment extends far beyond food to encompass all the ways the child's being receives what it needs to thrive and grow.

In early development, this quality naturally flows through loving care, attuned presence, and the child's direct experience of being fed, not just physically but emotionally, spiritually, and essentially. The infant nursing peacefully experiences not just milk but the essential quality of nourishment itself, the sweet sustenance that feeds all levels of their being.

## How Nourishment Becomes Veiled

The transition from breast or bottle feeding to solid foods often marks the beginning of the child's disconnection from Essential Nourishment. As feeding becomes more mechanical and less relational, and as the child's oral needs become satisfied through increasingly processed foods rather than direct human connection, their relationship to nourishment can become externalized.

The cultural emphasis on independence in feeding, while developmentally appropriate, can sometimes come at the cost of the deeper nourishment that flows through relationship and presence. Additionally, oral patterns established in infancy significantly influence how the child later receives not just food but all forms of nourishment, including learning, love, and spiritual sustenance.

As personality development proceeds, the child may lose touch with their authentic hungers and what truly nourishes them, replacing these with compensatory patterns of wanting, consuming, or rejecting that attempt to satisfy deeper needs through surface substitutes.

**The Subtle Trajectory of Hidden Qualities**

Unlike the more dramatic rises and falls of Essential Strength, Will, and Joy shown in our graph, these hidden qualities tend to follow a more gradual pattern of diminishment. They typically don't show pronounced peaks during specific developmental phases; rather, they provide a steady background presence that slowly fades as personality structures mature.

This gradual veiling makes these qualities particularly vulnerable because their loss often goes unnoticed. Parents may not realize that their child's natural sense of inherent worth is being replaced by performance-based self-esteem, or that their settledness is being crowded out by mental activity, or that their spacious awareness is being filled with self-consciousness.

Yet the cumulative impact of losing these foundational qualities contributes significantly to the overall pattern illustrated in our graph. A child who maintains a connection to Essential Value, Peace, Space, and Nourishment will exhibit a different trajectory of development—one where personality structures can develop without completely obscuring the essential foundation.

**Supporting the Hidden Qualities**

While these qualities don't require the same targeted developmental support as the more prominent essential qualities, parents can create conditions that help preserve their natural flow:

- **For Essential Value:** Offer recognition that acknowledges the child's inherent preciousness rather than only their achievements. "I love spending time with you," "You bring such light to our family," "I'm grateful you exist," communicate value independent of performance.
- **For Essential Peace:** Create regular periods of unhurried time, free from stimulation and agenda. Allow for moments of simple being together, comfortable silence, and the spaciousness in which Peace naturally arises.
- **For Essential Space:** Be mindful of not filling every moment with activity, instruction, or conversation. Support your child's natural rhythms of engagement and withdrawal, as well as their activity and rest.
- **For Essential Nourishment:** Approach feeding, whether physical, emotional, or spiritual, with presence and attention. Create mealtimes and other forms of care that nourish multiple levels of the child's being simultaneously.

## Foundation Beneath Development

These hidden qualities remind us that development occurs not in a vacuum but within a field of essential qualities that provide the foundation for healthy growth. While our graph shows the natural divergence between essence and personality, understanding these subtler qualities helps parents recognize what can be preserved even as necessary development proceeds.

The child who maintains some conscious connection to value, peace, space, and nourishment will develop personality structures that remain more permeable to essence. Their sense of worth won't depend entirely on achievement; their capacity for stillness won't be completely replaced by mental activity; their awareness won't be entirely filled with self-consciousness; and their ability to receive what they need won't be wholly externalized.

These hidden qualities flow like underground streams beneath the more visible landscape of development, providing essential nourishment for the child's deepest being even as they navigate the necessary challenges of growing up. By understanding their subtle presence and gradual veiling, parents can better support the full spectrum of their child's essential nature during these crucial formative years.

# Chapter 25
## When Essence Becomes Holes

*A hole is nothing but the absence of a certain part of our essence… When we are not aware of our Essence, it stops manifesting. This results in a sense of deficiency.* —A.H. Almaas

**Inevitable Geography of Loss**

A certain diminishment of conscious connection to one's essence is a natural and necessary part of human development. Yet within this general pattern lies a more specific process that A.H. Almaas calls the "Theory of Holes," a framework that explains how particular essential qualities become lost to consciousness and replaced by compensatory personality structures.

This process reflects a fundamental truth about human development: as each aspect of essence becomes lost to conscious awareness, what Almaas calls "a particular hole or deficient emptiness" is created. This hole is then filled by the development of a specific sector of personality, designed to compensate for the missing essential quality. In this way, each characteristic of personality can be understood as a false substitute for an essential quality, not inherently pathological, but a creative adaptation to the loss of direct, essential connection. The personality that develops isn't simply a neutral psychological structure but often functions in opposition to essence, viewing the emergence of essential qualities as potentially disorganizing to its established patterns and sense of identity.

Understanding this process helps parents recognize the difference between healthy personality development and the formation of rigid defensive patterns. While some degree of essence veiling is inevitable as children develop the structures needed to function in the world, the quality of early relationships and environmental responses significantly influences which essential qualities remain accessible and which become "holes," or areas of deficient emptiness that the personality attempts to fill through various strategies and substitutes.

The Theory of Holes reveals that what we often consider normal childhood difficulties, such as tantrums, defiance, withdrawal, or excessive neediness, may represent the child's creative attempts to manage the absence of essential qualities that have become lost to their direct experience. By understanding this dynamic, parents can respond more skillfully to challenging behaviors while working to preserve their child's connection to their essential nature.

**The Anatomy of a Hole**

In the Diamond Approach framework, a hole represents any part of the child's essential nature that has been lost to consciousness. This isn't a physical absence but a psychological and energetic gap where direct experience of a particular essential quality should be. When children lose conscious connection to qualities like Value, Strength, Will, or Joy, they experience what Almaas calls "deficient emptiness," a felt sense that something is fundamentally missing or wrong.

Every baby arrives complete with no holes in their essential nature. The innocent delight of the newborn, their natural strength in asserting needs, their inherent sense of worth, and their capacity for peaceful contentment all flow freely through their being. Yet as development proceeds and personality structures mature, certain essential qualities may become detached from conscious experience.

This abandonment occurs because the developing personality structure requires unconsciousness to maintain its patterns and conditioning. As the child increasingly identifies with learned behaviors, defensive strategies, and self-concepts, the personality begins to view essence as foreign or even threatening to its established sense of self. What was once the child's natural way of being becomes progressively excluded from their experience, not because essence disappears but because the personality structure that develops to fill the resulting holes actively maintains barriers against essential recognition. This is why reconnecting with essential qualities later in life often requires working through the very personality structures that developed to compensate for their absence.

**Holes Form in Early Development**

The formation of holes follows predictable patterns related to the developmental trajectory shown in our graph. As essential qualities naturally begin to diminish between 18 and 36 months, environmental responses significantly influence whether they recede into the background of awareness or become actively suppressed and replaced by compensatory structures.

- **The Value Hole:** Essential Value—the amber-colored sense of inherent preciousness—can become a hole when the child's worth becomes consistently tied to performance, appearance, or behavior. If love and approval primarily flow when the child meets certain standards, they may lose touch with their intrinsic value and develop what is experienced as a sense of worthlessness. This hole gets filled with efforts to achieve worth through accomplishment, appearance, or pleasing others.

- **The Strength Hole:** When Essential Strength—the red fire of vitality and autonomous capacity—is consistently suppressed or punished, children may lose connection to their natural power and develop what feels like fundamental weakness or powerlessness. This hole often gets filled with either aggressive compensation (forcing and controlling) or collapses into dependency and helplessness.
- **The Will Hole:** Essential Will—the grounded capacity for authentic self-direction—can become a hole when children's genuine preferences and intentions are consistently overridden or ignored. This creates what Almaas calls the "castration" experience, a felt sense of lacking inner support and personal confidence. The Will Hole often gets filled with either rigid willfulness (stubborn opposition) or passive compliance that avoids the anxiety of self-direction.
- **The Hole of Joy:** When Essential Joy—the spontaneous effervescence of being—meets with consistent dampening or conditional approval, children may lose touch with causeless delight and develop patterns of depression or forced cheerfulness. This hole gets filled with strategies for manufacturing happiness through external sources or performing enthusiasm to gain approval.

**Formation of False Qualities**

When essential qualities become holes, the personality doesn't simply leave them empty. Instead, it develops what Almaas calls "false qualities" or "pseudo-feelings," imitations that attempt to fulfill the function of the missing essential quality while avoiding the vulnerability of its direct experience.

These false qualities can be remarkably sophisticated, often fooling even the child who develops them. False strength may manifest as aggression or controlling behavior. False will appears as stubborn willfulness or people-pleasing. False joy becomes performance-based enthusiasm or manic excitement. False value shows up as achievement orientation or superiority.

The key difference between essential qualities and their false substitutes lies in their felt sense and sustainability. Essential qualities feel natural, effortless, and nourishing both to the child and those around them. False qualities require constant effort to maintain and often feel hollow or exhausting over time. Essential Joy bubbles up spontaneously and includes others; false joy feels forced and may exclude or compete with others' happiness.

Parents can learn to distinguish between these by paying attention to the quality of their child's expression rather than just its content. A child expressing Essential Strength moves through the world with natural confidence and consideration for others. A child compensating for the Strength Hole may exhibit either aggressive control or a collapsed and dependent behavior, both of which represent strategies for managing the underlying sense of powerlessness.

**Developmental Timing of Hole Formation**

Our graph reveals that the period from 18 to 36 months represents a particularly vulnerable window for hole formation. As essential qualities naturally begin to diminish and personality structures rapidly solidify, environmental responses have a maximum impact on which qualities remain accessible versus which recede further from conscious awareness.

The accelerated superego formation during this period creates additional vulnerability. As children internalize standards and expectations, they may begin suppressing essential qualities that don't align with family or cultural values. A family that prioritizes compliance may inadvertently create a hole of will. A culture that values achievement over being may contribute to a sense of deficient self-worth. Gender socialization often creates different patterns of hole formation, with boys frequently developing holes around emotional expression and vulnerability, while girls may develop holes around strength and assertiveness.

The rapprochement crisis, with its complex emotional demands, can overwhelm the child's developing capacity to integrate essential qualities with emerging personality structures. Suppose parents respond to this challenge with excessive control, dismissal, or emotional unavailability. In those cases, the child may abandon essential qualities that feel too risky to maintain in the face of perceived threats to crucial relationships.

**Environmental Factors That Contribute to Hole Formation**

Several environmental factors commonly contribute to the formation of holes during early development:

- **Conditional Love and Approval:** When acceptance depends on the child expressing only certain qualities while suppressing others, the unsupported qualities may become holes. The child learns that parts of their essential nature are unacceptable and gradually loses conscious connection to them.
- **Overwhelm or Misattunement:** When caregivers consistently respond to the child's essential expressions with overwhelming intensity or complete misattunement, the child may abandon these qualities as unsafe or ineffective. A parent who becomes anxious when their child expresses natural strength may inadvertently teach the child to suppress this quality.
- **Cultural and Familial Prejudices:** Explicit or implicit messages about which qualities are valuable versus problematic significantly influence hole formation. Families that view assertiveness as "selfish" or joy as "frivolous" may inadvertently create corresponding holes in their children.
- **Trauma and Disruption:** Significant disruptions to attachment relationships, family stability, or physical safety can create holes as the child's system prioritizes survival over essential expression. A child who experiences early loss may abandon qualities like trust or openness that feel too vulnerable in an uncertain world.
- **Projection of Parental Holes:** Perhaps most significantly, parents unconsciously tend to suppress in their children the essential qualities they have lost connection to. A parent with a lack of personal value may struggle to reflect their child's inherent worth. A parent who is overly identified with weakness may feel threatened by their child's natural power.

**Hidden Gifts of Compensatory Patterns**

While holes represent a loss of direct essential connection, it's important to recognize that the compensatory patterns children develop often contain remarkable creativity and adaptation. These structures aren't simply pathological but represent the child's brilliant attempts to maintain some version of essential function while protecting themselves from further loss.

The child who develops aggressive patterns to compensate for the loss of Essential Strength is attempting to maintain some sense of power and agency. The people-pleasing child with a weak will is trying to maintain connection while avoiding the anxiety of authentic self-direction. These patterns, while ultimately limiting, represent the personality's creative solutions to impossible developmental dilemmas.

Understanding this helps parents respond to challenging behaviors with greater compassion and effectiveness. Rather than simply trying to eliminate difficult patterns, parents can recognize them as indicators of underlying essential needs and work to address the holes that drive them. This approach tends to be more sustainable than behavioral management alone because it addresses the root cause rather than just the surface manifestation of the issue.

**Recognizing Holes Versus Essential Expression**

One of the most crucial skills parents can develop is distinguishing between their child's essential expressions and the compensatory patterns that fill holes. This discrimination requires attention to the qualitative feel of the child's behavior rather than just its content.

**Signs of Essential Expression:**

- Feels natural and effortless
- Includes consideration for others
- Sustainable over time without forcing
- Brings out the best in others
- Contains joy even during challenges
- Responsive to changing circumstances
- Emerges from present-moment awareness

**Signs of Compensatory Patterns:**

- Requires effort or force to maintain
- Often excludes or competes with others
- Exhausting or unsustainable over time
- May trigger reactivity in others
- Lacks authentic joy or satisfaction
- Rigid and inflexible
- Based on past conditioning or future fears

Learning this distinction allows parents to support genuine essential expression while providing appropriate guidance around compensatory patterns. This doesn't mean immediately attempting to eliminate all defensive structures, which would be neither possible nor wise; instead, it means gradually creating conditions where essential qualities can reemerge naturally.

**Working with Holes Without Pathologizing**

The Theory of Holes provides a framework for understanding childhood difficulties. Still, it's crucial not to pathologize normal developmental processes or become overly concerned about every instance of struggle or compensation. Some degree of hole formation is inevitable as children navigate the complex demands of growing up in an imperfect world.

The goal is not to prevent all holes, which would be impossible, but to minimize unnecessary ones while supporting the child's natural resilience and capacity for essential reconnection. This balanced approach recognizes that:

- **Some Defensive Structures Are Necessary:** Children need psychological defenses to function in complex social environments. The goal is to support defenses that remain permeable to essence rather than rigid barriers against it.
- **Holes Can Be Opportunities:** When approached with awareness, holes can become doorways to deeper understanding and connection. A child's struggle with a particular issue may reveal an opportunity to support the reemergence of an essential quality.
- **Timing Matters:** Attempting to address holes in a child's personality structure before they have developed adequate structure can be overwhelming. The work of essence reconnection is most effective when there is sufficient ego strength to tolerate the vulnerability involved.
- **Environmental Support Is Crucial:** The same hole may resolve naturally in a supportive environment while becoming more entrenched in a hostile one. Creating conditions that welcome essential expression remains the most powerful intervention.
- **Parents' Holes Influence Their Children:** Perhaps most importantly, parents' relationship with essential qualities directly impacts their capacity to support their children. Working on one's holes often proves more effective than focusing exclusively on the child's patterns.

## The Path Back to Wholeness

While hole formation represents a natural part of development, the qualities that become holes are never permanently lost. Essential nature remains intact beneath whatever compensatory structures have formed. Under the right conditions, typically involving safety, support, and appropriate challenge, children can reconnect with qualities that seemed irretrievably lost.

This reconnection often happens naturally during periods of security and growth. A child who developed a Hole of Joy due to early depression in the family may rediscover spontaneous delight when placed in an environment that welcomes and celebrates essential joy. A child with a Strength Hole may reconnect with their natural power when given appropriate challenges and support within safe boundaries.

The process typically involves first recognizing and accepting the compensatory patterns without judgment, then gradually creating space for the underlying essential quality to reemerge. This may occur through play therapy, family therapy, changes in family dynamics, or simply the natural maturation process, all of which can be supported by conscious parenting.

## Supporting Essential Wholeness

Understanding the Theory of Holes helps parents approach their children's development with greater wisdom and compassion. Rather than seeing challenging behaviors as problems to be eliminated, parents can recognize them as valuable information about their child's essential needs and the compensatory patterns they've developed to manage losses.

This perspective transforms parenting from primarily managing behavior to supporting the child's wholeness, both their developing personality and their essential nature. By creating environments that welcome the full spectrum of essential qualities, parents help minimize "loss of essence" while supporting their child's natural capacity for integration and growth.

The child who grows up with fewer rigid compensatory patterns and more access to their essential qualities develops what we might call "flexible resilience," the capacity to adapt to life's challenges while remaining connected to their authentic nature. This foundation serves them well not only in childhood but throughout their lives as they face the ongoing task of balancing the demands of living in the world with the call of their essential being.

As we conclude our exploration of essential qualities and their development, we return to a fundamental truth: **Every child arrives complete, carrying within them all the qualities needed for a life of meaning, connection, and authentic expression.** While some veiling of essence is inevitable as children develop the structures necessary to function in a complex world, conscious parenting can significantly influence how much essential connection is preserved and how readily it can be reaccessed when required.

The goal is not perfection, but awareness, helping our children develop personalities that serve their essential nature rather than obscuring it. This creates families and communities that welcome the full spectrum of human potential and support each child's unique path toward integration and wholeness.

## Chapter 26
## The Integrated Child

*The goal is not to preserve essence as a museum piece from childhood, but to support its integration with a maturing personality that serves rather than obscures our deepest nature..* —
A.H. Almass

### Living Tapestry of Essential Development

As we conclude our exploration of childhood development, we find ourselves not at an end, but at a beginning —the recognition that essence and personality development need not be opposing forces, but can become partners in the child's unfolding wholeness. Throughout this section, we've examined individual essential qualities like separate threads in a tapestry. Still, the living child experiences them as an integrated, dynamic whole that shifts and flows according to developmental needs and environmental conditions.

The child who maintains connection to this integrated essence doesn't live in a state of constant bliss or exhibit all essential qualities simultaneously. Instead, they retain what we might call "essential fluidity," the capacity to access different qualities as life circumstances call for them, while remaining grounded in their fundamental sense of wholeness and authenticity.

Watch a four-year-old engaged in deep play: Essential Joy bubbles through their absorption in discovery, Essential Will focuses their attention with effortless determination, Essential Strength provides the grounded confidence to persist through challenges, while the hidden qualities of Value, Peace, Space, and Nourishment create the background conditions that make such integrated expression possible. The Merging Essence of early infancy has evolved into a more mature capacity for connection that doesn't require the dissolution of boundaries but can include others in their delight and discovery.

This is the integrated child—not perfect, not without personality structures or adaptive strategies, but maintaining enough connection to their essential nature that these structures remain permeable rather than becoming opaque barriers to authentic being.

**Dance of Preservation and Development**

Our journey through essential qualities reveals a fundamental truth: The task of conscious parenting is not to choose between supporting development and preserving essence but to understand how they can enhance each other rather than diminish either. Each essential quality we've explored demonstrates this possibility when environmental conditions support integration rather than forcing separation.

- **Essential Strength** shows us that true power enhances rather than threatens relationship when it arises from authentic being rather than compensatory patterns. The child who maintains connection to the red fire of vitality can assert their preferences, explore their boundaries, and develop their capacities without becoming oppositional or aggressive. Their strength serves their authentic expression rather than defending against perceived threats.
- **Essential Will** reveals that authentic self-direction naturally includes consideration for others and realistic assessment of circumstances. The child operating from this grounded determination doesn't need to choose between autonomy and relationship; they can maintain their authentic center while remaining responsive to the needs and boundaries of their environment.
- **Essential Joy** demonstrates that genuine delight naturally wants to include and celebrate others rather than excluding or competing with them. The child expressing authentic joy becomes a catalyst for aliveness in their family and community, showing that essential qualities serve not just individual development but collective flourishing.
- **Merging Essence** establishes in infancy the template for connection that transcends the later false choice between independence and relationship. The child who experiences authentic unity in their earliest months carries within them the understanding that true autonomy enhances, rather than threatens, genuine connection.

Even the hidden qualities—Value, Peace, Space, and Nourishment—contribute to this integration by providing a stable foundation from which the more dynamic essential qualities can emerge and express themselves. A child who maintains some connection to their inherent worth doesn't need to prove themselves through performance. One who retains access to inner peace doesn't become overwhelmed by the intensity of development. Connection to essential spaciousness prevents the child's awareness from becoming crowded with defensive thoughts and self-monitoring.

**Recognizing the Integrated Child**

Learning to recognize integration versus compensation in your child requires developing sensitivity to the quality of their presence rather than focusing solely on behaviors or achievements. The integrated child displays certain unmistakable characteristics that transcend specific actions or expressions:

- **Present-Moment Responsiveness:** Rather than operating from automatic patterns or reactive conditioning, the integrated child responds freshly to each situation from their authentic nature. Their behavior emerges from a genuine assessment of current circumstances rather than from defensive habits or compensatory strategies.
- **Natural Consideration:** Integration doesn't require teaching the child to consider others. It naturally includes empathy and realistic assessment of impact. The child operating from essence doesn't need constant reminders about how their actions affect others because their essential qualities naturally include such awareness.
- **Effortless Authenticity:** Perhaps most characteristically, integration has a quality of ease and naturalness. The child isn't working to be authentic or struggling to maintain essential connection; it flows as their natural way of being. This doesn't mean they never experience difficulty, but that they meet challenges from their authentic center rather than from defensive patterns.
- **Flexible Resilience:** The integrated child can adapt to changing circumstances without losing their essential center. They develop what we might call "transparent structures," personality patterns that serve their essential expression rather than hiding or distorting it. When faced with stress, disappointment, or challenge, they may temporarily lose connection to specific essential qualities but retain the capacity to reconnect rather than becoming rigidly defended.
- **Inclusive Aliveness:** Perhaps most beautifully, the integrated child's aliveness enhances rather than threatens the well-being of others. Their joy evokes rather than exhausts, their strength supports rather than dominates, and their will includes rather than excludes others' legitimate needs.

**Parents' Essential Work as Foundation**

Throughout our exploration of essential qualities, a consistent theme has emerged: the child's capacity to maintain essential connection depends significantly on the parent's relationship with these qualities. This isn't about perfect parenting or achieving some ideal state before having children, but about ongoing willingness to recognize and work with our patterns of connection to essence and disconnection.

- **Recognizing Our Holes:** When we understand the Theory of Holes—how essential qualities become lost and replaced by compensatory patterns—we can begin to recognize where our essential connection may have been compromised during our development. The parent who lost connection to Essential Joy may unconsciously dampen their child's exuberance. The parent with a Strength Hole may feel threatened by their child's natural power. This recognition isn't for self-judgment, but for increasing our capacity to respond to our children from an essential presence rather than an unconscious reaction.
- **Working with Our Inner and Soul Child:** Understanding these developmental structures helps us recognize when we're operating from childhood patterns rather than essential presence. The parent who can distinguish between their Inner Child's need for approval and their essential capacity for authentic relationship creates more space for their child's natural development.
- **Essential Modeling:** Children learn not primarily from what we tell them about being authentic but from witnessing authentic being in action. When parents maintain their connection to essential qualities—expressing genuine enthusiasm rather than a performance, demonstrating grounded strength rather than forced effort, and showing authentic consideration for others—they provide powerful modeling for integrated development.
- **Creating Fields of Essence:** Perhaps most importantly, parents who maintain their essential connection create what we might call "fields of essence," environmental conditions where essential qualities can flow more freely. This isn't something we achieve through techniques or strategies, but rather by being present with our essential nature amidst family life.

**Supporting Integration Through Daily Life**

The cultivation of integrated development happens not through special programs or extraordinary interventions but through the quality of presence we bring to ordinary moments. Understanding essential qualities transforms how we approach the daily rhythms of family life:

- **Seeing Beyond Behavior:** When we understand essential qualities, we can recognize the vital needs and capacities beneath challenging behaviors. The toddler's tantrum may represent Essential Will attempting to maintain autonomy amid overwhelming circumstances. The preschooler's defiance might reflect Essential Strength asserting itself when it feels suppressed or ignored. This recognition allows us to address underlying essential needs rather than merely managing surface behaviors.
- **Creating Essence-Supporting Rhythms:** Family routines can be structured to support the natural flow of essential qualities. Unhurried morning transitions allow Peace and Spaciousness to remain accessible. Regular periods of unstructured play create opportunities for Joy and authentic expression. Consistent bedtime rituals that include presence and connection support the child's integration of daily experiences.
- **Essential Mirroring in Real Time:** Throughout the day, parents have countless opportunities to reflect the essential qualities they observe in their children. "I notice how determined you are to figure that out," acknowledges Essential Will in action. "Your joy is just bubbling up right now," helps the child recognize and value their authentic delight. This mirroring helps maintain conscious connection to essential qualities even as personality structures develop.
- **Distinguishing Essential Expression from Compensation:** Perhaps most crucially, parents can learn to discern when their children are operating from authentic essential qualities versus compensatory patterns designed to fill holes where essential connection has been lost. Essential expressions feel natural, effortless, and sustainable. Compensatory patterns require effort to maintain and often feel hollow or performative.

**Developmental Spiral of Integration**

Integration doesn't happen once and remain fixed. It unfolds as a developmental spiral where children periodically reconnect with essential qualities at deeper levels as their capacity for consciousness and self-awareness matures. The three-year-old's expression of Essential Will differs qualitatively from that of the seven-year-old, which in turn differs from the expressions of the teenager and the adult. Yet when development proceeds with consciousness and support, each spiral reveals greater integration and maturity rather than simply greater disconnection.

- **Early Integration (Ages 3-7):** During the Soul Child years, integration involves maintaining the aliveness and responsiveness of essence while developing basic personality structures needed for social functioning. The child learns to establish appropriate boundaries without losing their essential openness, develops language skills without compromising direct contact with experience, and begins to understand social expectations without sacrificing their authentic nature.
- **Middle Childhood Integration (Ages 7-12):** As cognitive capacities expand and social awareness deepens, integration involves maintaining essential connection while developing a more sophisticated understanding of others' perspectives, complex social relationships, and abstract thinking. The child learns to channel essential qualities appropriately for different contexts without suppressing them entirely.
- **Adolescent Integration (Ages 12-18):** The teenage years present the challenge of maintaining essential connection while developing an independent identity, adult capacities, and preparation for leaving the family system. Rather than requiring the abandonment of essential qualities, healthy adolescent development involves the mature expression of these qualities through the expansion of responsibilities and the development of relationships.
- **Adult Integration (18+):** The culmination of conscious development involves what Almaas calls "Personal Essence," the integration of essential being with functional personality that allows the person to access essential qualities as needed while maintaining the capacity for effective action in the world.

This developmental perspective enables parents to maintain realistic expectations while supporting their child's natural progression toward greater integration and consciousness throughout their development.

**Ripple Effects of Essential Connection**

When children maintain connection to their essential nature while developing healthy personality structures, the benefits extend far beyond the individual child to influence families, communities, and ultimately the larger society. The integrated child becomes what we might call an "essence catalyst," someone whose authentic being naturally evokes similar qualities in others.

- **Family Transformation:** The child who maintains essential connection often awakens dormant essential qualities in other family members. Their authentic joy can rekindle a parent's lost capacity for delight. Their natural strength can remind siblings of their power. Their peaceful presence can calm family anxiety. This mutual awakening creates what we might call "essence resonance" that supports the growth and healing of the entire family system.
- **Educational and Social Impact:** Children who maintain essential connection while developing appropriate social skills often become natural leaders and healers in their peer groups. They demonstrate through their presence that authenticity and social effectiveness can coexist, providing modeling for other children who may have learned to choose between being themselves and being accepted.
- **Cultural Evolution:** Perhaps most significantly, raising children while maintaining essential connection contributes to the evolution of human consciousness itself. Each child who grows up without completely losing their authentic nature represents a step toward a more conscious, compassionate, and integrated human culture.

## Transparent Structures Serving Essence

The ultimate vision that emerges from our exploration of essential qualities is not the elimination of personality structures, which would leave children unable to function effectively in the world, but the development of what we might call "transparent structures." These are personality patterns that allow essential expressions rather than obscuring them, adaptive strategies that enhance rather than limit authentic being, and social skills that support rather than suppress the child's deepest nature.

The child who develops transparent structures maintains access to essential qualities while gaining the tools needed for effective functioning in complex social environments. They can be appropriate in formal settings without losing their spontaneity, can meet others' legitimate needs without abandoning their authenticity, and can adapt to changing circumstances without losing their essential center.

This isn't a utopian fantasy but a real possibility supported by conscious parenting that understands both the necessity of development and the value of essential preservation. It requires neither perfect parents nor ideal children, but rather an ongoing commitment to supporting the child's wholeness, even as they navigate the inevitable challenges of growing up in an imperfect world.

**The Continuing Journey**

As we conclude this exploration of essential qualities and their development, we recognize that this is not an ending but a beginning. Each child's journey of integration is unique, unfolding according to their particular temperament, family circumstances, and environmental conditions. There is no single path or predetermined outcome, but rather an ongoing dance between essence and personality that continues throughout life.

For parents, understanding essential qualities provides not a rigid framework but a flexible compass, a way of orienting toward what matters most while remaining responsive to the unique needs and circumstances of their particular child and family. It offers tools for recognition and support rather than techniques for control or manipulation.

Most importantly, it provides hope: the hope that development need not require the sacrifice of what is most precious in human nature, that growing up can enhance rather than diminish our connection to our deepest being and that each child carries within them the possibility of becoming a fully functioning human being who remains connected to the essential qualities that make life meaningful and joyful.

The work of nurturing essence while supporting healthy development is neither easy nor perfect, but it is perhaps the most critical work we can do as parents and as human beings. In supporting our children's integration of essence and personality, we contribute not only to their flourishing but also to the evolution of consciousness itself, helping to create a world where authenticity and effectiveness, individuality and community, development and essence can coexist and mutually enhance one another.

The integrated child we nurture today becomes the integrated adult who can support others in their essence tomorrow, creating ripples of consciousness and authenticity that extend far beyond our families into the broader human community. This is the ultimate gift of conscious parenting: not just raising successful children but supporting the emergence of human beings who can remain connected to their essential nature while making a meaningful contribution to the world's healing and evolution.

In the end, the preservation of essence through conscious parenting isn't just about supporting our children; it's about supporting the continued presence of essential qualities in our world, ensuring that what is most precious in human nature continues to flow through future generations, illuminating the path toward a more conscious, compassionate, and integrated human presence on Earth.

# Chapter 27
## When Development Becomes Emergence

*We have walked through the stages of development. Now we pause at the threshold—not to conclude but to listen for what has always been moving beneath it all...*

### Implications of Human Development and Essence

There is something in us that does not need to be built or fixed, yet it has a developmental process. In the Diamond Approach, this is known as the Pearl, or the Personal Essence. It is not a structure but a living presence, uniquely individual. The Pearl is the essence of personhood: the real person who can function, relate, and create, not out of adaptation but from presence. It is who we are when we are not trying to be someone, not relying on history to define us.

### What if development as we know it is incomplete?

This book has explored how personality forms, how ego structures stabilize experience, and how early development prepares us to meet the world. But these psychological achievements are only the outer layer of a deeper movement: the soul's effort to express its native coherence through the form of a human being.

### Where does the drive for integration come from?

From the outside, ego development appears to be a process of assembling what's fragmented into some sense of unity, a whole person. But underneath that drive is not fragmentation but a movement to express something already unified. The soul is not striving to become something new. It moves from essential fullness toward essential embodiment, toward expression through body, heart, and mind. The impulse is not to acquire coherence but to live the coherence already inherent in Being.

### What arrests that movement?

The soul becomes stalled when it identifies with the ego. What began as scaffolding becomes mistaken for identity. The structures meant to support expression become structures of containment. Psychological development halts, not because of failure but because the self becomes crystallized around the adaptation that has occurred. What was once a vehicle becomes a cage.

**What reactivates essential development?**

Not insight or technique but longing. The longing for something gone missing. Not a yearning born of lack but of remembrance. This longing is the soul's signal calling itself back. It does not seek a better version of self; it seeks emergence into lived experience. Essential development begins where psychological growth levels off. It is not about building a self. It is about allowing what has been quietly present all along to come forward.

**Is the ego a distorted echo of a deeper intelligence?**

Yes. The ego's strategies to connect, relate, and function mimic what the personal essence does naturally. While the ego tries to construct a person, the Pearl is the original blueprint. It is formed not through adaptation but as a direct expression of Being.

The personal essence is the soul's innate capacity to live as a whole person. By the time we gain the power of abstract thought and self-reflection, our essence is hidden beneath the persona we've constructed. This is not a flaw in development; it's a necessary phase. Like a caterpillar dissolving within the chrysalis, ego development creates the ground for a transformation it cannot complete. What is required is not perfection of the ego but surrender to the process of emergence.

**What role do the body and mind play in this expression?**

The body and mind were never meant to be the source of identity. They are instruments of the soul—organs of perception, expression, and participation. When they are relieved of the burden of selfhood, they return to their proper function: to bring presence into contact with life.

**What does it mean to become a real human being?**

It means allowing the soul's unity to reveal itself through the complexity of living. To relate, act, and create, not out of strategy but from Being. A real human being is not someone who has arrived but someone whose presence is sincere, undivided, and responsive to objective reality.

This is the more profound implication of development. Human development, if it culminates in ego identity, remains incomplete. But if it continues, if it opens beyond this separate self-identity, it becomes the flowering of essence in time.

We do not need to become something other. We are never missing what matters.

This is not a return to innocence. It is the conscious embodiment of essence, a person in the world but not of it. A soul moving through a body, with a mind, as a human being.

Not development toward wholeness but development as the revelation of what was whole from the beginning.

# In Conclusion

## Dance Between Becoming and Being

The journey of childhood development is often likened to a magnificent symphony, where the physical, cognitive, emotional, and social domains contribute distinct melodies. But beneath this familiar composition lies a quieter, more ancient song, one that is easily missed in the rush of milestones and expectations. This is the song of essence: a child's innate joy, strength, will, merging, and presence.

As the scaffolding of personality assembles—through language, mirroring, boundaries, and adaptation—these essential qualities don't disappear. They fade from conscious access like stars in the morning sky. The louder melody of becoming someone often drowns out the silent resonance of simply being. And yet, that background music never stops playing.

This book has mapped both stories: the child's visible development across stages and domains and the more subtle arc of their essential nature—how it emerges, how it gets obscured, and how it can be preserved. Through the combined insights of our ten guides—Piaget, Vygotsky, Bandura, Kohlberg, Mahler, Erikson, Freud, Winnicott, Bowlby, and Almaas—we've explored both the architecture of the self and the light that fills it.

A central paradox emerges: The very developments that enable a child to function in society—the inner narrative, the superego, and adaptation to the social mirror—also risk distancing them from their essence. This is not failure. It's the natural unfolding of human life. But how steep that descent becomes is profoundly influenced by parenting.

The task is not to resist development but to guide and support it in ways that remain permeable to essence. The goal is not perfection but presence, not mastery but awareness.

Supporting this integration requires a parent willing to mirror essence, not just behavior. To reflect the strength in persistence, the will behind a firm no, the joy behind wild play. It means speaking the language of experience, not just evaluation, offering guidance that connects morality to meaning, not just authority, holding space for the child to discern which reflections of themselves to keep and which to let fall away.

The child's journey through Merging, Strength, Joy, and Will mirrors that of the parent. Supporting the child's essence begins with reconnecting to our own. When parents engage their histories, meet their lost places with kindness, and commit to their unfolding, they naturally create the kind of space in which a child's essence stays alive and accessible.

Over time, this dance of development and essence gives rise to something more profound: a mature integration known in the Diamond Approach as the Personal Essence, or Pearl. This is not simply a return to childhood purity but the emergence of an authentic adult who is both capable and whole, who lives from their center rather than from their conditioning.

And from such children, something extraordinary radiates. They become quiet catalysts. Not performers of essence but expressions of it. They evoke presence in others. They stir the dormant truth in their communities. They carry forward not just inherited genes but awakened being.

Parenting, then, is not simply about raising a child who functions well in the world. It is about nurturing a being who can remain in contact with what is most true. This is not an easy path. But it is a sacred one.

It begins anew in every moment we remember to pause, to meet what is here, and to recognize the quiet spark behind the eyes of the child before us. Not as something to protect or perfect but as something to honor, over and over again.

In doing so, we don't just raise a child.

We raise consciousness itself.

*Through your grace, the world will heal.*

# Glossary

**Attachment:** A deep emotional bond between a child and caregiver that forms the foundation for trust, safety, and later relationships. Developed through consistent, responsive care, this bond is the cornerstone of Bowlby's Attachment Theory.

**Attachment Patterns:** Specific relational styles formed in infancy (secure, avoidant, ambivalent, disorganized) that shape how a child responds to comfort, separation, and connection.

**Authentic Self / True Self:** The spontaneous, creative, and genuine expression of being that emerges when a child's inner reality is mirrored and welcomed. Central to Winnicott's work.

**Basic Trust:** A nonverbal, existential confidence in the goodness and support of reality, arising from early, consistent attunement. In Erikson's model, this results from successful navigation of the first psychosocial stage: trust vs. mistrust.

**Body Cathexis:** The process by which the soul's awareness gradually identifies with the physical body, anchoring a sense of "I am" in early development.

**Centration:** A cognitive limitation (Piaget) where a child focuses on a single aspect of a situation, ignoring other relevant features.

**Cognitive Development:** The progression of thinking, problem-solving, language, and understanding. Piaget and Vygotsky offer foundational models.

**Compensatory Structures:** Personality traits developed to cover the absence of contact with essence (e.g., willfulness for Essential Will). Often form in response to early deficiency or misattunement.

**Conditional Acceptance:** When a child perceives love is earned by compliance or performance rather than given unconditionally. Leads to suppression of authentic qualities.

**Developmental Domains:** Broad areas of human growth: physical, cognitive, emotional, and social.

**Developmental Milestone:** A typical skill (e.g., walking, speaking, empathizing) achieved within a predictable age range.

**Diamond Approach:** A spiritual and psychological framework developed by A.H. Almaas. It integrates essence, ego development, and phenomenological inquiry.

**Differentiation:** The early stage of Mahler's separation-individuation process, where the infant begins distinguishing self from other.

**Ego:** The structure of personality formed through adaptation, memory, and social interaction. Useful for survival, but can obscure essence.

**Egocentrism:** A child's early inability to understand another's perspective. A hallmark of Piaget's preoperational stage.

**Emotional Development:** The unfolding capacity to feel, identify, express, and regulate emotions, as well as develop empathy.

**Empathy:** The ability to attune to and feel what another is experiencing. Gradually develops through secure attachment and mirroring.

**Essence:** The inherent, unconditioned presence that precedes personality: qualities like joy, strength, will, peace, and love. Central to the Diamond Approach.

**Essential Qualities:** Specific felt qualities of essence (e.g., Essential Joy, Will, Strength, Peace), each with its own developmental appearance and role.

**Essential Mirroring:** The act of reflecting back a child's essential presence (not merely behavior or achievement), affirming their inner being.

**False Self:** A compliant adaptation developed to gain approval or avoid rejection. Protects the true self when the environment is misattuned.

**False Qualities:** Personality-level imitations that replace veiled essential qualities (e.g., arrogance for Essential Value).

**Good Enough Parenting:** Winnicott's concept that consistent, responsive but not perfect caregiving fosters healthy development and resilience.

**Holding Environment:** A term from Winnicott describing the physical and emotional safety provided by a caregiver that supports authentic development.

**Holes:** Absences in experience where essence has been lost from awareness. These holes are often filled by compensatory patterns.

**Inner Child:** The sum of early ego structures and strategies developed to navigate dependency, vulnerability, and survival in childhood.

**Initiative vs. Guilt:** Erikson's third stage in which children test their capacity to act and create. Support fosters initiative; dismissal breeds guilt.

**Internal Working Model:** Mental blueprints for relationships formed through early caregiver interactions. Affects all future relational dynamics.

**Magical Thinking:** The belief (normal in early childhood) that thoughts or wishes can control reality. Reflects limited causality understanding.

**Merging Essence:** The essential quality felt in early infancy as oneness and golden fusion with the caregiver. Supports bonding and primal trust.

**Mirroring:** Reflecting back the child's feelings, gestures, or essential nature. Builds self-recognition and self-worth.

**Object Constancy:** The ability to sustain an emotional connection with a caregiver even when they are absent or frustrating. Central to Mahler's final subphase.

**Object Permanence:** A Piagetian milestone when the infant realizes objects/people exist even when unseen.

**Observational Learning:** Learning by watching others, particularly in social or emotional domains. Core to Bandura's theory.

**Personality:** The construct of identity formed by adaptation, memory, defenses, and learned behaviors. Often mistaken for the self.

**Personal Essence:** A mature integration of personality and essence, enabling authentic functioning in the world.

**Practicing Subphase:** Mahler's phase (10–16 months) is marked by exploration and joyful autonomy. Children return for emotional refueling.

**Preoperational Stage:** Piaget's cognitive stage (~2–7 years) of symbolic thought, language use, and egocentrism, with limited logic.

**Private Speech:** Self-directed talk by children during tasks; seen by Vygotsky as a transitional form of thinking.

**Psychosocial Stages:** Erikson's framework of eight life stages, each defined by a core developmental task (e.g., trust vs. mistrust).

**Rapprochement:** Mahler's phase (16–24 months), where the child experiences both autonomy and longing for closeness, often with emotional ambivalence.

**Scaffolding:** Temporary support provided by a caregiver or teacher to help a child achieve something just beyond current ability. Concept from Vygotsky.

**Secure Base:** A caregiver who provides consistent emotional safety, allowing the child to explore while feeling grounded.

**Self-Efficacy:** A belief in one's ability to act effectively. Formed through encouragement, mastery, and modeled resilience (Bandura).

**Separation–Individuation:** Mahler's overall process describing how a child becomes a distinct self while remaining emotionally connected.

**Sensorimotor Stage:** Piaget's first cognitive stage (birth to ~2 years), where learning is through sensation and movement.

**Social Development:** The maturing of relational capacities, including cooperation, empathy, role-taking, and emotional regulation.

**Social Mirror:** The way children come to see themselves through the reflected responses and expectations of caregivers and peers.

**Soul Child:** A term for the ego structure that carries the memory of the soul's purity and vitality. Acts as a bridge back to essence.

**Superego:** Freud's internalized moral structure, often experienced as inner judgment, guilt, or idealized standards.

**Symbolic Play:** Using objects or actions to represent others in play. Indicates symbolic thinking and cognitive maturation.

**Transitional Object:** An item (blanket, stuffed toy) that provides comfort as a child moves between dependence and independence.

**Transparent Structures:** Personality patterns that have become aligned with essence, allowing full human expression without distortion.

**Trust vs. Mistrust:** Erikson's first stage, whereby an infant learns whether the world is safe based on caregiver attunement.

**Will:** An essential quality representing inner determination, presence, and intention, not control. Supports autonomy and choice.

**Zone of Proximal Development (ZPD):** Vygotsky's term for the range between what a child can do alone and what they can do with guidance. Learning flourishes here.

# The Enneagram World of the Child

At the heart of parenting is a silent question every child asks: Am I welcome as I am? **The Enneagram World of the Child** takes this question seriously—and explores how your presence, your patterns, and your past all shape the answer. This companion book extends beyond personality theory to explore how the earliest years of life lay the groundwork for self-image, resilience, and relational patterns. It's not about typing children's personality. It's about understanding how the emotional atmosphere of your home—shaped by your and your spouse's Enneagram (personality) type—impacts the inner world of your child and their developing sense of self – who they are becoming.

If *Nurturing Essence* is your compass for essential parenting, *The Enneagram World of the Child* is the map that reveals the hidden terrain. Whether you're a parent, teacher, coach, or therapist, it offers powerful insight into how early life experience echoes through adulthood—and how greater awareness can interrupt old patterns and create space for something new to emerge.

## EnneagramWorldoftheChild.com

## About the Author

John Harper is a Diamond Approach® teacher, Enneagram guide, and a student of human development whose work bridges psychology, spirituality, and deep experiential inquiry. He is the author of *The Enneagram World of the Child: Nurturing Resilience and Self-Compassion in Early Life* and *Good Vibrations: Primordial Sounds of Existence,* available on Amazon.

Reviews, social posts, and word-of-mouth are greatly appreciated!

HarpGnosisBooks@gmail.com

# Nurturing-Essence.com

www.ingramcontent.com/pod-product-compliance
Lightning Source LLC
Chambersburg PA
CBHW080726230426
43665CB00020B/2631